Data Strategy

Data Strategy

Sid Adelman
Larissa T. Moss
Majid Abai

⋀⋁Addison-Wesley

Upper Saddle River, NJ • Boston• Indianapolis • San Francisco
New York • Toronto • Montreal • London • Munich • Paris • Madrid
Capetown • Sydney • Tokyo • Singapore • Mexico City

The publisher offers excellent discounts on this book when ordered in quantity for bulk purchases or special sales, which may include electronic versions and/or custom covers and content particular to your business, training goals, marketing focus, and branding interests. For more information, please contact:

U. S. Corporate and Government Sales
(800) 382-3419
corpsales@pearsontechgroup.com

For sales outside the U. S., please contact:

International Sales
international@pearsoned.com

Visit us on the Web: www.awprofessional.com

Library of Congress Catalog Number: 2005923029

ISBN 0-321-24099-5
Text printed in the United States on recycled paper at R.R. Donnelly in Crawfordsville, IN
First printing, June, 2005

Dedication from Sid:
To my sister Roz Kraus.

Dedication from Larissa:
To Leia, in loving memory.

Dedication from Majid:
To Mona, Mateen, and Sheila: The center of my universe
and the universe that keeps me centered.

Contents

Chapter 3: Data Quality   47

Chapter 4: Metadata   73

Chapter 6: Organizational Roles and Responsibilities   133

Acknowledgments

A book is not just a product of its authors, but also a product of colleagues, business associates, clients, reviewers, publishers, friends, and even family members who put some of their personal needs on hold during the writing process.

Our special thanks go to our colleague and good friend, Steve Hoberman, for his major contribution to the "Data Modeling" chapter. We thank NCR/Teradata for letting us reuse the white paper, "The Importance of Data Modeling as a Foundation for Business Insight," written by Larissa Moss and Steve Hoberman. We also thank our numerous colleagues who have been our "sounding boards" for years and with whom we have a chance to regularly brainstorm about problems, ideas, solutions, and innovations. We want to thank our clients, whose struggles with too much data and not enough usable information spurred us on to write this book, and who have allowed us to learn from their mistakes (as well as our own), enabling us to provide a roadmap for delivering a true data strategy for organizations.

We would like to express our special gratitude to the following reviewers and colleagues who gave us their ideas, critiques, and suggestions for topics: Charles Angione; Joyce Bischoff; Charles Finch; Tom Haughey; Dirk Herreman; Sean Ivoghli; Chuck Kelley; David Loshin; David Marco; Simon Nazarian; Kim Nevins; Steven Palmer; Clay Rehm; Mike Schmitz; Mike Scofield; Mark Da Silva; Ann Marie Smith; Kim Stanick; Greg Tomaino; Adriaan Veldhuisen; Donna Welch; Ka-Yiu Yu; and Dale Zinkgraf.

We would also like to thank our publishing staff for their efforts in converting our drafted materials, which were not always consistent in terms of layout, into a perfectly formatted and professionally illustrated book. Our thanks go to: Jeff Pepper, Mary Kate Murray, and Paul Petralia; Michelle Vincenti, Ginny Bess Munroe, and Steven Heim; and The Scan Group, Inc.

We would also like to take turns thanking our families and friends:

Sid: I'd like to thank my wife Melinda Smith who is the funniest woman I've ever met and a pretty good dance partner.

Larissa: My endless thanks go to my soul mate Donald Sherman who has patiently supported me through four books, always cautiously asking if "this is the last one." I also thank Claudia Acri, one of the most phenomenal Jazzercise teachers I've met in all my travels, for getting and keeping me in such good shape both physically and mentally. Her exercise and dance instructions, her positive outlook on life, and her embracing personality were the main sources of my wellbeing throughout the writing of this book.

Majid: My thanks to my wife and best friend Sheila for putting up with the late nights and weekends while I was researching, writing, and rewriting the material for the book.

I'd also like to thank my parents, David and Sara, and my brothers, Masoud and Mike, who have always been my mentors, guiding lights, and biggest supporters. And thanks to Behnam who's been a life-time friend and a long-time business partner and who continues to be a great sounding board, an excellent voice of reason, and a pretty cool guy to hang out with.

About the Authors

Sid Adelman is a principal in Sid Adelman & Associates, an organization specializing in planning and implementing data warehouses, in data warehouse and BI assessments, and in establishing effective data architectures and strategies. He is a regular speaker at the Data Warehouse Institute and IBM's DB2 and Data Warehouse Conference. Sid also speaks often at DAMA conferences. He chairs the "Ask the Experts" column on www.dmreview.com.

Sid is a founding member of the Business Intelligence Alliance. Its members include Colin White, Herb Edelstein, Larry English, David Foote, Douglas Hackney, Pieter Mimno, Neil Raden, and David Marco. Sid is also a frequent contributor to journals that focus on data warehouse and data-related topics. He co-authored *Data Warehouse Project Management* with Larissa Moss. He is the primary author of *Impossible Data Warehouse Situations with Solutions from the Experts*.

Sid can be reached at sidadelman@aol.com. His web site is www.sidadelman.com.

Larissa Moss is president of Method Focus Inc., a corporation specializing in enterprise information management. She frequently lectures at data warehouse and data quality conferences worldwide on the topics of data warehousing, business intelligence, and other enterprise architecture and data strategy topics, such as data integration, data modeling, data quality, and metadata.

Larissa is a senior consultant of the Cutter Consortium and a member of Friends of NCR-Teradata and the IBM Gold Group. Her present and past associations also include membership in DAMA, part-time faculty member at the Extended University of California Polytechnic University Pomona, associate of the Relational Institute and the Codd & Date Consulting Group, and lecturer for TDWI, DCI, MIS Training Institute, and PESG.

Larissa has authored and co-authored numerous books, white papers, and articles on business intelligence, project management, information asset management, development methodologies, data quality, and organizational realignments. She can be reached at methodfocus@earthlink.net. Her website is www.methodfocus.com.

 **Majid Abai** is President of Seena Technologies, a Santa Monica, California consultancy dedicated to delivery of holistic data and enterprise solutions to various organizations. Majid's two decades of IT experience have been primarily focused on solution architecture, data strategies, and business intelligence systems for organizations facing challenges with the management of massive amounts of data. Majid has developed and teaches a class in Business Intelligence at the University of California, Los Angeles (UCLA) and several other seminars and lectures for national and international corporations. He can be reached at majid@seenatech.com. Seena Technologies website is www.seenatech.com.

Foreword

Data strategy is one of the most ubiquitous and misunderstood topics in the information technology (IT) industry. Most corporations' data strategy and IT infrastructure were not planned, but grew out of "stovepipe" applications over time with little to no regard for the goals and objectives of the enterprise. This stovepipe approach has produced the highly convoluted and inflexible IT architectures so prevalent in corporations today. This architecture—or rather the lack thereof—creates a significant stumbling block because it is exceedingly time consuming and costly to modify existing systems. In fact, I have seen situations in which a chief marketing officer could not initiate a desired marketing campaign because the opportunity to do so would have grown stale by the time the systems were modified to implement the new campaign.

Besides inflexibility, the lack of enterprise IT planning has lead to epidemic levels of data redundancy. In my experience, most major corporations and large government organizations have three- to four-fold "needless data redundancy"—data that exists for no other reason than failure to properly plan and implement. This issue has become so pressing that it has entered into the chief executive officer (CEO)'s key corporate objectives. I have personally witnessed several CEOs declare that their organization must simplify its IT portfolio, so that redundant data and applications can be removed.

Many organizations target enterprise data strategy as one of the key initiatives to reduce data redundancy, simplify IT portfolios, and ease the strain on the architectures of applications. Through meta data management, an enterprise data strategy identifies how data should be constructed, what data exists, and what the meaning of that data is. This helps organizations address data redundancy by showing when a proposed new system will replicate existing applications. This is a critical aspect of data strategy because many companies want to consolidate existing redundant applications, but processes are not in place to prevent new redundancy from entering the IT environment. Thus, an effective enterprise data strategy can save organizations that currently operate as the proverbial sinking ships whose crews are bailing water, but cannot plug the leaks. A sound enterprise data strategy not only "bails water" by affording IT staff the means and methods for reducing existing redundant data, but it can "plug the leaks" by ensuring that new redundancies stop flowing into the organization.

Sid Adelman, Larissa Moss, and Majid Abai's book represents an outstanding achievement in defining the key activities for implementing a successful enterprise data strategy. Their real-world experience assisting companies shines throughout the book and makes it a must read for any IT professional.

—David Marco, President of EWSolutions

Introduction

A chief financial officer (CFO) was approached by the chief executive officer (CEO) and asked for an accounting of the company's financial assets. The CFO gave a vague response indicating a lack of knowledge of the corporate bank accounts, had little idea what was in each account, and had no idea about the status of accounts receivable. The board of directors asked the CEO about the intended use of the corporate assets and was told, "There is no plan for their use." The CFO and the CEO were soon pursuing new personal interests.

A primary asset in IT is data, and when most chief information officers (CIOs) are asked about the assets under their control, most are forced to respond that there are no plans for the use of this primary asset. They would have to admit that there is no inventory of data, little is known about what data is in which database, they have no idea about the quality of the data, and they would have to admit that "there is no plan for the productive use of this asset." Interestingly, the turnover in CIOs is also high, albeit not for the same reason.

CURRENT STATUS IN CONTEMPORARY ORGANIZATIONS

Very few organizations, large or small, have a well defined data strategy. If asked, some will point you to dusty and outdated volumes of database standards, usually geared specifically to a database management system (DBMS). The more advanced organizations have a subset of standards and perhaps a documented strategy on portions of what should be included in an overall strategy.

In most organizations, the value of data is not well understood. Data is considered the province of the department that creates it, and this data is often jealously guarded by that department, often under the guise of data ownership, which, to the mind of the department head means secreting the data from all others in the organization. Some of the more astute people in your organization may recognize that data and the information derived from that data translates into real power, and control of that data can be the stepping stone to advancement.

A data strategy is usually addressed piecemeal. A company launches an effort to choose its preferred DBMS or attacks a database performance problem when response time becomes excessive. Rarely do organizations work from the big picture, and as a result they suboptimize solutions, introduce programs that may have a deleterious effect on the overall enterprise, cause inconsistencies that result in major efforts for interfacing, or develop systems that cannot be easily integrated.

As application packages or enterprise resource programs (ERPs) are introduced, they bring with them a plethora of diverse standards, naming conventions, codes, and DBMS platforms. Modifying these packages to conform to the organization's standards is unthinkable and so the "Tower of Babel" data becomes even more unmanageable.

Organizations also make terrible choices of underlying technology infrastructure. For example, if a platform (operating system and DBMS) does not scale or will not support the organization's service level agreements, projects will usually fail after millions are spent, years are wasted, and credibility and careers are dissipated. An interesting fallacy holds that after the failure has occurred, the guilty (and some of the innocent) are sacrificed, the organization learns and therefore never makes the same mistakes (or any other mistakes), and success is assured the second time around. There are countless instances of the second or the third time around also being failures, either making the same mistakes or making new and equally catastrophic decisions. The absence of a sound data strategy provides fertile ground for yet another disaster. The voice of reason is often ignored, those with an understanding of the potential problems are discouraged from voicing their opinions, and anyone who disagrees with a well-intentioned but unviable architecture is known as "not being a team player."

Most organizations have rogue databases and stealth applications. These are often on Excel or on Access, but they can also be on SQL Server or on another DBMS. The existence of these applications is often unknown (and purposely undisclosed) to IT. They came into existence because a department needed an application and users were unwilling to wait for IT to deliver, the department wanted total control, or the department did not want to conform to IT's standards. These departments either developed the applications themselves or hired an outside consultant to write the applications. The choice of the platform, the DBMS, and the development language was usually determined by the skills of those writing the application. There was almost no thought to conforming to organizational standards and certainly no consideration for integrating with other applications.

WHY A DATA STRATEGY IS NEEDED

Working without a data strategy is analogous to a company allowing each department and each person within each department to develop its own financial chart of accounts. This empowerment allows each person in the organization to choose his own numbering scheme. Existing charts of accounts would be ignored as each person exercises his or her own creativity. Even to those of us who don't wear green eye shades, the resulting chaos is obvious and easy to predict.

The chaos without a data strategy is not as obvious, but the indicators abound: dirty data, redundant data, inconsistent data, the inability to integrate, poor performance, terrible availability, little accountability, users who are increasingly dissatisfied with the performance of IT, and the general feeling that things are out of control.

Without a data strategy, the IT people in the organization have no guidelines for making the decisions that are absolutely crucial to the success of the IT organization. In addition, the absence of a strategy gives a blank check to those who want to pursue their own agendas, including attachment to certain technologies or Machiavellian aspirations of power. This includes those who want to try a new DBMS, new technologies (often unproven), and new tools that may or may not be appropriate. This type of environment provides no checks or validation for those who might pursue a strategy that has no hope for success.

A data strategy should result in the development of systems with less risk and a much higher success rate. It should also result in much higher quality systems. A data strategy provides a chief technology officer (CTO) and CIO with a rationale to counter arguments for immature technology and data management approaches that are inconsistent with existing strategies.

Value of Data as an Organizational Asset

Organizations keep data on their customers, their suppliers, and transactional data that captures the heart of the business, the purchases, sales, customer calls, activities, as well as financial data. This data has value, which means it is an asset that is just as important, if not more important than the buildings, the parts inventory, accounts receivable, and equipment assets of the organization. Some organizations that sell data carry it as an asset on their books and may consider it intellectual capital. When a company gets evaluated for acquisition, evaluated as a merger candidate, or appraised by Wall Street, the notion of a going concern includes the value of the data as an asset. The Europeans have already adopted the notion of "fair-value accounting," and the United States is supposed to adopt this method of accounting by the end of 2006. This means organizations will account for assets, previously unrecognized assets, and the organizations will place those assets on the balance sheet. An asset has future value and an organization's data certainly has future value, but this value has rarely been reflected on a company's books. However, it is lurking there sometimes as sound management, excellent technology, and goodwill, and sometimes it is reflected in the price of the stock. It is difficult to properly value this asset, especially data that has been in the organization for some time.

Why would we need to assign value to data when an organization cannot exist without the data that supports its applications? The reason is that budgets and resources are limited, and it may be difficult for the person attempting to get the needed budget and the right people resources. By showing the business value of data, the budget and the right staff should be easier to acquire.

New federal regulations require the CEO and the CFO to certify the accuracy of what is reported to the investment community and to governmental regulators. Such certification would be greatly improved if the organization had a strong and viable data strategy.

VISION AND GOALS OF THE ENTERPRISE

The vision of a data strategy that fits your organization has to conform to the overall strategy of IT, which in turn must conform to the strategy of the business. Therefore, the vision should conform to and support where the organization wants to be in 5 years.

Every organization, be it a publicly traded company, a private for-profit company, a non-profit organization, a governmental agency, or a quasi-governmental entity all have strategic goals. At minimum, the for-profit companies want to increase profits, and most organizations have customer service among its goals as well as high levels of financial integrity.

Your goals are unique because your organization is unique. Arriving at these goals and gaining consensus is time-consuming and will cause some dissension, but this is not a task to avoid; it must be addressed. Without the goals and the principles that follow, there will be little direction for the decisions you will make.

The following is a set of primary goals of IT:

• Deliver systems faster.

• Improve the relationship with the business community.

• Improve the quality of delivered systems.

• Reduce the risk and reduce the failures in application development.

• Reduce costs.

• Attract and retain good people.

• Increase the productivity of application development.

• Provide controls for the IT environment.

• Improve the productivity of the people who use the data.

These goals should *not* be accepted without extensive discussion and the requisite commitment needed to make them work. None of these goals come free. Each has a cost.

Support of the IT Strategy

The target data environment does not exist in a vacuum. It is relevant only in the context of an overall IT strategy. This strategy, in turn, has been established to support the business of the organization, both for the existing environment and for the future plans of the business. Some organizations are unable to pursue business opportunities because IT is unable to support them in a timely manner.

Although we discuss the data environment, it is critical to recognize that a supporting infrastructure or architecture must be in place to support a robust data environment.

COMPONENTS OF A DATA STRATEGY

There are a number of key components in a data strategy, and each aspect is covered by a chapter in this book. The components are as follows:

• Data integration

• Data quality

• Metadata

• Data modeling

• Organizational roles and responsibilities

• Performance and measurement

• Security and privacy

• DBMS selection

• Business intelligence

• Unstructured data

• Business value of data and ROI

Data Integration

Data integration has continued to elude most organizations. They have not been able to integrate business data, and understanding the customer continues to be a problem. Organizations have been taxed with massive volumes of data redundancy and plagued with the difficulties of integration because the data has resided on different DBMSs for decades, and no thought has ever been given to the need for eventual integration.

Legacy data is the data on which most organizations run operational systems. Organizations need to address how they plan to inventory data, the redundancy factor, and the evaluation of the legacy data for its use and quality. Organizations must decide what to do with much of legacy data. Should they migrate it to another platform? Is it possible to dispose some of this data (it's expensive to keep it)? How should it best be archived? Historical data is required for some business intelligence (BI) operations and for some operational systems. Legal requirements and the threat of legal action demand certain and selected data retention.

The benefits of integrating your data are:

- Minimizing data redundancy. A reduction in redundant data means less hardware and software required, less program maintenance, and less time reconciling inconsistent reports.

- Providing a comprehensive view of your key subject areas, such as customer, patient, member, and supplier.

- Minimizing the effort and the potential for error when data needs to be pulled together from multiple sources.

Data Quality

Almost every organization overestimates the quality of data. Most organizations recognize quality problems, but do not realize the magnitude of the problems. Data quality is multifaceted; there are so many aspects of this quality. As you discuss data quality in your organization, it's important to be clear about which portions you address.

Data quality is clearly a key component of the data strategy. Management awareness and support for data quality continues to be a problem. The quality of the data must be evaluated, and you must be able to identify data quality problems. This includes which source data is the most correct, the valid values (domains), which business rules should be implemented (for instance, the number of dependents cannot be negative), data types (for example, hexadecimal, packed decimal, integer, and so on), missing data (completeness), inappropriate defaults (for example, if gender is missing, code the person as "male"), fields used for multiple purposes (for example, a birth date of 9999 means the person is deceased), and inaccurate data.

Data quality includes standardization and availability of historical data. (Over time, codes change and some data is new; for example, the data might not have been captured prior to 1999.) Data quality also includes the following:

• Timeliness of data. (How current is the data?)

• Validation of the extract, transform, load (ETL) process in the data ware-houses. (Has the target database been created correctly?)

• The cost of cleansing. Some cleansing efforts might not be worth the expense.

• Prioritization of the cleansing effort (the order in which data will be cleansed).

• The responsibility for data quality. It's not enough to say that data quality is everyone's responsibility.

The benefits of improving data quality are:

• Less time manually correcting problems

• Less time and effort checking for data inconsistencies

• Greater trust from the user community

• Fewer public relations problems

• Less time in the "big house" for the CEO and CFO

Metadata

A metadata strategy is another key component of a data strategy. Metadata is information about data that normally includes business definitions, valid values (domains), business rules for creating the data, transformation and aggregation rules, security, ownership, source, timeliness, and data format. Few organizations work to capture much of these metadata and those that have captured the metadata have not made effective use of it. Management support for metadata is critical, including which metadata to capture; the responsibility for capturing metadata; the responsibility for maintenance, business metadata, technical metadata, process metadata, and usage metadata; how metadata is captured;

how metadata is used; tools that generate metadata; and software tools to capture and maintain metadata.

The benefits of building and maintaining enterprise-wide metadata are:

- Metadata provides for impact analysis, which results in less time to research the programs to be maintained.

- Metadata provides for a better understanding of the meaning of the information derived from the data.

- Metadata research reveals the availability of needed data, creating less redundancy of data.

Data Modeling

Data modeling is an important component of a data strategy. Data modeling has been around for many decades, but most organizations have not seen the types of benefits that were promised by the modeling tool vendors. Data modeling standards need to include the tools, the creation and use of metadata in data modeling, the control and inventory of data models, how and where the models should be developed and used, and industry models (Finance, Health Care, Insurance, and so on).

The benefits of developing and using data models are:

- Construction of the Single Version of the Truth (a 360-degree view of your organization)

- A better understanding of the data

- A better process to gather user requirements

- Improved communication within the IT organization and between IT and the user community

- The minimization of redundant efforts

- The minimization of redundant data

- An initial point for capturing metadata

Organizational Roles and Responsibilities

The people involved will make or break even a proper data strategy. Organizational roles and responsibilities include to whom various roles should report and the data-related roles and responsibilities that include the database administrator (DBA), data administrator (DA), data quality administrator, security officer, and the system architect. Data ownership and data stewardship have continued to be contentious issues involving the creation, access, and security of the data.

The benefits of building a strong framework for organizational roles and responsibilities to support your data strategy are:

- Having the right resources to do the job

- Making the most effective use of the training budgets

- Supporting the organization's service level agreements (SLAs)

- Effectively using people resources

Performance and Measurement

Performance is almost always an issue with high-volume systems and large databases. It is also a factor that is often considered far too late in the cycle of a system's implementation. We have seen systems that have been significantly delayed or even cancelled when, at roll-out, transaction response time was unacceptable (more than 15 seconds on average, for example), when the addition of a few more users brought the system to its knees, or when historical data could not be kept for longer than 6 months due to severe performance degradation. We have seen query response time measured in days.

A data strategy includes the need to understand performance requirements and the capabilities of the hardware, operating system, and DBMS. The performance implications should be understood before a line of code is written and before an application package is purchased. Performance includes capacity planning, monitoring and measuring, and service level agreements (SLAs) for performance. It also includes tuning, roles and responsibilities for performance, reporting performance, the perception of performance by management and user departments, and proactive versus reactive modes of dealing with performance issues.

Tom DeMarco paraphrasing Lord Kelvin said, "If you can't measure it, you can't manage it." We must first begin with an understanding of why we measure. We measure for the following reasons:

- Measurement helps you to identify problems that can then be addressed.

- Measurement helps prioritize the projects to improve the systems.

- Measurement allows you to be proactive and deal with problems before the users are even aware of them.

- Measurement allows you to report to management on the status of the system including usage, response time, availability, and customer satisfaction.

- If you charge costs back to the users, you need a fair and accurate way to measure resources used.

Measurement and metrics include tools and the roles and responsibility for measuring. These measurements are critical in your ability to manage the environment. The measurements should support your SLAs, especially for performance and availability.

Security and Privacy

Security and privacy is becoming more and more important as organizations globalize, and as they give access to their data to people outside of the organization. Security of data within the organization is an obvious requirement as organizations face problems with insider trading and public relation fiascos. Governmental regulation makes security issues critical for publicly traded companies and for every organization dealing with customer data. Healthcare organizations are closely regulated because they deal with patient privacy issues. Critical aspects involve the responsibility for determining security and privacy, the mechanism for establishing security and privacy, the audit of security, and regulatory issues. Data sharing is another contentious issue. Finally, there are issues related to the standards for data sharing as well as issues of motivation and incentives to share.

The benefits of establishing and implementing strong security and privacy policies are:

- The company complies with governmental regulations.

- You can assure customers and suppliers that you are protecting their privacy.

• You have fewer public relations problems.

• You spend money and resources protecting the right areas.

DBMS Selection

Your organization will have to decide which DBMSs will be the standard, which operating system (OS/390, UNIX, or Windows) will be used, and which business applications (OLTP, ERPs, BI/DW, and so on) will drive the DBMS. Without a standard, a consultant might push his own favorite or the DBMS he knows the best. Without a standard, a marginally superior application package requiring a new DBMS might be chosen without giving thought to the attendant costs and disruptions. Without a standard, an organization has more DBMSs than needed and the cost is high. The complexity associated with multiple DBMSs is challenging because anomalies and inconsistencies in format and rules make integration difficult and interface programs necessary. This does not mean that new DBMSs should not be embraced; however, it does mean that one needs to be justified. The selection of a DBMS standard should encompass a process that establishes the choice as a standard.

Application package and ERP vendors concentrate on function and are not as concerned about the performance implications of architectures and designs. Application packages and ERP systems usually come with the designation of allowable DBMSs, which means that there are often choices the organization can make in selecting a DBMS. The impact of an application package on architecture, capacity requirement, performance, and availability can swamp and overwhelm a DBMS standard.

The benefits of standardizing on one or more DBMSs are as follows:

• Less money is spent on DBMS software licenses and associated utility, maintenance, and upgrade licenses.

• There are fewer interfaces among the DBMSs.

• There is greater leverage with the DBMS vendor.

• The DBAs have more in-depth knowledge of the DBMS and the attendant utilities.

• The training costs are lower.

• There is a better chance of achieving the SLAs.

Business Intelligence

Business intelligence (BI), including data warehousing (DW), has become critical for an organization's capability to make intelligent tactical and strategic decisions. BI includes the DW infrastructure, the DW data, the DW tools, the methodology, as well as the organization and training. The data strategy profoundly affects BI because it addresses performance, security, data modeling, data integration, and metadata.

The benefits of a BI platform are:

- **Revenue enhancement**—Improved marketing can produce more revenue per customer, resulting from increased spending and a greater share of the customer's wallet. Selling higher margin products, focusing on the more profitable customers, and turning unprofitable customers into profitable ones enhance revenue.

- **Analyst productivity**—In the past, analysts and knowledge workers had to spend 80 percent of their time gathering data with only 20 percent left over to perform the analysis. With some data warehouses, those numbers are reversed. Depending on the degree of consolidation, the integration of the data, and the availability of useful metadata, analysts now may spend only 20 percent of their time gathering the data.

- **Cost containment**—In contrast to revenue, which must be balanced with the cost required to produce that revenue, cost savings flow directly to the bottom line. The data warehouse can help control costs in a number of areas. Costs can be reduced by minimizing inventory, minimizing promotional mailers, and using more cost-effective channels to deliver services.

- **Fraud reduction**—The DW and specifically data mining have been used to detect fraudulent insurance claims and fraudulent credit card usage. Analysis of claims has identified fraudulent health and workers' compensation claims coming from specific doctors and lawyers. The types and patterns of the claims alert the investigators, who then conduct a more thorough audit to uncover fraud and abuse.

- **Customer conversion rates**—Better understanding the customers and targeting the prospects with the right products, channels, and incentives can dramatically improve the conversion of shoppers to buyers.

- **Customer attrition/retention rates**—By knowing which customers are likely to leave and knowing their relative profitability, you can take appropriate action to minimize customer attrition.

Unstructured Data

All organizations have unstructured data types including text, video, paper documents, audio, pictures, and other types of unstructured, internal, and external documents. The volume of the unstructured data always far exceeds the volume of the structured data that is stored in traditional databases.

The benefits of establishing standards and processes to deal with unstructured data are:

- You can actually use the data that has been difficult to utilize.

- You minimize the cost and effort in duplication of the vast amount of unstructured data.

- You gain the ability to search for and locate the unstructured data components.

- You achieve compliance with governmental regulations.

Business Value of Data and ROI

An organization's data has value that is just as important, if not more important than its other assets, such as buildings, the inventory, accounts receivable, and equipment. The final chapter in this book is necessary because developing and implementing a data strategy will cost money and will take significant and valuable resources. In addition, the money and people will be made available only if management believes there is real value in the project.

Because the project will take many months, or even years to accomplish, and because the strategy must be maintained in perpetuity, cost justification is an absolute requirement to support the project and sustain the necessary management commitment to protect it from cost cutters and from short-term solutions that would undermine the strategy.

Measuring return on investment (ROI) is relevant because organizations cost justify potential applications. It is also relevant for post-implementation evaluation. Many of the same procedures and equations can be used for both purposes. Expected ROI should be a major determinant in evaluating options and making decisions about which architectures to employ, which vendors to choose, and which projects to pursue, and how these projects should be prioritized. Some companies measure their managers' performance based on the success of projects, and bonuses are often tied to the ROI of these projects.

HOW WILL YOU DEVELOP AND IMPLEMENT A DATA STRATEGY?

The only way a data strategy can be developed and then implemented is with the strong support of the CIO and business executives, who must be educated on the criticality and impact of a good data strategy. It also requires that business managers understand and concur with the goals and with the process; their cooperation is essential. A small team of dedicated (dedicated means full time with no other duties) people who concentrate on building the data strategy and then on selling and implementing the strategy is necessary. The ideal team is composed of the CTO, who will lead the project or at least be a major contributor to the project, a data administrator, a strong DBA, and a business analyst who comes from the business side. All these people should have a strong track record of accomplishment and a good relationship with key members of both IT and the business. They should also be intimately familiar with the business and the data that supports the organization. The team has to sell the strategy and should be authorized to create the strategy and implement it. Again, this means strong support from the CIO, senior directors, and the business executives, and this support must be communicated to everyone involved. A data strategy may attract many would-be assassins and the only thing that will keep them at bay is an understanding that the strategy will happen because it is mandated by senior management.

Data Environment Assessment

Orienteering (the British call it "cunning running") features cross-country running with a map and a compass. When learning to use a map and compass, the first exercise is to determine where you are on the map. Without this knowledge, you are absolutely lost. So it is with establishing a target data environment under the umbrella of a data strategy. First you must determine where you are today. This includes an assessment of your existing DBMSs, internal skills, culture, and legacy systems. Table 1.1 is a Data Environment Assessment Questionnaire that should give you an initial analysis of your existing data environment.

TABLE 1.1 DATA ENVIRONMENT ASSESSMENT QUESTIONNAIRE

The purpose of this questionnaire is to assist your organization in gathering basic information about its current data environment.

1. Organization

    1.1 Data Administration (DA)

        1.1.1 How many people are in data administration?

        1.1.2 What are their skill levels and what kind of training have they had?

        1.1.3 What is the charter of the department?

        1.1.4 Is the DA centralized or decentralized (is the DA assigned to specific lines of business)?

        1.1.5 Where does the DA report in the organization?

        1.1.6 Does the DA set naming standards? If not, who does? Are naming standards enforced? How are they enforced?

        1.1.7 Does the DA keep track of all synonyms and homonyms in the system? How do they track them? What do they do to prevent new synonyms and homonyms from being created?

        1.1.8 Is the DA responsible for metadata or do you have a metadata administration function?

    1.2 Database Administration (DBA)

        1.2.1 How many people are on the DBA staff?

        1.2.2 What are the skill levels of the staff and what training has the staff had?

1.2.3 What is the charter of the department?

1.2.4 Which DBMSs does the department support?

1.2.5 Is the DBA staff centralized or decentralized?

1.2.6 Where do the DBAs report in the organization?

1.2.7 Do the DBAs or do the programmers design the databases?

2. Application Production Environment

2.1 Mainframe

2.1.1 What DBMSs are used?

2.1.2 Which applications use which databases?

2.1.3 Which are operational and which are decision support?

2.2 Midrange

2.2.1 What DBMSs are used?

2.2.2 Which applications use which databases?

2.2.3 Which are operational and which are decision support?

2.3 Servers

2.3.1 What DBMSs are used?

2.3.2 Which applications use which databases?

2.3.3 Which are operational and which are decision support?

2.4 PC Workstations

2.4.1 What DBMSs are used?

2.4.2 Which applications use which databases?

2.4.3 Which are operational and which are decision support?

2.4.4 Is the data stored in spreadsheets? On Access databases? Are they shared? Who maintains them?

2.4.5 Are spreadsheets used for operational or decision support purposes?

2.4.6 How many people in the organization have access to those spreadsheets or Access databases?

2.5 Is there a strategic plan for using the DBMSs?

2.6 Are there plans to move legacy databases to relational DBMSs?

continues

2.7 How much redundant data is in the systems today? How do you measure the redundancy? Are there plans to reduce data redundancy?

2.8 What problems has redundancy created? How do you measure the problems?

2.9 How integrated are the databases? Are there plans for future integration?

2.10 Are there plans for the use of subject databases?

2.11 Is there an accurate inventory of data? If so, what mechanisms are in place to maintain this inventory? Who maintains this inventory? The DAs? The metadata administrators?

3. Application Development Environment

3.1 Is there a standard for the "buy versus build" decision?

3.2 Which application packages are being used? How extensively? What databases or access methods are associated with these application packages (for example, DB2 with SAP or Oracle with PeopleSoft)?

3.3 Are industry data models being employed? Are these logical, physical, or both?

3.4 Do your application vendors provide you with data models (database views)? If so, how are they being used?

3.5 Do you use logical data models in your application request for proposal/price (RFPs) to clarify your requirements to the vendors?

3.6 Application Delivery: Analysis Phase

3.6.1 What experience does the staff have with data analysis?

3.6.2 What experience does the staff have with data modeling? Is experience limited to database design or does it include business modeling?

3.6.3 Are these activities part of the System Development Life Cycle (SDLC) methodology? Are these activities separate from design activities?

3.7 Application Delivery: Design Phase

3.7.1 What experience does the staff have with database design?

3.7.2 What experience does the staff have with data modeling in terms of logical database design?

3.7.3 Are these activities part of the SDLC methodology? Are these activities separate from analysis activities?

3.7.4 Are data modeling tools used in the design process? Which ones? How are they used?

3.7.5 How are the data models mapped (logical data model from analysis to physical data model from design)?

3.8. Application Delivery: Production Phase

3.8.1 Is DDL generated automatically? How? What tools are used?

3.8.2 Are separate data request modules used? Where are the reusable modules stored? Do all programmers know about them and use them?

3.8.3 Are physical data models used to reflect the physical DB design? How are they used?

3.9 Application Delivery: Maintenance Phase

3.9.1 Are you reverse engineering from legacy databases when you enhance existing systems?

3.9.2 Are tools being used to reverse engineer? What tools are used?

4. Metadata

4.1 Is metadata an integral part of application development?

4.2 What role does metadata play in your organization?

4.3 What metadata tool (if any) is used?

4.4 Who uses your metadata?

4.4.1 Who inputs the metadata?

4.4.2 Who extracts the metadata?

4.4.3 What training is given to metadata users?

4.4.4 Who controls the metadata?

4.5 How accurate and current is the information in your metadata repository?

4.6 Are there plans for changes in the use of metadata?

continues

4.7 What additional capabilities do you require to make metadata significant and productive?

4.8 Is metadata retrieved and displayed as part of a database query?

4.9 Is business metadata mapped to technical, process, and usage metadata? Where is it mapped? Who does the mapping?

4.10 Is business metadata, as it pertains to data, mapped and synchronized with the logical data models?

4.11 Is technical metadata, as it pertains to data, mapped and synchronized with the physical data models and the corresponding DDL?

4.12 Is process metadata, as it pertains to processes, mapped and synchronized with the various tools that use it (ETL, OLAP, data mining, and so on)?

4.13 Is usage metadata collected? How is it captured?

5. Distributed Data

5.1 Describe the current and planned strategy for both centralized and decentralized data.

5.2 Will data be distributed to support your clients, desktops, and so on?

5.3 How are distributed databases managed? Who controls the data redundancy? How is it controlled?

5.4 How does data naming remain centralized to avoid creation of synonyms and homonyms? Does the DA play a role in controlling the naming process? If not, who does?

5.5 How is metadata managed in the distributed environment?

5.6 Is metadata distributed as well? Is the distribution by data subject area or by user department? Is the distribution accomplished through mirrored metadata repositories or through XML-enabled metadata retrieval directly from tools?

5.7 Who maintains the meta-meta model over the distributed metadata implementation?

6. Data Quality

6.1 How would you characterize the quality of your data?

6.1.1 How important is the data? Do you know which data is critical to the organization? Which data is important but not absolutely critical? Which data is relatively insignificant?

6.1.2 Is the data available when your users need it?

6.1.3 How timely is the data?

6.1.4 How accurate is the data?

6.1.5 How complete is the data?

6.1.6 How many overloaded data fields exist (fields that store values of different domains, such as Master-Code A, B, C, and D, where the values A and B describe a customer and C and D describe a product)?

7. Enterprise Issues

7.1 Is data viewed as a vital corporate resource? Who in your organization has this opinion?

7.2 Does your organization have data owners and data stewards? Do you know who they are?

7.3 Is there an existing data strategy that guides the application development process? Who is responsible for creating and maintaining the data strategy?

7.4 Are data standards in place (naming, security, and database recovery)? Who creates them? Who enforces them?

7.5 Do you have a target application development environment (where you want to be in 3 years)? What is it? Whose vision is it (CIO, CTO, or DBA, and so on)?

REFERENCES

"When you can measure what you are speaking about and express it in numbers, you know something about it; but when you cannot measure it, when you cannot express it in numbers, your knowledge is of a meager and unsatisfactory kind." —Lord Kelvin, Scottish Physicist, 1884

CHAPTER 2

Data Integration

"Computing is not about computers anymore. It is about living."

—Nicholas Negroponte

If you ask ten knowledgeable people for their definition of integration, you are likely to get ten different answers. Most of the answers will be an interpretation of Webster's dictionary definition for integration, which is, "to make whole or complete by adding or bringing together parts." This can mean anything from two systems passing data back and forth (loosely coupled) to a shared data environment in which all data elements are unique and non-redundant and are reused by multiple applications (tightly coupled).

For example, when creating an integrated view of a customer, you might start by bringing together customer-related data elements from multiple sources, such as:

- What the customer fills out on a loan application.

- Transactions this customer performs with your organization, which is captured as data when the customer swipes an infinity or loyalty card at the supermarket or casino slot machine.

- Demographic data on the customer that is available from external vendors.

• Data from sales force automation or order management applications.

• Information gathered when the customer calls a customer service department or asks for information on a website.

Unfortunately, a lot of customer data is usually duplicated in several of these source systems. As a result, the redundant data is often inconsistent. Thus, just bringing together parts (the inconsistent data) to "make whole" the image of the business entity CUSTOMER is obviously not the only thing we strive for with data integration. Therefore, we have to refine Webster's definition into a more complete definition for data integration: "To make a business entity or subject area whole or complete by adding or bringing together its unique data elements and storing them nonredundantly so that they can be reused consistently by multiple applications." This adds a new level of complexity to data integration, which technology solutions alone cannot adequately address.

INEFFECTIVE "SILVER-BULLET" TECHNOLOGY SOLUTIONS

When they realize that data integration is the key to thriving in the fast-paced, information-oriented economy, company leaders look for the silver-bullet solution to data integration problems. However, they quickly discover that the real issues underlying the current *dis*integrated data chaos cannot be solved by technology solutions without fundamentally changing the way they manage their data assets overall.

Enterprise Resource Planning (ERP)

ERP solutions are a collection of functional modules used to integrate operational data to support seamless operational business processes for the enterprise. ERP products were meant to solve the redundant and inconsistent operational data mess by consolidating operational data into ERP modules. Good idea—if properly implemented. Properly implemented meant performing extensive research on the data to be converted into the ERP modules. This was rarely, if ever, done due to time constraints. Extensive research normally includes analyzing *all* data elements for definitions, contents, semantics, and business rules. This extensive business analysis activity usually also includes finding and fixing gaps in business knowledge and lost data interrelationships. Performing extensive research and correcting existing data impairments should have been a mandate for every ERP conversion. Instead, most ERP conversion projects were performed the old-fashioned way—using traditional sources to target mapping, which does not include extensive data domain (content) analysis, such as:

- Finding data elements that have multiple meanings and are used for multiple purposes.

- Finding missing relationships between business entities.

- Finding and resolving duplicate keys.

- Validating data content among dependent data elements across files.

- Deciphering, separating, and translating one-byte or two-byte codes.

- Finding and extracting processing logic embedded in the data values.

Therefore, as a result of performing a traditional conversion, the promises of the ERP technology solution to solve data integration and data quality problems did not materialize to the extent expected. A summary of explicit and implicit ERP promises and ERP realities is listed in Table 2.1.

Table 2.1: ERP Promises Versus Realities

ERP Promises	*ERP Realities*
Data integration.	Cross-organizational integration is limited to the operational functions converted to the ERP package.
No more redundancy.	Reduced data redundancy is limited to the converted operational systems.
Consistency of data content.	Data content is almost as consistent or inconsistent as it was on the old legacy systems because it is rarely changed or cleaned during conversion.
Improved data quality.	Data quality is usually as good or as bad as it was on the old legacy systems because only limited or no data cleansing was performed during conversion.
Easy reporting.	Poor quality or unusable reports (often the reason for a data warehouse initiative).
Easy maintenance.	Complicated and costly maintenance.

Data Warehousing (DW)

Another serious attempt at integrating data has been without question, the drive toward data warehousing. The definition of data warehousing speaks to this attempt: "A DW delivers a collection of integrated data used to support the decision making process for the enterprise." A solution at last, and a sound plan—if properly implemented. Again, properly implemented meant extensive analysis of the operational data to find the data redundancy and data inconsistency problems and to correct them. This detailed analysis had to be performed on all data elements within the scope of the DW to deliver a pool of nonredundant, clean, consistent, and integrated data. This type of analysis cannot be magically performed by a tool, but requires business analysts who have the knowledge to define the organization in business terms and with a cross-organizational scope. These business analysts should be business people who are either data owners, data stewards, or data consumers, guided by a skilled IT data analyst who documents the results of the analysis.

In reality, few DW projects have the necessary user involvement to perform such rigorous analysis. Users are still trapped in the habit of expecting IT to build a customized silo system just for them. IT is still trapped in obliging. Both are trapped by not understanding the real issues or choosing to ignore them. As a result, DW initiatives are more often than not little more than silo data mart projects on a new platform, and many of the data integration problems remain to the dismay of disappointed users, as itemized in Table 2.2.

Table 2.2: DW Promises Versus Realities

DW Promises	DW Realities
Data integration.	Stove-pipe data marts, each with its own extract/transform/load (ETL) staging area.
No more redundancy.	Continued, sometimes even increased data redundancy.
Consistency of data content.	Data is still inconsistent among data marts (no central staging area, no reconciliation).
Improved data quality.	Little improvement to data quality.
Historical enterprise data.	Historical data is limited to departmental views.
Unlimited, ad-hoc reporting.	Limited, ad-hoc reporting (too complicated, missing relationships, and poor performance).

DW Promises	DW Realities
Reliable trend analysis reporting.	Inconsistent trend analysis reports among data marts.
Faster data delivery and data access.	Drill-down capabilities are slow.
Business intelligence (BI) capabilities.	BI capabilities compromised by inconsistent and unreliable key performance indicators (KPIs).

Customer Relationship Management (CRM)

CRM attempts to integrate customer information with product information through related business functions, such as sales, marketing, and order fulfillment. Over the last two decades, CRM has metamorphosed into a sophisticated set of tools and applications. Unfortunately, as with ERP systems, too many CRM conversions follow the traditional habits of source-to-target mapping without extensive data analysis and little data cleansing. Data is usually moved "as-is" into the new CRM modules with the unreasonable expectation of magically having clean, consistent, and integrated customer data in their CRM package. Again, simply using new technology is not the whole solution, as is demonstrated by the comparison between the CRM promises and CRM realities listed in Table 2.3.

Table 2.3: CRM Promises Versus Realities

CRM Promises	CRM Realities
Data integration.	More stove-pipe systems; most CRM modules are not integrated, especially when purchased from different vendors.
No more customer redundancy.	Still no single, cross-organizational view of customer; different departments continue to keep and utilize redundant customer files and databases.
Improved data quality.	Customer data is often still as dirty as it was on the old legacy files.
Customer profitability analysis and customized product pricing.	Customers often still have multiple keys, which makes profitability analysis difficult.
Customer intimacy.	Privacy issues and government regulations override customer intimacy requirements.
Knowing your competition.	Information about competition is still illusive.
Geographic market potential and increased customer wallet share.	Customer wallet share is difficult to estimate; external customer data is incomplete or dirty.

Enterprise Application Integration (EAI)

The need for integration increases only when more competitive demands are placed on organizations. Data integration must happen by hook or by crook, and it must happen quickly. EAI vendors understand this pressure placed on organizations. They also realize that organizations have a colossal investment in existing systems, which should be leveraged if at all possible. EAI middleware technology provides that leverage by allowing the unrestricted sharing of data and business processes among *any* connected applications and data sources in the organization. The obvious advantage of EAI technology is that existing data and existing processes can be shared without having to make any changes to existing systems and without having to build new ones (such as a DW). This can be a cost-effective solution to solve data access and data integration problems across heterogeneous systems and platforms, if—and only if—the disparate data is nonredundant, or at least consistent and if it is reasonable performance-wise to expect sharing and collaboration.

The reality is that EAI tools eliminate writing customized bridges between existing systems only. The tools do not affect the quality of the data in the existing systems, nor do they help the end users interpret the data. For example, the data element Annual Income Amount can be stored redundantly in 45 customer files, and in 30 of the 45 files, these "duplicate" amount fields have a different value. EAI is of no value in determining which of these amount fields is correct. Thus, what starts as an easy and cost-effective solution to the data integration problem usually ends with unfulfilled promises, as shown in Table 2.4.

Table 2.4: EAI Promises Versus Realities

EAI Promises	EAI Realities
Fast and automated system integration by reusing existing data.	Existing data can be reused, but it is the same dirty, inconsistent, and unreliable legacy data.
Bridge islands of automation through middleware.	Systems are bridged, not integrated—there is no true integration, and the islands of automation still exist.
Keep cost of data integration down by leveraging investment in existing systems.	Same high data redundancy and process redundancy and the same cost to maintain it, which in many cases is higher than the cost of integration.
Faster data delivery and data access through easy, cross-system reporting.	Access to data might be faster, but the analysis to wade through it takes just as long as before because of redundant and dirty data.

GAINING MANAGEMENT SUPPORT

Integrating data is difficult, expensive, and requires top management support. To gain that support, senior management must recognize the value of data integration and understand that the reasons for it are to support basic organizational goals and objectives. Common goals and objectives include reducing overall costs, increasing revenue, improving the supply chain, reducing product development time (products and services), providing better customer service, complying with information legislation, gaining better control of corporate assets, and most importantly, being a driver of business transformation. Integrated data contributes to every one of these goals:

- **Reducing overall costs**—Integrated data minimizes supplier costs, reduces programming costs associated with building interfaces and maintaining redundant applications, reduces fraud, and minimizes the effort required to reconcile inconsistent reports. The cost savings associated with a single customer database include reducing administrative effort, reducing time spent switching between applications, not having to make multiple updates in disparate customer records, and not having to correct data inconsistency errors.

- **Increasing revenue**—Integrated data gives you a better perspective of each of your products and how much money you make or lose on each one of them. You can determine which products sell well in what geographic regions and to what type of customers, and you can determine which products do not sell well. By integrating data about your competitors, you can then compare your market share to theirs. This comparative analysis exposes opportunities to hone your marketing and sales strategy, thereby increasing your revenue.

- **Improving the supply chain**—A popular business intelligence (BI) application at manufacturing and retail organizations is the supply chain intelligence (SCI). SCI applications have proactive alert capabilities to notify supply chain managers and analysts via e-mail, pager, or cell phone about low inventory levels or shipment delays. This type of capability requires the integration of product data, inventory levels, order placements, and shipments. Some of these organizations already use radio frequency identification (RFID) technology to improve supply chain operations.

- **Reducing product development time**—Increasing the efficiency of your business processes and your daily business activities ultimately decreases your time to market. Bringing your products or services to market before your competition does increases your customer base and thus increases revenue—assuming your products and services are high quality and price-competitive. BI applications such as business performance management (BPM) and business activity monitoring (BAM) need an integrated set of metrics about your business processes, your organization, your suppliers, and your customers.

- **Providing better customer service**—Integrated customer and sales data gives your support personnel a more accurate view of your customers and their purchases. This enables your support staff to provide a more tailored solution, which should raise customer satisfaction. Satisfied customers are usually more receptive to cross-selling attempts made by customer representatives during a service call. Therefore, improving your customer service allows you to better market to your customers with the right products at the right time using the right channels while also resolving the customer's inquiry or complaint. It means that your customers do not have to deal with multiple points of contact or receive multiple solicitations and legal letters of notification, such as privacy policy letters.

- **Complying with information legislation**—A number of new laws mandate complete, consistent, and accurate information that can be realized only with data integrated from multiple areas in the organization. As an example, Section 302 under Title III of the U.S. Sarbanes-Oxley Act of 2002 (Public Company Accounting Reform and Investor Protection Act) mandates (among other things) the following:

  - Periodic statutory financial reports must fairly represent the financial condition of the organization in all material respects.

  - The reports cannot contain untrue statements, misleading statements, or material omissions.

  - The reports must include certifications of accuracy signed by the company officers who have reviewed the reports.

  - The signing officers are responsible for internal data quality controls.

Violations of the Sarbanes-Oxley Act not only lead to fines, but can result in the imprisonment of the signing officers. This might be the strongest reason for organizations to take data integration and data quality seriously.

- **Improving control of corporate assets**—A pool of integrated information about corporate assets is a necessary component of an organization's *business quality*. Market analysts use business quality metrics in their evaluation of stock prices and their recommendations to shareholders. Analysts look for ongoing reduction of inventory costs, quality control, a stream-lined supply chain with more effective purchasing and stocking, improved reusability of fixed assets, better utilization of personnel, and so on.

- **Being a driver of business transformation**—Effective use of information should lead to business process improvements, such as moving to a real-time business environment, developing productive and cost-saving part-nerships with suppliers and customers, streamlining internal business operations, and actually driving up productivity and superior customer service.

Business Case for Data Integration

Data integration is costly, but the cost of the effort is almost always justified if the integration project is properly managed. It also requires that the integration process goes to completion. If the project is cancelled half way through, most of the money expended will be lost. The justifications are numerous and com-pelling and should be reiterated at every meeting with senior management. Some compelling reasons for data integration are:

- **Reduced risk of litigation**—A prime example of cost-justifying a data integration project is the need for accuracy, consistency, and completeness in patient data. In the event that lab results indicate a life-threatening situ-ation, such as the signs of a heart attack, the healthcare provider should not only have access to those lab results, but also to other diagnostic data in the patient's medical record. All information about that patient needs to be accurate, consistent, and complete, so that the health care provider can prescribe the proper treatment, avoiding a potential malpractice lawsuit and the death of the patient.

- **Reduced risk of compliance failures**—The benefit of risk reduction should be considered as the cost of insurance. What would the organiza-tion be willing to pay to reduce the risk of a fine, perhaps a downgrade by Moody's and the investment community, and the unfavorable publicity that often accompanies compliance failure?

- **Retirement of legacy systems**—An integrated database can provide the opportunity to retire old legacy files and databases that store the data redundantly. This also allows the retirement of the maintenance and interface programs that support those databases.

- **Increased business agility**—In a climate in which speed is of the essence, many organizations don't understand why it takes IT so long to deliver information. And when IT finally produces the requested reports, the data on the reports is often inconsistent. Data integration leads to a reduction in databases and programs maintaining those databases, and it results in a more flexible and responsive IT infrastructure. This gives IT the ability to respond to information requirements more quickly, which gives the organization the capability to respond faster to the changing business environment and to competitive threats.

- **Fraud detection**—Another benefit of data integration is detection of fraud and abuse. For example, data mining applications can uncover transactions with stolen credit cards or fraudulent insurance claims connected with specific doctors and lawyers. The potential losses to a business from undetected fraud and abuse can easily justify any cost associated with data integration.

DATA INTEGRATION OPPORTUNITIES BY INDUSTRY

There are numerous data integration opportunities in every industry. The most common major subject areas are:

Consumer Goods
- Customers
- Suppliers
- Products
- Stores
- Inventory

Distribution
- Customers
- Assets
- Supply chain
- Warehousing
- Inventory

Finance and Banking
- Customers
- Accounts
- Products
- Branches

Government and Education
Federal Government
- Citizens
- Taxpayers
- Terrorists
- Visas

State and Municipal Government
- Citizens
- Taxpayers
- Service recipients

Universities
- Students
- Instructors
- Courses
- Enrollments
- Facilities
- Classrooms
- Exams and testing

Hospitality
- Guests
- Services
- Stays
- Facilities
- Locations
- Loyalty programs

Insurance
- Policies
- Policyholders
- Incidents

- Properties
- Claims
- Beneficiaries

Healthcare
- Patients
- Suppliers
- Treatments
- Hospitals
- Doctors
- Nurses
- Medication

Health Insurance
- Policies
- Policyholders
- Groups
- Claims
- Claimants
- Providers (doctors, hospitals)
- Services

Manufacturing and Distribution
- Customers
- Suppliers
- Distributors
- Products
- Parts
- Inventory

Retailers
- Customers
- Loyalty programs
- Suppliers
- Products
- Orders
- Inventory

Telephony
- Customers
- Products
- Services
- Equipment

Transportation
- Customers
- Suppliers
- Vehicle inventory
- Transportation routes

Utilities
- Customers
- Suppliers
- Services
- Installations
- Utilization (meters)

INTEGRATING BUSINESS DATA

As previously mentioned, integrating data is much more than connecting a few databases, building bridges among applications, or consolidating disparate data into one database. It also addresses the high percentage of data inconsistency and redundancy found in every organization. Integrating data is not a rote task that can be relegated to a tool. It is an important, precise, detailed, and rigorous analysis process performed by business analysts and data administrators. This process produces an inventory of data (either as logical data models or physical databases) in which all data is integrated within a common business context and appropriately deployed for maximum use in supporting the business information needs of the organization. This task is not without challenges.

Know Your Business Entities

Each organization has key business entities that are the heart of its business. Automobile manufacturers have dealers, distributors have suppliers, mortgage loan companies have brokers, and almost every organization has customers of one type or another (policyholders, depositors, borrowers, students, patients, citizens, nonprofit contributors, convicts, and so on). To effectively compete and be successful, organizations must understand these entities to the point of knowing their profiles including who they are; how they shop; what they buy; what services they use; what channels they prefer; their preferences for receiving marketing information; price sensitivities; service-level requirements; and quality requirements. The information about these entities must be integrated in a fashion that allows the organization to take clever and the most effective actions. For example, a banking customer can choose to use an automated teller machine (ATM), the bank's website, a voice response unit (VRU), a customer service representative (CSR), or the teller at the counter in the bank. The choice of customer channels has a major impact on the cost to the bank. Speaking to a CSR costs the bank between $6.00 and $10.00, whereas a Web inquiry costs only pennies.

Mergers and Acquisitions

When organizations are merged and businesses are acquired, the normal process is to integrate the two companies. The potential for cost savings related to the integration is usually one of the primary justifications for the merger. The operative word is *potential*. The reality can be quite different and it is up to the IT folks to determine just how technically difficult it will be for the two organizations in question to merge. Following are some of the difficulties involved in the process:

- Duplicate records—A customer might belong to the two companies that are merging.

- Duplicate keys—Even if primary keys are unique in each company's system, there might be overlapping numbers between the two companies.

- Different data types and different field lengths are used by the two companies.

- Data elements with the same names have different meanings.

- Data elements with the same meaning have different names.

- Corresponding data elements have different data values.

- Corresponding data elements have different business rules.

- If the two companies use different database management systems (DBMSs), there might be technical or design incompatibilities.

Many companies resolve only the two or three items that are technical hurdles to physical data integration, but they rarely address the other items that have a business impact, but not a technical impact. Sometimes, the reason given for the lack of rigorous data analysis is that expectations from the end users are difficult to manage. Managers and end users think that the integration process should be easy and fast (unless they have been through it before).

Data Redundancy

Data redundancy is rampant in almost every organization. It is not at all uncommon to find data repeated 10, 20, or even more times within the organization, and nobody knows which file is the system of record and which copy of the data most accurately reflects the real world. Although there are legitimate reasons for consciously maintaining controlled redundant data (such as performance, legal, and security reasons), *un*controlled redundant data contributes significantly to the costs of developing and maintaining multiple redundant databases and applications. The costs include programmer efforts, disk and machine costs, the reconciliation of inconsistent results, and the need to update (sometimes manually) multiple systems. Redundant data results in a loss of control, misunderstandings, and a continuing bad reputation for IT. The goal is to minimize data redundancy and have a single version of the true and accurate data.

How did the data get there and why is it redundant and different? It might have started off with the same raw data, but it was filtered, transformed, and had different business rules applied. A redundant set of data might have been created if the application developer for a new system was unaware of the existing data. The redundant data might have been consciously created when the owner of the new system did not want the political burdens of having to rely on another data owner.

Data Lineage

Webster's definition for lineage is "the direct descent from an ancestor." Data lineage is therefore the process of tracking the descendent data elements from their origins to their current instantiations. Because most organizations have a plethora of redundant data, it is important to know where the data came from to determine which data is the most reliable. Documenting the data lineage for each data element in a data dictionary or a metadata repository provides the origin and subsequent alterations and duplications of each data element. This data inventory is an invaluable data management resource. Not only does it provide guidance for correctly using data elements, but it is also extremely useful for impact analysis. One has to only remember the immense effort of Y2K impact analysis because most companies didn't—and still don't—track data lineage.

Establishing data lineage for each data element is a monumental effort given the fact that organizations have millions of data elements in thousands of files and tables. Being overwhelmed by the scope of the effort, most organizations do nothing. Rather than taking the all or nothing approach, a good place to start is on a DW project. For example, you can capture data lineage for the subset of data elements used by your DW with the metadata in the ETL tool. The tool tracks what data is sourced, how the data is transformed, and where it is stored for access. In addition to the ETL tool vendors, most BI and DW software vendors have some metadata capability to trace data lineage built into their products. This is an untapped resource that should be exploited.

Multiple DBMSs and Their Impact

Having multiple DBMSs can be an obstacle to data integration, especially when the same system is required to access these multiple DBMSs. Multiple DBMSs require more interface programs, which can get expensive. There will probably be integration problems including incompatible formats and data definitions. If data from multiple DBMSs needs to be joined, the optimizers are sure to be fooled, although some DBMS vendors claim omniscience and omnipotence for their optimizers. In addition, having multiple DBMSs also means more product expense to buy and maintain the software.

DECIDING WHAT DATA SHOULD BE INTEGRATED

Data integration is performed in two layers: logical and physical. Logical data integration is the process of building an enterprise logical data model—not all at once, but one project at a time as new systems are developed or old systems are converted. This process is described in greater detail in Chapter 5, "Data Modeling." Physical data integration is the process of filtering redundant data, retiring redundant files and databases, and combining data elements for the same business entity into one physical database. This process also includes stopping uncontrolled data propagation where data originates from a single provider application and then is propagated to individual, subscriber applications.

Data Integration Prioritization

You cannot boil the ocean; you have to prioritize your data integration deliverables. An enterprise-wide data integration effort must be carved up into small iterative projects, starting with the most critical data and working down to the less significant data. The business people working with the data integration team must determine which data is most appropriate for integration. Some data might not be suitable for integration at all, such as department-specific data, highly secured data, and data that is too risky to integrate. The team also needs to look at historical data and decide how much of it to include in the data integration process. This is especially true for DW and BI projects. The following points should be considered when determining which data to include in the integration process:

- **How will the data be used?**—This question can be answered by a process of gathering and comparing the information requirements of all the business units. In addition, the business units should be periodically pinged to determine if there is new data that should be integrated. It's also important to measure what data is accessed and how it is used. If that data is used by only one operational or decision support application, the integration effort on this data should be reconsidered because integrating data on a continual basis is expensive.

- **Political issues**—Some data owners might not want the data they control to be integrated and brought under the control of another data owner or made available to the entire enterprise. Information is a major source of power and many line-of-business managers recognize this and are loath to give it up. This data-retentive attitude can be solved only by the CEO who must clearly state that these data sources *will* be integrated and made available to the entire enterprise.

- **Security issues**—Some managers justify withholding the data based on security considerations, which may or may not be legitimate. They use the argument that they, and only they, can truly understand and interpret the data, and to let this data out of their control would be to invite the disaster of the unwashed running amok with incorrect conclusions and taking adverse actions. Many of those claims are bogus and should be overruled by the CEO. However, there are legitimate situations that require restrictions to data access on a need-to-know basis.

- **Regulatory and legal issues**—Some industries require a firewall between the vertical functions of their business. For example, Wall Street firms must have a separation between underwriting and brokerage. To comply with security and privacy laws (as well as internal policies), it might be against the law to have all the integrated information about a customer available to the marketing department. In the healthcare industry, HIPAA regulations deal with the restriction of a patient's private health information by placing strict limitations on who can access that data, although there are no general restrictions on integrating that data.

Risks of Data Integration

A number of risks are associated with data integration, such as lack of management commitment, cost and effort, sustainability, external data, data selection, and validation. These and the following should be considered carefully before the integration process begins, so that the investment in data integration is not wasted:

- **Management commitment**—For any significant data integration initiative to be successful, senior management must be committed to a long-run project for the initial implementation and must support the continued sustenance of the initiative. If management is short-term oriented or always focuses on the sexy, new application, it lacks the desire and ability to support a meaningful data integration initiative. To those immediate-gratification executives, data integration sometimes appears to provide few immediate demonstrable benefits. Management doesn't realize that the benefits include consistency across reports, such as the financial reports required by the Sarbanes-Oxley Act, recognition of a single, authoritative source of data, and uniform visibility across functional business units. Perhaps most importantly, management does not understand that data integration is a prerequisite to execute BI applications on any of the sought-after sexier architectural paradigms, such as service-oriented architectures.

- **Cost and effort**—We keep pointing out that integrating data is expensive. It requires an infrastructure including hardware and software. The software might already be in place, but there is no shortage of vendors who are eager to sell you their integration software. In addition, you need dedicated and smart internal personnel with strong analytical and technical skills who know the internal systems, know the important internal people, and are respected by those people. You might also want to consider bringing in consultants for the initial stages of the data integration project, but don't depend too much on them and don't put them in the role of the subject matter experts.

- **Sustainability**—The integrated data must be kept reasonably current. The level of currency should be based on how the data is used and the user requirements for currency. For example, a requirement for near real-time integrated data means the data must be close to up-to-the minute. Near real-time and especially real-time data requires a more demanding process for maintaining currency, which usually involves more sophisticated data movement techniques, such as messaging systems or database replication.

In a DW or BI environment, you have additional challenges. If data is integrated near-real-time for a DW, you need an ETL tool with "trickle-feed" processing capabilities. In addition, when source systems change, the ETL process must be modified to incorporate these changes before they are implemented in the operational systems. This can be a challenge if the DW staff does not have effective communication and notification procedures established with the operational systems people.

- **External data**—You will most likely bring data in from suppliers, distributors, and trading partners. If you are integrating customer data, you will be purchasing data from companies that specialize in capturing customer demographic data. Most organizations underestimate the difficulty of integrating this external data. It is often incomplete, less than clean, difficult to match to your data, out-of-date, and often poorly documented. You will probably be bringing in the data periodically, perhaps once a month or once a quarter, and the data supplier will often change the format, the meaning, or some other characteristic of the data, and that will cause problems.

- **Data selection and validation**—Validation has more to do with data quality, but it is relevant in selecting which data to use for the integration process and which data to filter. The dirtier the data, the more difficult it is to integrate. To state the obvious, be sure to first profile (evaluate) the different data sources, and then, if all other factors are reasonably similar, select the source with the cleanest data.

CONSOLIDATION AND FEDERATION

Data consolidation and data federation are alternatives to true data integration. The commitment to enterprise-wide data integration is usually found in organizations with a higher level of data management maturity than organizations that stop with data consolidation or data federation.

Data Consolidation

Many people confuse data integration with data consolidation. Consolidating data simply means gathering data elements that describe the same business entity (such as CUSTOMER) from multiple source databases and storing them in one database. Enterprise information integration (EII) tools, EAI products, and other messaging middleware can be used instead of, or in addition to, ETL tools to accomplish this data migration. Integrating data goes beyond that. In addition to consolidating data, integration enforces data uniqueness by standardizing the business data, enforcing business rules, and eliminating (or reducing and controlling) data redundancy. Integration also means that data is formally named, unambiguously defined, well architected, and its lineage is properly documented.

Many organizations choose to consolidate operational data into ERP products and in the process, attempt to standardize on one DBMS. Other organizations consolidate operational data into DW environments, either on the same DBMS as the operational systems or on a different DBMS platform. The impetus for both types of consolidation is two-fold: cost and control. Although data consolidation does not identify and eliminate every redundancy at the data element level, benefits are still realized because every old database that can be retired should result in cost savings for hardware (servers and disks), software (DBMS license and annual maintenance fees), and personnel (technicians who administered the old database and maintained the programs that kept the database current).

Data Federation

In a federated approach, data does not have to be consolidated or moved to a common, integrated database. A simplistic definition of data federation is leaving the data where it is, installing middleware (such as EAI or EII), and providing metadata to make people aware of the existence of the data, how current the data is, and how to get to it. This eliminates the need to convert, match, filter, and merge the data, and it avoids the struggles with data anomalies during the integration process. However, this approach requires complete and current metadata as well as clean and consistent business data, not to mention good quality processes to promote and allow federation.

The federated approach is not mutually exclusive with consolidation or integration. If the data is infrequently accessed, federation makes more sense because you don't have to pay for the effort of migrating this occasionally accessed data and changing all the programs affected by the migration.

Data Integration Strategy Capability Maturity Model

Similar to the data quality maturity levels explained in Chapter 3, "Data Quality," the generic capability maturity model (CMM) can be adapted to a company's data integration strategy, as summarized in Table 2.5.

Table 2.5: Data Integration CMM Levels

Level 1	Limited data federation; often with redundant and inconsistent data.
Level 2	Limited data consolidation; documenting redundancies and inconsistencies.
Level 3	Data integration initiated; new "*dis*integration" is discouraged.
Level 4	Data integration widely adopted; "*dis*integration" is penalized.
Level 5	Enterprise-wide data integration and other data strategy principles practiced by all departments in the organization.

On a scale of one to five, leaders of an organization at Level 1 wouldn't even be reading this book because they don't think they need a data strategy and data integration is not on their radar screen. At best, this organization might engage in some limited data federation, paying little or no attention to its redundant and inconsistent data. In an organization at Level 2, some isolated business units or individuals recognize the enormous business benefits of data integration. They are trying to raise awareness with their senior management while IT is attempting to at least consolidate some of its data into a DW environment. At Level 3, true data integration is discussed and an initiative is launched to create a data integration team, prioritize the data sources to be integrated, and set up policies and procedures to be followed to avoid further data *dis*integration. At Level 4, all projects in the organization comply with data integration policies and procedures, data redundancy is tightly controlled, and managers are held accountable for any intentional data *dis*integration. Leaders of organizations at Level 5 are probably also not reading this book because they have been practitioners of solid data strategy principles for a number of years.

GETTING STARTED

One of the first steps to get started with a data strategy in your organization is to assess the current state of your data assets. Only then can you come up with a strategy and a tactical implementation plan that addresses your specific problems in a sequence that has the highest payback for your organization. Take the following steps to create and implement a data strategy:

- **Measure**—Start by measuring the costs associated with the "*dis*integrated" data in your organization. Although most realize that they have data problems, few take the time to quantify the costs associated with those problems.

- **Educate**—Show the costs of your "*dis*integrated" data to your executives and business managers. Give specific examples that they will be familiar with and care about. Tie your findings to the bottom line of the company's profit and loss statement.

- **Get sponsorship**—Data integration initiatives can be sustained only with strong executive sponsorship. You have to secure at least one sponsor, preferably several. The sponsor must be a business person—not just the CIO or CTO—who is heavily committed to the data integration project. He or she should be a senior executive who is well respected and influential in your organization.

- **Prioritize**—Find out which data your business people consider to be the most critical and which data is used by many of them. Also determine what types of regulations affect your data (for example, SEC regulations or security and privacy laws).

- **Research**—Data integration requires an in-depth knowledge of your business data. You need to know the semantics of the data, how the data was derived, any security and privacy considerations, who the data owners are, the data domains, the business rules, and how the data is processed (entry and exit points) in your organization.

- **Recruit**—Data integration, like data quality, should be a business-driven activity. Recruit business people, such as business analysts and subject matter experts, who will actively participate on data integration projects, if not lead them. You also need technicians who know the source systems, the files and databases, the data element names, data types and field lengths, and who can read the programs that create and manipulate the data. Every member on this data integration team must be dedicated to the integration project. This is not a part-time activity.

- **Plan**—Have the data integration team assess and discuss the different approaches, tools, and architectures to determine how to best integrate data in your environment. Try to weave yourself into ongoing projects and use that opportunity to educate the masses and arrest any further proliferation of data redundancy. This is not a lightweight activity.

- **Execute**—After you have a tactical plan for data integration, data consolidation, and, or data federation, execute it. Measure your results! Are the benefits being realized? Did you overestimate or underestimate the cost? What are you hearing from the business people? Do you have to make any adjustments to your plan or your approach? Report the results to management.

- **Adapt**—Nothing should be cast in concrete. With every project, you learn more about the business data, your business people, their information requirements, your platform capacity, and so on. Be flexible and adapt your plan as well as your approach, so that they make the most sense and have the highest benefit for your organization.

CONCLUSION

Data integration is a topic that is well publicized, much talked about, and heavily hyped by many tool vendors. It is a complicated topic that requires considerable effort if implemented to its fullest extent. The alternatives to data integration are data consolidation and data federation. EII and EAI middleware technology can and should be utilized when appropriate and cost-effective, but realize that true data integration cannot be achieved by technology alone. It requires a strategy, a plan, a team, skills, sponsorship, and an ongoing commitment from the end users.

REFERENCES

Brackett, Michael H. *The Data Warehouse Challenge: Taming Data Chaos.* New York: John Wiley & Sons, 1996.

Hall, Curt. BI Advisory Service, Executive Update, Vol. 4, No. 6. Andover, MA: Cutter Consortium, 2004.

Levy, Evan. Baseline Consulting Group. "Architectural Alternatives for Data Integration," TDWI FlashPoint, September 22, 2004.

Linthicum, David. *Enterprise Application Integration.* Boston, MA: Addison Wesley, 2000.

CHAPTER 3

Data Quality

"Virtually everything in business today is an undifferentiated commodity, except how a company manages its information. How you manage information determines whether you win or lose."

—Bill Gates

Everybody wants better quality of data. Some organizations hope to improve data quality by moving data from legacy systems to enterprise resource planning (ERP) and customer relationship management (CRM) packages. Other organizations use data profiling or data cleansing tools to unearth dirty data, and then cleanse it with an extract/transform/load (ETL) tool for data warehouse (DW) applications. All of these technology-oriented data quality improvement efforts are commendable—and definitely a step in the right direction. However, technology solutions alone cannot eradicate the root causes of poor quality data because poor quality data is not as much an IT problem as it is a business problem.

Other enterprise-wide disciplines must be developed, taught, implemented, and enforced to improve data quality in a holistic, cross-organizational way. Because data quality improvement is a process and not an event, the following enterprise-wide disciplines should be phased in and improved upon over time:

- A stronger personal involvement by management

- High-level leadership for data quality

- New incentives

- New performance evaluation measures

- Data quality enforcement policies

- Data quality audits

- Additional training for data owners and data stewards about their responsibilities

- Data standardization rules

- Metadata and data inventory management techniques

- A common data-driven methodology

CURRENT STATE OF DATA QUALITY

We repeatedly run into a common example of data quality problems when trying to speak with a customer service representative (CSR) of a bank, credit card company, or telephone company. An automated voice response system prompts you to key in your account number before passing your call to a CSR. When a person finally answers the call, you are asked to repeat your account number because the system did not pass it along. Where did the keyed-in data go?

Another more serious data quality problem involves a report in 2003 about the federal General Accounting Office (GAO) not being able to tell how many H-1B visa holders worked in the U.S. The GAO was missing key data and its systems were not integrated. This presented a major challenge to the Department of Homeland Security, which tried to track all visa holders in the U.S.

According to Gartner, Inc., Fortune 1000 enterprises may lose more money in operational inefficiency due to data quality issues than they spend on data warehouse and CRM initiatives. In 2003, the Data Warehouse Institute (TDWI) estimated that data quality problems cost U.S. businesses $600 billion each year.

At an Information Quality Conference in 2002, a telecom company revealed that it recovered over $100 million in "scrap and rework" costs, a bank claimed to have recovered $60 million, and a government agency recovered $28.8 million on an initial investment of $3.75 million. Clearly, organizations and government are slowly realizing that data quality is not optional.

Many companies realize that they did not pay sufficient attention to data while developing systems during the last few decades. While delivery schedules have been shrinking, project scopes have been increasing, and companies have been struggling to implement applications in a timeframe that is acceptable to their business community. Because a day has only 24 hours, something has to give, and what usually gives is quality, especially data quality.

RECOGNIZING DIRTY DATA

When asked to define "data quality," people usually think of error-free data entry. It is true that sloppy data entry habits are often the culprit, but data quality is also affected by the way we store and manage data. For example, old file structures, such as flat files, did not have strong data typing rules, and it was common practice to use REDEFINE and OCCURS clauses with those structures. A REDEFINE clause allows you to change the data type of a data element or a group of data elements. For example, a character name field can be redefined and reused as a numeric amount field or a date field. An OCCURS clause allows you to define an array of repeating data elements. For example, an amount field can occur 1–12 times, if you were capturing monthly totals for January through December. Relational database management systems and the new generation of object-oriented programming practices no longer encourage such untidy data typing habits, but they do not provide any deterrence for other types of data abuse, such as some extensible markup language (XML) document type definition (DTD) usage that propagates into the relational databases. Many of the dirty data examples described in the following list can be found in relational databases as often as they can be found in flat files:

- **Incorrect data**—For data to be correct (valid), its values must adhere to its domain (valid values). For example, a month must be in the range of 1–12, or a person's age must be less than 130. Correctness of data values can usually be programmatically enforced with edit checks and by using lookup tables.

- **Inaccurate data**—A data value can be correct without being accurate. For example, the state code "CA" and the city name "Boston" are both correct, but when used together (such as Boston, CA), the state code is wrong because the city of Boston is in the state of Massachusetts, and the accurate state code for Massachusetts is "MA." Accuracy of dependent data values is difficult to programmatically enforce with simple edit checks or lookup tables. Sometimes it is possible to check against other fields or other files to determine if a data value is accurate in the context in which it is used. However, many times accuracy can be validated only by manually spot-checking against paper files or asking a person (for instance, a customer, vendor, or employee) to verify the data.

- **Business rule violations**—Another type of inaccurate data value is one that violates business rules. For example, an effective date should always precede an expiration date. Another example of a business rule violation might be a Medicare claim for a patient who is not yet of retirement age and does not qualify for Medicare.

- **Inconsistent data**—Uncontrolled data redundancy results in inconsistencies. Every organization is plagued with redundant and inconsistent data. This is especially prevalent with customer data. For example, a customer name on the order database might be "Mary Karlinsky," the same name on the customer database might be "Maria Louise Karlinsky," and on a downstream customer-relationship, decision-support system the same name might be spelled "Mary L. Karlynski."

- **Incomplete data**—During system requirements definition, we rarely bother to gather the data requirements from down-stream information consumers, such as the marketing department. For example, if we build a system for the lending department of a financial institution, the users of that department will most likely list Initial Loan Amount, Monthly Payment Amount, and Loan Interest Rate as some of the most critical data elements. However, the most important data elements for users of the marketing department are probably Gender Code, Customer Age, or Zip Code of the borrower. Thus, in a system built for the lending department, data elements, such as Gender Code, Customer Age, and Zip Code might not be captured at all, or only haphazardly. This often is the reason why so many data elements in operational systems have missing values or default values.

- **Nonintegrated data**—Most organizations store data redundantly and inconsistently across many systems, which were never designed with integration in mind. Primary keys often don't match or are not unique, and in some cases, they don't even exist. More and more frequently, the development or maintenance of systems is outsourced and even off-shored, which puts data consistency and data quality at risk. For example, customer data can exist on two or more outsourced systems under different customer numbers with different spellings of the customer name and even different phone numbers or addresses. Integrating data from such systems is a challenge.

DATA QUALITY RULES

There are four categories of data quality rules. The first category contains rules about business objects or business entities. The second category contains rules about data elements or business attributes. The third category of rules pertains to various types of dependencies between business entities or business attributes, and the fourth category relates to data validity rules.

Business Entity Rules

Business entities are subject to three data quality rules: uniqueness, cardinality, and optionality. These rules have the following properties:

- **Uniqueness**—There are four basic rules to business entity uniqueness:

    - Every instance of a business entity has its own unique identifier. This is equivalent to saying that every record must have a unique primary key.

    - In addition to being unique, the identifier must always be known. This is equivalent to saying that a primary key can never be NULL.

    - Rule number three applies only to composite or concatenated keys. A *composite key* is a unique identifier that consists of more than one business attribute. This is equivalent to saying that a primary key is made up of several columns. The rule states that a unique identifier must be minimal. This means the identifier can consist only of the minimum number of columns it takes to make each value unique— no more, no less.

    - The fourth rule also applies to composite keys only. It declares that one, many, or all business attributes comprising the unique identifier can be a data relationship between two business entities. This is equivalent to saying that a composite primary key can contain one or more foreign keys.

- **Cardinality**—Cardinality refers to the degree of a relationship, that is, the number of times one business entity can be related to another. There are only three types of cardinality possible. The "correct" cardinality in every situation depends completely on the definition of your business entities and the business rules governing those entities. You have three choices for cardinality:

  - One-to-one cardinality means that a business entity can be related to another business entity once and only once in both directions. For example, a man is married to one and only one woman at one time, and in reverse, a woman is married to one and only one man at one time, at least in most parts of the world.

  - One-to-many (or many-to-one) cardinality means that a business entity can be related to another business entity many times, but the second business entity can be related to the first only once. For example, a school is attended by many children, but each child attends one and only one school.

  - Many-to-many cardinality means that a business entity can be related to another business entity many times in both directions. For example, an adult supports many children, and each child is supported by many adults (in the case of a mother and father supporting a son and a daughter).

- **Optionality**—Optionality is a type of cardinality, but instead of specifying the maximum number of times two business entities can be related, it identifies the minimum number of times they can be related. There are only two options: either two business entities must be related at least once (mandatory relationship) or they don't have to be related (optional relationship). Optionality rules are sometimes called reference rules because they are implemented in relational databases as the referential integrity rules: cascade, restrict, and nullify. Optionality has a total of five rules; the first three apply to the degree of the relationship:

  - One-to-one optionality means that two business entities are tightly coupled. If an instance of one entity exists, then it must be related to at least one instance of the second entity. Conversely, if an instance of the second entity exists, it must be related to at least one instance of the first. For example, a store must offer at least one product, and in reverse, if a product exists, it must be offered through at least one store.

- One-to-zero (or zero-to-one) optionality means that one business entity has a mandatory relationship to another business entity, but the second entity does not require a relationship back to the first. For example, a customer has purchased at least one product (or he wouldn't be a customer on the database), but conversely, a product may exist that has not yet been purchased by any customer.

- Zero-to-zero optionality indicates a completely optional relationship between two business entities in both directions. For example, the department of motor vehicles issues drivers licenses and car licenses. A recently licensed driver may be related to a recently licensed car and vice versa, but this relationship is not mandatory in either direction.

- Every instance of an entity that is being referenced by another entity in the relationship must exist. This is equivalent to saying that when a relationship is instantiated through a foreign key, the referenced row with the same primary key must exist in the other table. For example, if a child attends a school and the school number is the foreign key on the CHILD table, then the same school number must exist as the primary key on the SCHOOL table.

- The reference attribute does not have to be known when an optional relationship is not instantiated. This is equivalent to saying that the foreign key can be NULL on an optional relationship.

Business Attribute Rules

Business attributes are subject to two data quality rules, not counting dependency and validity rules. The two rules are data inheritance and data domains:

- **Data inheritance**—The inheritance rule applies only to supertypes and subtypes. Business entities can be of a generalized type called a supertype, or they can be of a specialized type called a subtype. For example, ACCOUNT is a supertype entity, whereas CHECKING ACCOUNT and SAVINGS ACCOUNT are two subtype entities of ACCOUNT. There are three data inheritance rules:

  - All generalized business attributes of the supertype are inherited by all subtypes. In other words, data elements that apply to all subtypes are stored in the supertype and are automatically applicable to all subtypes. For example, the data element Account Open Date applies to all types of accounts. It is therefore an attribute of the supertype

ACCOUNT and automatically applies to the subtypes CHECKING ACCOUNT and SAVINGS ACCOUNT.

• The unique identifier of the supertype is the same unique identifier of its subtypes. This is equivalent to saying that the primary key is the same for the supertype and its subtypes. For example, the account number of a person's checking account is the same account number, regardless of whether it identifies the supertype ACCOUNT or the subtype CHECKING ACCOUNT.

• All business attributes of a subtype must be unique to that subtype only. For example, the data element Interest Rate is applicable to savings accounts, but not checking accounts, and must therefore reside on the subtype SAVINGS ACCOUNT. If the checking accounts were interest bearing, then a new layer of generalization would have to be introduced to separate interest-bearing from noninterest-bearing accounts.

• **Data domains**—Domains refer to a set of allowable values. For structured data, this can be any of the following:

  • A list of values, such as the 50 U.S. state codes (AL … WY)

  • A range of values (between 1 and 100)

  • A constraint on values (less than 130)

  • A set of allowable characters (a … z, 0 … 9, $, &, =)

  • A pattern, such as a date (CCYY/MM/DD)

Data domain rules for unstructured data are much more difficult to determine and have to include meta tags to be properly associated with any corresponding structured data. Unstructured data refers to free-form text (such as web pages or e-mails), images (such as videos or photos), sound (such as music or voice messages), and so on. We describe unstructured data in more detail in Chapter 11, "Strategies for Managing Unstructured Data."

Data Dependency Rules

The data dependency rules apply to data relationships between two or more business entities as well as to business attributes. There are seven data dependency rules: three for entity relationships and four for attributes:

- **Entity-relationship dependency**—The three entity-relationship dependency rules are:

  - The existence of a data relationship depends on the state (condition) of another entity that participates in the relationship. For example, orders cannot be placed for a customer whose status is "delinquent."

  - The existence of one data relationship mandates that another data relationship also exists. For example, when an order is placed by a customer, then a salesperson also must be associated with that order.

  - The existence of one data relationship prohibits the existence of another data relationship. For example, an employee who is assigned to a project cannot be enrolled in a training program.

- **Attribute dependency**—The four attribute dependency rules are:

  - The value of one business attribute depends on the state (condition) of the entity in which the attributes exist. For example, when the status of a loan is "funded," the value of Loan Amount must be greater than ZERO and the value of Funding Date must not be NULL. The correct value of one attribute depends on, or is derived from, the values of two or more other attributes. For example, the value of Pay Amount must equal Hours Worked multiplied by Hourly Pay Rate.

  - The allowable value of one attribute is constrained by the value of one or more other attributes in the same business entity or in a different but related business entity. For example, when Loan Type Code is "ARM4" and the Funding Date is prior to 20010101, then the Ceiling Interest Rate cannot exceed the Floor Interest Rate by more than 6 percent.

  - The existence of one attribute value prohibits the existence of another attribute value in the same business entity or in a different but related business entity. For example, when the Monthly Salary Amount is greater than ZERO, then the Commission Rate must be NULL.

Data Validity Rules

Data validity rules govern the quality of data values, also known as data domains. There are six validity rules to consider:

- **Data completeness**—The data completeness rule comes in four flavors:

  - *Entity* completeness requires that all instances exist for all business entities. In other words, all records or rows are present.

- *Relationship* completeness refers to the condition that referential integrity exists among all referenced business entities.

- *Attribute* completeness states that all business attributes for each business entity exist. In other words, all columns are present.

- *Domain* completeness demands that all business attributes contain allowable values and that NULL values can be differentiated from missing values.

- **Data correctness**—This rule requires that all data values for a business attribute must be correct and representative of the attribute's:

  - Definition (the values must reflect the intended meaning of the attribute)

  - Specific individual domains (list of valid values)

  - Applicable business rules

  - Supertype inheritance (if applicable)

  - Identity rule (primary keys)

- **Data accuracy**—This rule states that all data values for a business attribute must be accurate in terms of the attribute's dependency rules and its state in the real world.

- **Data precision**—This rule specifies that all data values for a business attribute must be as precise as required by the attribute's:

  - Business requirements

  - Business rules

  - Intended meaning

  - Intended usage

  - Precision in the real world

- **Data uniqueness**—There are five aspects to the data uniqueness rule:

  - Every business entity instance must be unique, which means no duplicate records or rows.

  - Every business entity must have only one unique identifier, which means no duplicate primary keys.

- Every business attribute must have only one unique definition, which means there are no homonyms.

- Every business attribute must have only one unique name, which means there are no synonyms.

- Every business attribute must have only one unique domain, which means there are no overloaded columns. An overloaded column is a column that is used for more than one purpose. For example, a Customer Type Code has the values A, B, C, D, E, F, where A, B, and C describe a type of customer (for example, a corporation, partnership, or individual), but D, E, and F describe a type of shipping method (for example, USPS, FedEx, or UPS). In this case, the attribute Customer Type Code is overloaded because it is used for two different purposes.

- **Data consistency**—Use the following two rules to enforce data consistency:

  - The data values for a business attribute must be consistent when the attribute is duplicated for performance reasons or when it is stored redundantly for any other reason, such as special timeliness requirements or data distribution issues. Data should never be stored redundantly because of departmental politics, or because you don't trust the data from another user, or because you have some other control issues.

  - The duplicated data values of a business attribute must be based on the same domain (allowable values) and on the same data quality rules.

DATA QUALITY IMPROVEMENT PRACTICES

Many organizations still sidestep long-term data quality improvement practices in favor of achieving short-term goals. However, an increasing number of organizations realize that the consequences of not addressing the poor quality of data may result in adverse effects, such as customer attrition or severe loss in market share. Analyst firms, such as the Gartner Group, have warned of consequences as grave as total business failures.

Data Profiling

The first step in improving data quality is to uncover your data defects through data profiling, sometimes called data archeology, which is the process of analyzing the data for correctness, completeness, uniqueness, consistency, and reasonability. Once a difficult and tedious task requiring dozens of SQL and 4GL/5GL programs searching through every record on every file or database to find data anomalies, data profiling, data cleansing tools now have the capability to profile the data for you.

Similarly, you may be able to leverage some functions of your data mining tool to assess your data quality. For example, Teradata's data mining tool Warehouse Miner has two functions that can be used for source data analysis. Their "values analysis" function identifies characteristics of the data values, such as ZEROs, NULLs, and number of unique values, whereas their "overlap analysis" function identifies the number of overlapping keys that the tables share, which is helpful for data mart consolidation. Histograms and scatter plots allow you to visually detect outliers. In addition, the SQL generated by the tool can be run against the entire database to quickly differentiate the aberrant value deviations from the norm.

Data Cleansing

After the extent of "dirty data" is known, the easiest place to start the data quality improvement process is by cleansing operational data at the time it is moved into DW databases where it is used for cross-organizational reporting. However, data cleansing is a labor-intensive, time-consuming, and expensive process, and cleansing all the data is usually neither cost-justified nor practical. On the other hand, cleansing none of the data is equally unacceptable. It is therefore important to carefully analyze the source data and to classify the data elements as critical, important, or insignificant to the business. Then, concentrate on cleansing all the critical data elements, and as time permits, cleanse as many of the important data elements as practical, leaving the insignificant data elements unchanged. In other words, you do not need to cleanse all the data, and you do not need to do it all at once.

Another factor that will influence your ability to cleanse the data is whether the correct data still exists or whether it can be recreated with a minimal amount of manual or automated effort. There are situations where values are so convoluted or disparate—even with different and opposing meanings to the same fact—that any attempt to decipher such data might produce even worse results. In that case, it might be best to just leave the data alone.

Another decision to make is *how* to cleanse what can reasonably be cleansed. Can the data cleansing products on the market today handle most of the common data quality problems? The answer is yes. Are the data cleansing and extract/transform/load (ETL) products on the market capable of resolving all of the complicated and unique "dirty data" situations on all of your platforms, and will they ever be? The answer is probably no. Therefore, if you are truly serious about creating value-added information out of the dirty data, then you will probably have to invest in writing some procedural code to supplement the capabilities of your tools.

Data Defect Prevention

The next decision to make is how to prevent future "dirty data" from being entered. That begins by identifying the root causes for the data defects, which can be a combination of the following:

- Defective program logic

- Not enough program edits

- Not understanding the meaning of a data element

- No common metadata

- No domain definitions

- No reconciliation process

- No data verification process

- Poor data entry training

- Inadequate time for data entry

- No incentive for quality data entry

The owners of the operational systems should plan to improve their programs and edit checks, unless the effort is unreasonably high. For example, if the corrective action requires changing the file structure, which means modifying (if not rewriting) most of the programs that access that file, then the cost for such an invasive corrective action on the operational system is probably not justifiable—especially if the bad data does not interfere with the operational needs of that system. This type of decision cannot—and should not—be made by IT alone. Downstream information consumers must negotiate with the data originators about justifying and prioritizing the data quality improvement steps.

A data governance group should be established at the enterprise level, which should be staffed with data administrators, metadata administrators, and data quality stewards:

- **Data administrators**—These people are responsible for the enterprise logical data model, for establishing and maintaining naming standards, and for capturing data-related business rules.

- **Metadata administrators**—These people are responsible for loading, linking, managing, and disseminating metadata to facilitate the common understanding of data and to encourage data reuse. Metadata is the contextual information about the data. Metadata components include data names, data definitions, business rules, data content (domains), data type, data length, data owner, data transformations, degree of cleanliness, and so on.

- **Data quality stewards**—These people are charged with preventing the propagation of inferior quality data throughout the enterprise, and thus, the decision-making processes. Therefore, it is their responsibility to perform regular data audits on business data, metadata, and data models, and to be involved in data reconciliation efforts by helping to identify and resolve the root causes of data quality issues. The findings of the audits and reconciliation efforts should feed back into a continuous data quality improvement cycle.

Data quality training should be instituted to address poor data entry habits. Not all data rules can be enforced through edit checks or by the features of relational databases, such as strong data typing, referential integrity, use of look-up tables, and the use of stored edit procedures. Many data violations can still occur because of human error, negligence, or intentionally introduced errors. For example, if an end user needs a new data element but must wait six months for IT to change the database, then the end user might simply decide to *overload* an existing column and use it for dual (or triple) purposes, such as putting the date of the last promotion into the Account Closed Date column.

ENTERPRISE-WIDE DATA QUALITY DISCIPLINES

Organizations have a number of data quality disciplines at their disposal, but rarely will they implement all disciplines at once because improving data quality is a process and not an event. This process is measured on a data quality maturity scale of 1–5. Depending on how fast an organization advances through the data quality maturity levels, it will either institute stringent, light, or no disciplines.

Data Quality Maturity Levels

An easy way to determine your organization's level of data quality maturity is to look at your current data quality improvement activities. Figure 3.1 shows the common data quality improvement activities in each of the five data quality maturity levels based on Larry English's adaptation of the capability maturity model (CMM) to data quality. The five levels are:

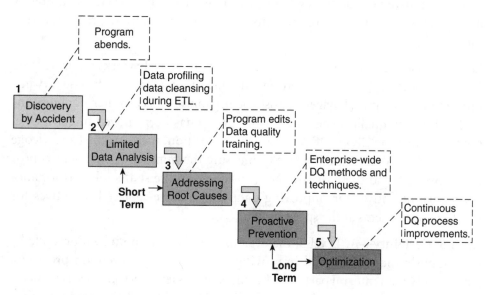

Figure 3.1: Data Quality Improvement Activities

Level 1: Uncertainty—At Level 1, the organization is stumbling over data defects as its programs abend (crash) or its information consumers complain. There is no proactive data quality improvement process, no data quality group, and no funding. The organization denies any serious data quality problems and considers data analysis a waste of time. Or the CIO is ready to retire and doesn't want anything to disrupt it. Basically, the organization is asleep and doesn't want to be awakened.

Level 2: Awakening—At Level 2, the organization performs some limited data analysis and data correction activities, such as data profiling and data cleansing. There still is no enterprise-wide support for data quality improvement, no data quality group, and no funding. However, a few isolated individuals acknowledge their dirty data and want to incorporate data quality disciplines in their projects. These individuals can be data administrators, database administrators, developers, or business people.

Level 3: Enlightenment—At Level 3, the organization starts to address the root causes of its dirty data through program edits and data quality training. A data quality group is created and funding for data quality improvement projects is available. The data quality group immediately performs an enterprise-wide data quality assessment of their critical files and databases, and prioritizes the data quality improvement activities. This group also institutes several data quality disciplines and launches a comprehensive data quality training program across the organization.

Level 4: Wisdom—At Level 4, the organization proactively works on preventing future data defects by adding more data quality disciplines to its data quality improvement program. Managers across the organization accept personal responsibility for data quality. The data quality group has been moved under a chief officer—either the CIO, COO, CFO, or a new position, such as a chief knowledge officer (CKO). Metrics are in place to measure the number of data defects produced by staff, and these metrics are considered in the staff's job performance appraisals. Incentives for improving data quality have replaced incentives for cranking out systems at the speed of light.

Level 5: Certainty—At Level 5, the organization is in an optimization cycle by continuously monitoring and improving its data defect prevention processes. Data quality is an integral part of all business processes. Every job description requires attention to data quality, reporting of data defects, determining the root causes, improving the affected data quality processes to eliminate the root causes, and monitoring the effects of the improvement. Basically, the culture of the organization has changed.

Standards and Guidelines

Data quality does not happen by accident. Organizations must establish standards and guidelines for all personnel to follow to ensure that data quality is addressed during the entire lifecycle of a system. For example, standards should be established for defining the data, naming the data, establishing domains and business rules, and modeling the data. Guidelines should be in place for data entry, edit checking, validating and auditing of data, correcting data errors, and removing the root causes of data contamination. Training and familiarization with the standards and guidelines should be required of all data entry staff, developers, data stewards, and information consumers.

Standards and guidelines should also include policies and procedures, such as operating procedures, change-control procedures, issue management procedures, and data dispute resolution procedures. Additional policies and procedures should be considered for the communication processes, estimating guidelines, roles and responsibilities, and standard documentation formats.

Development Methodology

A development methodology is a common roadmap that provides a complete list of all the major activities and tasks to be performed on projects. The trouble with traditional methodologies is that they do not support cross-organizational data integration activities because operational systems were rarely designed with integration in mind. But increasing demand for integrated systems (including ERP, CRM, and DW) requires a new type of data-driven methodology that includes the appropriate data quality improvement tasks. For example, the methodology must have a separate development step for incrementally building the enterprise logical data model and enforcing data standardization across all projects.

Data Naming and Abbreviations

Data naming and abbreviation standards provide consistency and a common look and feel that are useful for both developers and business people. Proven standards can be applied, such as the convention of name compositions using prime words, qualifiers or modifiers, and class words. Data administrators are usually trained in the various industry-standard naming conventions.

Abbreviations are part of naming standards, but they apply only to physical names, such as column names, table names, or program names. Business names should always be spelled out for clarity and understanding regardless of how long they are. You should publish a standard enterprise-wide abbreviations list that includes industry-specific and organization-specific acronyms. Every project team should use these abbreviations and acronyms.

Metadata

Metadata is descriptive contextual information about architectural components. Metadata can be business metadata, technical metadata, process metadata, and usage metadata. Large amounts of business metadata can be collected about business functions, business processes, business entities, business attributes (data elements), business rules, and data quality. Technical metadata represents the physical architectural components, such as programs, scripts, databases, tables, columns, keys, and indices. Process metadata describes any type of program logic that manipulates data during data capture, data movement, or data retrieval. Usage metadata is statistical information about how systems are used by the business people. For example, what type of data is accessed, by whom, how often, and for what purpose.

You should set up standards or guidelines that govern who captures which metadata components and how, when, and where to capture them. The metadata repository should be set up in such a way that it supports the standards for metadata capture and usage. Metadata is discussed in more detail in Chapter 4, "Metadata."

Data Modeling

There is a difference between logical data modeling and physical data modeling. A logical data model is a normalized business model and a physical data model is a denormalized database design model, also known as a logical database design. These two different types of data models are described in Chapter 5, "Data Modeling." Data quality must be addressed in both sets of models. In addition, the data models themselves must meet data-modeling quality standards with respect to data policies and modeling rules, such as compliance with naming conventions, consistent use of data types and data domains for semantically equivalent attributes, and so on.

For the purpose of finding redundant and inconsistent data, logical entity-relationship modeling with complete data normalization is still the most effective technique because it is a business analysis technique that includes identification, rationalization, and standardization of data through business metadata. Because every business activity or business function uses or manipulates data in some fashion, a logical data model documents those logical data relationships and the business rules, regardless of how the data or the functions are implemented in the physical databases and applications.

Logical data models created for individual applications should be merged into one cohesive, integrated enterprise logical data model. This activity is usually performed by the data administration department, which might be part of the data quality group. The enterprise logical data model is the baseline business information architecture into which physical files and databases are mapped. You should establish standards for creating logical data models as part of system development activities and for merging the models into the enterprise logical data model.

Data Quality

Because most organizations have a lot of dirty data—too much to cleanse it all— they must establish guidelines about triaging (categorizing and prioritizing) dirty data for cleansing. Some data is critical to the organization, some is important but not critical, and some is nice to have but relatively insignificant to the business people. You should create standards that define acceptable data quality thresholds for each of these categories and specify how to measure data quality during and after database updates. Processing rules for error handling and suspending dirty data records for subsequent correction also should be part of the standards.

Testing

You should specify what types of testing should be performed during system development and who should participate in the various types of testing. Specific types of testing include unit testing, integration or regression testing, performance testing, quality assurance testing, and user acceptance testing. Guidelines should be established that describe the types of test cases required, how much regression testing to perform, and under what circumstances to regression test. Testing guidelines should include a brief description of a test plan, perhaps even a template, as well as instructions for how to organize and manage the various testing activities.

Reconciliation

Similar to testing, yet in a separate category, is reconciling the results of any data manipulation, which is the process of capturing, storing, extracting, merging, separating, copying, moving, changing, or deleting data. This is especially true for DW applications that extract data from multiple operational source files and merge the data into one target database. If your organization has adopted an architected data mart strategy, then the various data marts also have to be reconciled to each other to guarantee consistency. This includes having one central staging area with extensive reconciliation programming for every input-process-output module.

Security

Security guidelines apply to operational systems as well as decision-support systems. The only time data security can be slightly relaxed is in data marts where data is highly summarized and the ability to drill down to the details is not enabled. You should establish security standards to guide the project teams on what types of security measures are mandatory for what types of data exposure. The security standards should have guidelines for categorizing data sensitivity and risks of exposure for the organization. Security standards should cover application security, network security, database security, and Web security against intrusions, hackers, and viruses.

Data Quality Metrics

Data quality metrics ordinarily reflect the explicit as well as the implicit business principles of an organization. Business principles are explicit if stated in mission or vision statements, implicit if they are just "understood" by the staff. For example, if an organization rewards project managers for meeting deadlines even though their applications are full of errors, while it punishes project managers for missing deadlines even though their applications are flawless, then the implicit principle is "speed before quality." Therefore, when creating data quality metrics, the explicit as well as implicit business principles must be reviewed and changed, if necessary, to support the metrics.

Another important aspect to measuring data quality is setting goals. Organizations need to be clear on where they are today and what they're trying to achieve in the short term, medium term, and long term. What are the priorities in the organization? Should operational data be addressed or only analytical data? Should financial data be cleansed first or a specific subject area for an application, such as CRM? What is the plan for incrementally managing data quality improvements? What are the staffing requirements and what are the roles and responsibilities for a data quality improvement initiative? These questions must be answered to develop meaningful and actionable data quality metrics.

ENTERPRISE ARCHITECTURE

Creating and maintaining an enterprise architecture (EA) is a popular method for controlling data redundancies as well as process redundancies, and thereby reducing the anomalies and inconsistencies that are inherently produced by uncontrolled redundancies. EA is comprised of models that describe an organization in terms of its business architecture (business functions, business processes, business data, and so on) and technical architecture (applications, databases, and so on). The purpose of these models is to describe the actual business in which the organization engages. EA is applicable to all organizations, large and small. Because EA models are best built incrementally, one project at a time, it is appropriate to develop EA models on DW and BI projects, as well as on projects that simply solve departmental challenges.

EA includes at least five models, with the business data model and metadata repository being the two most important components for data quality.

- **Business Function model**—This model shows the hierarchy of business functions of an organization. In other words, it shows *what* the organization does. This model is used for organizing or reorganizing the company into its lines of business.

- **Business Process model**—This model shows the business processes being performed for the business functions. In other words, it shows *how* the organization performs its business functions. This model is used for business process reengineering and business process improvement initiatives.

- **Business Data model**—This model is the enterprise logical data model, also known as enterprise information architecture, that shows what *data* supports the business functions and business processes. This model contains:

    - Business objects (data entities)

    - Business activities involving these entities (data relationships)

    - Data stored about these entities (attributes)

    - Rules governing these entities and their attributes (metadata)

  In the real world, business objects and data about those objects are intrinsically unique. Therefore, they appear as entities and attributes once and only once on a business data model, regardless of how many times they are redundantly stored in physical files and databases. There should be only *one* business data model for an organization showing the "single version of the truth" or the "360-degree view" of the organization.

- **Application inventory**—The application inventory is a description of the physical implementation objects that support the organization such as applications (programs and scripts), databases, and other technical components. It shows *where* the architectural pieces reside in the technical architecture. You should always catalog and document your systems because such inventories are crucial for performing impact analysis.

- **Metadata repository**—Models have to be supported by descriptive information, which is called metadata. Metadata is an essential tool for standardizing data, for managing and enforcing the data standards, and for
  reducing the amount of rework performed by developers or users who are
  not aware of what already exists and therefore do not reuse any architectural components.

Data Quality Improvement Process

In addition to applying enterprise-wide data quality disciplines, creating an enterprise data model, and documenting metadata, the data quality group should
develop their own data quality improvement process. At the highest level, this
process must address the six major components shown in Figure 3.2. These
components are:

- **Assess**—Every improvement cycle starts with an assessment. This can
  either be an initial enterprise-wide data quality assessment, a system-by-
  system data quality assessment, or a department-by-department data quality assessment. When performing the assessment, do not limit your efforts
  to profiling the data and collecting statistics on data defects. Analyze the
  entire data entry or data manipulation process to find the root causes of
  errors and to find process improvement opportunities.

  Another type of assessment is a periodic data audit. This type of assessment
  is usually limited to one file or one database at a time. It involves data profiling as well as manual validation of data values against the documented
  data domains (valid data values). These domains should have already been
  documented as metadata, but if not, they can be found in programs, code
  translation books, online help screens, spreadsheets, and other documents.
  In the worst case, they be discovered by asking subject matter experts.

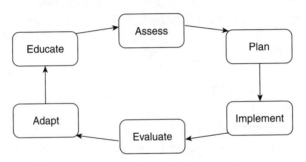

Figure 3.2: Data Quality Improvement Cycle

- **Plan**—After opportunities for improvement have been defined, the improvements should be analyzed, prioritized, approved, funded, staffed, and scheduled. Not all improvements have the same payback and not all improvements are practical or even feasible. An impact analysis should determine which improvements have the most far-reaching benefits. After improvement projects have been prioritized, approved, and funded, they should be staffed and scheduled.

- **Implement**—In some cases, the data quality group can implement the approved improvements, but in many cases, other staff members from both the business side and IT will be required. For example, a decision might have been made that an overloaded column (a column containing data values describing multiple attributes) should be separated in a database. That would involve the business people who are currently accessing the database, the database administrators who are maintaining it, and the developers whose programs are accessing it.

- **Evaluate**—The best ideas sometimes backfire. Although some impact analysis will have been performed during planning, occasionally an adverse impact will be overlooked. Or worse, the implemented improvement might have inadvertently created a new problem. It is therefore advisable to monitor the implemented improvements and evaluate their effectiveness. If deemed necessary, an improvement can be reversed.

- **Adapt**—Hopefully, most improvements do not have to be reversed, but some may have to be modified before announcing them to the entire organization or before turning them into new standards, guidelines, or procedures.

- **Educate**—The final step is to disseminate information about the new improvement process just implemented. Depending on the scope of the change, education can be accomplished through classroom training, computer-based training, an announcement on the organization's intranet website, an internal newsletter, or simple e-mail notification.

BUSINESS SPONSORSHIP

Without executive sponsorship from the business side, the data quality policies of the organization and the work habits of the staff will not change. The best data quality disciplines will have little effect if senior executives continue to reward their staff for speed rather than quality. Senior business executives must institute an incentive program for employees to follow the new data quality policies. The incentive program should be composed of two main parts. One should be public recognition of employees who make major contributions toward the data quality improvement process, and the other should be a monetary bonus. Only through strong business sponsorship and commitment can incentives be changed and a quality improvement process be enforced.

Business Responsibility for Data Quality

Data archeology (finding bad data), data cleansing (correcting bad data), and data quality enforcement (preventing data defects at the source) should be *business* objectives. Therefore, data quality initiatives are *business* initiatives and require the involvement of *business* people, such as information consumers and data originators.

Because data originators create the data and establish business rules and policies over the data, they are directly responsible to the downstream information consumers (knowledge workers, business analysts, and business managers) who need to use that data. If downstream information consumers base their business decisions on poor-quality data and suffer financial losses because of it, then the data originators must be held accountable. Data quality accountability is neither temporary nor application-specific. Thus, the business people must make the commitment to permanently accept these responsibilities.

Data originators, also known as information producers and data owners, are key players in data quality. They are usually business managers and staff responsible for a distinct function or operation of the business. Most operational systems are developed for them, thus, they are the ones who provide the original data requirements, data definitions, data domains, business rules, and process rules. During the requirements definition phase of a new system or during a conversion, data originators should involve downstream information consumers to collect and include the data requirements from these constituents. Information consumers are typically marketing people, the sales force, customer service representatives, or financial analysts.

Data originators are also responsible for participating in all testing activities as well as in retroactive data profiling and data assessment activities. If data defects are discovered, then the data originators should plan to address the root causes that reside in their systems or that resulted from their poor data-entry habits. Information consumers should know who the data originators are, so that they can take their data questions or data disputes directly to them for resolution.

Information consumers are the internal customers who need to consume business data for operational, tactical, or strategic decision-making purposes. They are usually business managers and staff who are responsible for resolving customer inquiries or disputes on the operational level, or for providing executive management with reports for strategic planning. Their data requirements are not the same as those of the data originators, but must be considered when a new system is developed.

Information consumers should participate during the requirements gathering activities for all systems from which they will eventually extract data for their own analytical use. They must participate in the data quality improvement process because they are frequently the first to discover data discrepancies that are not obvious to an operationally-oriented business person.

CONCLUSION

The time has come to acknowledge that an organization can no longer treat data as a byproduct of their systems. In the intelligent enterprise, information is the product and data is its raw material. Because the quality of the product can only be as good as the quality of its raw materials, organizations must bite the bullet and invest in data quality improvement practices. Although you can start small with limited data profiling and data cleansing activities, you must rapidly evolve into a robust data quality improvement program with focus on restoring the cross-organizational, 360-degree view of your business.

REFERENCES

Adelman, Sid and Larissa Terpeluk Moss. *Data Warehouse Project Management.* Boston, MA: Addison-Wesley, 2000.

Duncan, Karolyn and David L. Wells, "Rule-Based Data Cleansing." *The Journal of Data Warehousing*, Fall 1999.

English, Larry P. *Improving Data Warehouse and Business Information Quality.* New York: John Wiley & Sons, Inc., 1999.

English, Larry. "New Year; New Name; New Resolve for High IQ." *DM Review*, Volume 13, Number 1, January 2003.

Eckerson, Wayne W. "Data Quality and the Bottom Line." *TDWI Report Series*, 2003.

Loshin, David. "Customer Care, Consistency and Policy Management." *DM Review*, Volume 13, Number 8, August 2003.

Loshin, David. *Enterprise Knowledge Management—The Data Quality Approach.* San Francisco, CA: Morgan Kaufmann, 2001.

Moss, Larissa and Shaku Atre. *Business Intelligence Roadmap, The Complete Project Lifecycle for Decision-Support Applications.* Boston, MA: Addison-Wesley, 2003.

"TDWI Data Cleansing: Delivering High-Quality Warehouse Data." seminar, TDWI World Conference, San Diego, California: 2004.

Thibodeau, Patrick. "Data Problems Thwart Effort to Count H-1Bs." *Computerworld*: 6 October 2003.

CHAPTER 4

Metadata

"Common sense is not so common."

—Voltaire

Metadata is an integral part to data management because it provides the contextual information for business data. Business data without context has no meaning. For example, the perfectly valid and clean data values "24, 38, and 41" have no meaning by themselves and cannot be used to make business decisions. However, if you knew that the context for these data values was your company's annual gross sales in billions, then you could see that sales have increased. Examples of contextual information are:

• The meaning and content of the data

• Policies and business rules that govern the data

• Technical attributes of the data

• Transformations and calculations of the data

• Manipulation and usage of the data

• Lineage of the data

• Currency of the data

In this chapter, we explain why metadata is critical to a data strategy. We describe the various metadata categories and compare buying versus building a metadata repository. For those of you who will be building your own metadata repository, we review the six engineering stages of the metadata development lifecycle: justification, planning, analysis, design, construction, and deployment. Because implementing a metadata repository is only the beginning of a managed metadata environment (MME), we conclude this chapter with a discussion of the additional components you need for an MME.

WHY METADATA IS CRITICAL TO THE BUSINESS

No one will argue that data is critical to the business. We need it to identify our customers, track our sales and services, manage our employees, maintain our bookkeeping records, control our inventory, and so on. Data is so critical to the business that organizations are gathering more and more data not only about their own business but about their competitors as well. They are building data warehouses, buying business analytics solutions, and spending millions of dollars on business intelligence technology. Yet many of these organizations are drowning in data while still thirsting for valuable intelligence about their business. Data alone does not translate into business intelligence without metadata.

Metadata as the Keystone

Metadata is the keystone to business intelligence because it provides the context for business data. Metadata is not new; we used to call it documentation. We documented the data definitions in data dictionaries, the business rules in policy manuals and programming code, the location of files and databases in project manuals, the list of programs in system documentation, and the job streams in operating guides. Our documentation also included user manuals that described the data entry screens and the report layouts. Although our old and inefficient ways of documenting are outmoded in today's global companies with distributed workforces, the basic need for documentation remains.

Without contextual information (metadata), it is difficult for technicians to manage the systems and even more difficult for end users to use them. It is like entering a building filled with books but without a catalog and without any reference materials. It would take a very long time to find just the right book you were looking for, if you were not sure about its title, could not look up the name of the author, could not scan the descriptions of the books, and could not locate the right bookshelf or determine if any copies were left.

In today's fast-paced environment, we often skip this type of documentation and rely instead on people's memories (tribal knowledge) and on the abilities of technicians to trace through programs when questions arise. We think there is little value in spending time on documentation when business people push for 90–120 day deliverables. We think that documentation is mostly for the benefit of technicians and contributes little value to end users. Wrong. Being able to locate critical business data, understand its meaning, rely on its data values, trust its accuracy, know its source, and use it correctly is as important to a business person as it would be to you to be able to navigate easily through a large library of books. Furthermore, metadata might well play an increasing role in defending public statements and justifying operational compliance issues, as well as facilitating solid internal auditing practices. Noncompliance and shoddy audit practices can result in jail sentences for business executives.

Management Support for Metadata

Intuitively, business people understand the value of metadata because they suffer from the current data chaos more than the technicians. However, rather than support a managed metadata environment for their organization, many succumb to their other pressing needs for more data and more reports. When IT cannot deliver fast enough, some business units hire their own technicians under the guise of "business analysts" who add to the existing data chaos with thousands of Microsoft Access databases and Excel spreadsheets—all without metadata or "documentation." IT is in a difficult position to resist that wave of end user self-reliance, especially when so many organizations outsource IT functions. It can be debated whether it is even IT's job to save the end users from themselves.

Business data is a business asset just like financial assets, fixed assets, real estate assets, or human resource assets. Assets must be inventoried and managed. Metadata is the vehicle for inventorying and managing the business data assets. Therefore, metadata should be of extreme interest to end users. IT should not have to beg for funding, resources, and tools to capture and maintain metadata. Instead, the business should demand and support it because without metadata, it will become increasingly difficult to rely on the business data and to comply with government regulations. Some metadata industry experts predict that the average company in the Global 2000 will have 7–12 metadata management-related activities occurring at any one time. This includes point-solution metadata repositories in production, repositories that are in Excel or manually managed, and repositories that are attached to bigger projects, such as ERP or CRM.

Starting a Metadata Management Initiative

Managing metadata for the organization is as challenging as managing business data for the organization. At a minimum, metadata should be able to answer the following five questions:

- What physical data is currently in our files and databases?

- What does each data element mean in both business and technical language?

- Where is the data located (in what files and databases) and in how many different places is it located?

- How did it get into those files and databases? Through what process and what person did it get placed there?

- How can the data be accessed?

Other common contextual questions are:

- Who owns the data?

- Who makes the rules for it?

- Who is responsible for the content (domain)?

- When was the data last updated?

- Who updated it?

- How clean or reliable is it?

- What is its definition?

- Does each data element have a unique name?

- If each element does not have a unique name, what are the synonyms?

- What are the homonyms?

- What other users access it?

• How are they using it?

• Are there privacy and security restrictions?

• Is it an atomic data element? If not, how was it derived?

Metadata can answer all of these questions if it is collected, updated, integrated, and maintained.

You can start a metadata management initiative with the following four basic components:

- **A database**—A database for metadata is called a metadata repository. It is made up of tables and columns like any other relational database, only its tables represent metadata objects, such as ENTITY, TABLE, COLUMN, ATTRIBUTE, and PRIMARY KEY. Its columns represent meta metadata, which is contextual information about metadata, or metadata about metadata. Examples are Name, Definition, Type, Length, and Domain (Valid Values) of the metadata object.

- **A metadata administrator**—This is the person who creates and maintains the metadata repository. She collects, updates, and integrates the metadata from its various sources (for example, database modeling tool, DBMS data dictionary, or OLAP tool), produces metadata reports, and maintains the interfaces to the metadata repository. This person must have a solid data management and data analysis background in addition to technical skills.

- **A policy**—This is an assertion, a proclamation, or a rule to be followed. It is set by the business to achieve or support a specific business goal or business objective. The business objective for managing metadata is to have control over business data like any other business asset. A policy to support that objective would be that "every project deliverable must include a metadata deliverable." Another policy would be a "mandate to follow data naming standards."

- **Procedures**—These are processes and practices that people perform to ensure they follow the policies. Procedures are usually incorporated into system development lifecycle (SDLC) methodologies. An example might be the task of "writing a short definition for each data element and have it approved by the data owner, as well as the end users who use that data element." Another example might be the process of "capturing counts and diagnostic information about data errors during a program run."

METADATA CATEGORIES

To answer the questions listed in the previous section, you have to gather, link, and maintain a variety of metadata objects. Some of the most common data-related metadata components that organizations collect are:

- Business name

- Technical name

- Definition

- Owner

- Type and length

- Domain (allowable values)

- Data relationships (including cardinality)

- Business rules

- Business policies

- Privacy and security rules

- Data defect thresholds

- Data quality metrics

- Data applicability

- Timeliness

- Origin (data source)

- Physical location (database)

- Referential integrity (optionality)

- Transformations

- Derivations

- Aggregations

- Summarizations

- Volume

- Growth expectancy

- Utilization

- Table join patterns

- Access frequency

- Peak periods

Metadata can be grouped into four categories. Some metadata is *business-oriented*, such as business names, definitions, and business rules. Other metadata is *technical* in nature, such as table and column names, data types and lengths (for instance, CHAR 2), and referential integrity rules. Another large category of metadata is *process-related*, such as program names, transformation logic, refresh schedule, and error statistics. A fourth category is *usage* and it includes what data is accessed most frequently, by whom, when, and for what purpose (for example, which report or query).

Business Metadata

Business metadata is provided by the end users, not by technicians. Business metadata supplies the business meaning associated with data in flight to ensure that proper context is maintained as data is repurposed across applications. Thus, business metadata provides a semantic layer between IT systems and end users. Business metadata is documented in business terms in logical data models, business process models, and business policies. It should be captured in computer-aided software engineering (CASE) or modeling tools, such as Oracle Designer or ERwin Data Modeler.

The business names of data elements are fully spelled out and fully qualified. The names are not shortened or abbreviated and they do not contain hyphens or underscores. Names are composed of prime words, qualifiers, and class words.

- **Prime words**—These denote the business object being described. Prime words are usually kernel (fundamental) entities of a business, such as ACCOUNT, CUSTOMER, EMPLOYEE, and PRODUCT.

- **Qualifiers**—These are words that further describe "what kind of" entity it is. For example: *SAVINGS* ACCOUNT, *PROSPECTIVE* CUSTOMER, *RETIRED* EMPLOYEE, and *SOLD* PRODUCT. Qualifiers can also describe "what kind of" class word it is, such as *DAILY* BALANCE and *EFFECTIVE* DATE.

- **Class words**—These identify the data type and to some extent the data domain (allowable values) of the data element. You should publish a list of class words, which usually includes, but is not limited to, the following entries:

  - Amount
  - Balance
  - Code
  - Count
  - Date
  - Description
  - Identifier
  - Name
  - Number
  - Percent
  - Rate
  - Text

An example of a fully qualified and spelled out business name for a data element might be: Interest Bearing Checking Account Monthly Average Balance. "Account" is the prime word and "Balance" is the class word. "Average" and

"Monthly" qualify what type of balance, and "Checking" and "Interest Bearing" qualify what type of account.

Technical Metadata

Technical metadata is provided by the technicians or software tools, not by end users. It is documented in technical terms in databases, file descriptions, and programs. It is usually captured in developer tools, such as extract/transform/ load (ETL) or OLAP tools, in DBMS data dictionaries, or on CASE tools, such as Oracle Designer or ERwin Data Modeler.

The technical names of data elements (fields and columns) are abbreviated and underscored or hyphenated depending on the programming language (for example, SQL versus COBOL). The technical names are still made up of prime words, qualifiers, and class words, unless the name is too long, in which case the least significant qualifier can be dropped. In some cases, aliases and synonyms can be added if necessary.

You should create and publish a standardized list of approved abbreviations and acronyms that everybody is expected to use. Developers and end users should not make up their own abbreviations, nor should they spell out words that exist on the abbreviations list. This list must be maintained and expanded over time, which is usually done by a data administrator or the metadata administrator if you do not have a data administrator.

Continuing with the example of Interest Bearing Checking Account Monthly Average Balance, the technical name of the column would be INT_BRG_CHK_ACCT_MO_AVG_BAL. The technical names in existing files and databases will, most likely, not conform to your new standards. They should be documented as they are and linked to the business name Interest Bearing Checking Account Monthly Average Balance. This will allow the end users to see how many times this data element appears in the existing systems and under what names.

Process Metadata

Process metadata is also provided by the technicians, not by end users. It is documented as programming code in programs and in developer tools, such as program generators, testing tools, ETL tools, OLAP tools, reporting tools, EAI tools, and business process modeling tools. Process metadata usually describes an action taken by a program. The process can be an edit routine that verifies the accuracy of the data values; it can be the calculation of a derived column (for example, profit calculation); or it can be the transformation logic in an ETL tool for a data warehouse (for instance, converting PIC XX to CHAR 2).

Process metadata has traditionally been considered technical documentation serving only the technicians, who seldom bother to document their process logic because they are perfectly capable of reading their own programming code. The result is that many end users do not know what the programs do and cannot verify the validity of the process logic. How many times do you hear statements from end users similar to: "I have no idea what the program does, but it must be right because we have been using this for 10 years" or "I don't know how Bob (the programmer) does it, but it balances against GL." This is a sad situation because most of the process logic is written to implement some business rule. Knowing the business rules is a *business* responsibility, not Bob's. Defining the business rules as business metadata, and then linking it to the process metadata (the programming code that implements the business rules) allows business people to enforce and test that the business rules are implemented consistently for all business objects and all business data.

Usage Metadata

Usage metadata is collected by the technicians, not by the end users. It documents data access patterns and frequency of access by people and programs. Using utility tools, database administrators (DBA) and application developers can monitor how the data is used. They can track who accesses what data, how often, and when. They can trace user IDs, the time of day a table is accessed, and what program or tool does the accessing. They can also tell what columns are retrieved by what queries, what data is frequently joined, what type of calculations are performed, and how often.

Usage metadata is the least understood and utilized feature in metadata repository products. However, it is an important metadata category because knowing the utilization of data helps DBAs tune the databases, helps application developers tune their programs, and helps end users decide what data to keep at the atomic level, what data to summarize, and what data to archive. Managing data as an asset is not just managing the storage of data, but also managing the meaning, quality, and lifespan of the data. Metadata can be used as a tool for that.

METADATA SOURCES

Where does metadata come from? How does it get created? Where is it captured? Where will it be stored? As Figure 4.1 shows, metadata is captured by many people in a variety of ways. The purpose of the metadata repository is to link or integrate the related metadata. Integrating metadata is the responsibility of the metadata administrator who has to work with business people, business analysts, data administrators, DBAs, and application developers.

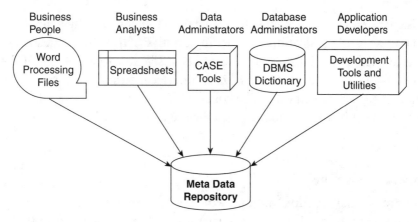

Figure 4.1: Metadata integration

- **Business metadata**—This must be gathered from business people and business analysts. This is usually done during data analysis and logical data modeling. As business objects are identified, they are captured as "entities." The data elements that describe these entities are captured as "attributes." The names, definitions, domains, and business rules are then created by the data administrator with the help of business people who know the most about the data, such as the data owners, subject matter experts, data stewards, or downstream information consumers. Business metadata is usually captured in a CASE tool, but it also can reside in word processing documents or spreadsheets.

- **Technical metadata**—This is usually created by the DBA and the developers during database and application design. Depending on the types of development tools available to them, DBAs usually capture the technical database-related metadata on a CASE tool or in a data definition language (DDL) script that is loaded into the database. The developers capture the technical programming-related metadata either directly in their programs or in the dictionary of their development tool.

- **Process metadata**—This is provided by the developers during application design and development. If they use formal programming specifications, the "structured English" instructions can be used for input into the metadata repository. Otherwise, the actual programming logic can be converted into "pseudo code." If a development tool is used, then the process logic, which is stored by the tool's dictionary, can be extracted from the tool directly.

- **Usage metadata**—This must be gathered manually with the help of database- and application-monitoring utilities. This activity is usually performed by the DBA, but it also can be assigned to a developer. If the metadata repository does not have an interface to the monitoring utility, then the usage metadata can be collected in a word processing file or a spreadsheet before it is loaded into the metadata repository.

METADATA REPOSITORY

Unlike traditional documentation, which was stored in text documents or spreadsheets, metadata is stored as structured data in a database so that it can easily be accessed and queried by business people and technicians. There are several options for implementing such a database, known as the metadata repository. You can build a metadata repository or you can buy one. You can implement a centralized or a distributed metadata repository. Or, you can go with an XML-enabled metadata repository solution.

Buying a Metadata Repository Product

The easiest metadata solution might be to simply buy a metadata repository product off the shelf. There are advantages and disadvantages to this approach:

- **Advantages**—The biggest advantage is that a purchased product can be installed and ready to use in a much shorter time than it would take you to design, code, and test a custom-built metadata repository with all of its interfaces and reports. Another advantage is that most metadata repository products come with a complete set of functionality and can be expanded further through their application program interfaces (API). In addition, if the product is certified for certain tools, whereby some of the metadata is captured, it will already have the necessary built-in interfaces for those tools. In addition, there is the ongoing support the vendors provide for the metadata sourcing and integration layers.

- **Disadvantages**—The biggest disadvantage with any purchased product is that the "vanilla" version rarely satisfies all the requirements. The product might not provide certain metadata components that you want to track or you might not like its user interface. Another disadvantage is the price for such products. The more sophisticated the product, the more expensive it is, and the cheaper products might not be as useful as you would like. One more disadvantage is the dependency on a particular vendor.

Building a Metadata Repository

If you consider building your own metadata repository, then you have to properly staff the project. Not only will you need staff to maintain the repository database, application, and content, but you will also need analysts, designers, and developers for the construction effort. Advantages and disadvantages to building your own customized metadata repository are:

- **Advantages**—The most obvious advantage for building your own metadata repository is that you can customize it to your requirements because your technicians have full control over design and functionality. Another advantage is that you can build and deploy the metadata repository capabilities in increments over time. This will allow you to start quickly without too much complexity or spending too much time on development. Another big advantage is the ability to customize your reports, end-user interfaces, tutorials, and any other usage of the metadata repository.

- **Disadvantages**—The disadvantage of a custom-built metadata repository is that you need full-time staff to build and maintain it. Not only does the repository database have to be designed, but the end-user access layer and the interfaces to the tool dictionaries from which the metadata will be extracted have to be designed and developed. As the metadata repository is enhanced, regression testing will take a lot of time, and keeping the metadata repository stable and in synch with the metadata in the tool dictionaries may be challenging. This means that your staff size will probably have to be larger than when you buy a product, assuming the product can do some of the work for you.

Centralized Metadata Repository

Many organizations prefer a centralized metadata repository solution over a distributed one. The advantages seem obvious, but there also are some disadvantages to this approach:

- **Advantages**—The strongest advantage to a centralized metadata repository is eliminating metadata redundancy, thus providing a single version of the truth. Because each unique metadata component is defined once, and only once, it ensures standardization and consistency. Another advantage is a reduction in maintenance because there is only one metadata repository database and one set of interfaces to maintain. In addition, metadata does not have to be kept in synch across metadata repositories or across tools.

- **Disadvantages**—One disadvantage of any type of centralized solution is that it requires a strategy, a plan, a flexible and expandable architecture, and dedicated resources to develop and maintain the centralized metadata repository. This is one major reason why so many data warehouse initiatives break up into a collection of nonarchitected, stand-alone data marts without a metadata solution. It is easier to develop something small and contained than to provide a cross-organizational solution. Another disadvantage is that the architecture of a centralized metadata repository can be complicated and requires a higher learning curve. This is especially true for purchased metadata repository products.

Distributed Metadata Repository

A distributed metadata repository implies that metadata is not stored in one central location, but is distributed across multiple databases. Although this is not a common metadata repository solution, and there are disadvantages, it should still be considered, especially when the alternative is to ignore metadata entirely because of its complexity or cost:

- **Advantages**—One advantage is that a smaller, customized metadata repository database, which was built to support only one specific application or department, is easier to use because it contains only the familiar metadata components for that application or that department. Another advantage is that the reports and interfaces of each metadata repository can be tailored to the needs of each set of end users. Also, each metadata repository can be maintained by separate technicians, thereby decreasing the *individual* metadata repository maintenance effort.

- **Disadvantages**—The biggest disadvantage is the cost. Although the cost for each *individual* metadata repository might be lower and absorbed by the various lines of business, cumulatively the overall costs to the organization are actually higher. In addition, controlling metadata redundancy across multiple repository databases and keeping the redundant metadata in synch is difficult. Another challenge is to link metadata across various repository databases, especially if the repositories are based on different database designs (different meta models). To build and maintain a gateway between these different repositories so that end users can access them transparently without having to switch from one to another can also be quite complicated. Finally, this is not an enterprise-wide approach, and it does not produce a single version of the truth.

XML-Enabled Metadata Repository

Another solution to metadata management is using XML and simple object access protocol (SOAP) to point to metadata at its source. In an XML-enabled metadata solution, the metadata can remain at its original location, such as the CASE tool, spreadsheet, or DBMS dictionary. A gateway then acts as the directory to those various locations where the metadata is stored. At the time of an end user's request, metadata is extracted and brought into the metadata delivery layer. There are advantages and disadvantages to pursuing an XML-enabled metadata repository solution, as follows:

- **Advantages**—The main advantage to an XML-enabled metadata solution is that metadata never has to be duplicated or moved from its original location to another metadata repository database. Instead, XML tags enable access to the metadata across any type of data storage (at least in theory—not always in practice). Another advantage is that standard web search engines can locate any tagged metadata in any location.

- **Disadvantages**—As promising as this new technology is, its main disadvantage is that not all tools and DBMSs are XML-enabled, so there is no way to tag all the metadata. Also, the initial tagging of metadata is a laborious process; the tags require additional disk space; and the tag names have to be managed as metadata, which adds another maintenance layer. In addition, DBMS and tool vendors must follow some metadata standards for XML tagging to enable seamless metadata access across all products. Currently, there are two main standards under development, one by the Meta Data Coalition, influenced by Microsoft, and the other by the Object Management Group, influenced by Oracle. The jury is still out on which of the two standards will be adopted as the metadata industry standard. Finally, not having the metadata physically integrated in one database prevents you from having a single version of the truth.

DEVELOPING A METADATA REPOSITORY

If the decision is made to build a metadata repository, a project team should be assembled. The team should have the combined skills of project management, business analysis, systems analysis, data modeling, database architecture, application design, knowledge of one or more development languages or development tools, and familiarity with one or more testing tools. Developing a metadata repository is not much different from developing any other application. The tasks and deliverables are similar.

The project team has to go through the six engineering stages of justification, planning, analysis, design, construction, and deployment. These stages are discussed in the following sections.

Justification

We mentioned earlier that management support for metadata is crucial. Therefore, make a business case to demonstrate the costs associated with the current data problems and to show how a metadata repository can help eliminate those problems. Prepare an assessment report that itemizes the costs of poor-quality data, lack of data standardization, and maintenance of redundant data and processes. The report should also include an estimate of the time wasted by technicians and business people trying to locate the right data, get access to the data, integrate the data, and reconcile inconsistencies found in the data. Most importantly, the report should highlight the risks and exposures to the organization, showing how the unmanaged data chaos affects the company's capability to compete effectively. The benefits of eliminating the costs, risks, exposures, and making the company more competitive should offset the costs for building or buying a metadata repository.

Planning

After a metadata initiative is approved, put together a project plan. Use a methodology that is tailored to building metadata repositories and define your project. Start with your project objectives and the project scope. You do not have to provide a complete metadata solution all at once. Instead, plan on implementation releases and prioritize which metadata components you want to implement immediately and which ones you want to add in future releases.

Then organize and staff your project. Remember to identify an executive business sponsor and business representatives who will work with your technical team. The support of a business executive who understands the business value of metadata is crucial in getting other business people and other IT development groups to participate in the metadata initiative. With your project team, develop a project plan and create a short project charter. The project charter should have the following components:

- Project objectives

- Budget

- Costs and benefits

- Project risks, constraints, and assumptions

- Roles and responsibilities

- Project team members including business representatives

- Scope (metadata components and functionality)

- Testing procedure

- Test plan template

- Change control template

- Issues management template

- Critical success factors

Analysis

During the analysis stage, the metadata requirements are finalized and documented in a logical meta model, which is the name for a logical data model that contains metadata components. The logical meta model is a requirements model, and the physical meta model is a database design model. Because the logical and physical meta models are often identical, the words "logical" and "physical" are usually dropped, and these models are commonly referred to as meta models. A meta model is usually a normalized entity-relationship diagram with associated meta metadata, which is metadata about metadata components. A meta model and meta metadata are best illustrated with the two examples shown in Figures 4.2 and 4.3.

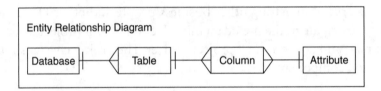

Figure 4.2: Small excerpt of a logical meta model

Name: Entity
Definition: A fully normalized business object.
Relationship: Related to one or many tables
Read by all, create/update/delete by the DA
Ownership: Data Administrator (DA)
Origin: ERwin
Physical Location: MDRSYSENT table
Cleanliness: 2 percent missing data
Applicability: Since November 1, 2003

Figure 4.3: Example of meta metadata

Design

The most common design of a metadata repository is the entity-relationship meta model that is created during the analysis stage. However, the second alternative is to use a more object-based architecture, which has a much higher level of abstraction. In this design, all entities and their relationships from the logical meta model are abstracted into three entities: OBJECT, OBJECT TYPE, and OBJECT RELATIONSHIP, as shown in Figure 4.4.

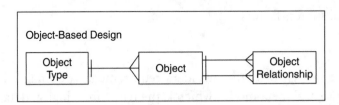

Figure 4.4: Example of an object-based physical meta model

The entity called OBJECT contains *all* metadata components. The entity called OBJECT TYPE identifies the type of metadata component (for example, entity, table, column, and attribute). The entity OBJECT RELATIONSHIP indicates what metadata components are related to each other. Although this streamlined design allows for maximum flexibility and expansion, accessing and reporting against such a database structure is not intuitive and requires many recursive joins. Therefore, very few metadata repositories use this type of architecture.

In addition to designing the repository database, you have to also design the metadata extraction process, the interfaces, the reports, and the online help function. The metadata has to be extracted from the sources where it originates (for instance, CASE tool, DBMS dictionary, and ETL tool) and loaded into the metadata repository. Then it has to be integrated or "linked." For example, the column INT_BRG_CHK_ACCT_MO_AVG_BAL has to be associated or linked with the attribute Interest Bearing Checking Account Monthly Average Balance. Because the metadata repository will be accessed by end users and technicians, you have to design the interfaces for them along with any predefined reports and an online help function.

Construction

Developing a metadata repository is not much different from developing a business application. You have to build a tool interface or a metadata ETL process to extract the metadata from the tool where it was captured, change it into a format that can be used to load into the metadata repository database, and then load the database.

The second major construction effort is that of the end-user access interface. You might even want to build two different types of access interfaces, one for end users and one for technicians, depending on how these two constituents plan to use the metadata repository. You also might want to give technicians and "power users" authorization to directly access the metadata repository database. If you have only one centralized metadata repository, then building these interfaces is relatively straightforward. However, if you choose a distributed or XML-enabled metadata solution, then your interfaces will be a lot more complicated. In either case, be sure you get frequent feedback from your end users during the construction process.

The third component you need to build is an online help function. This can be modeled after the familiar wizard screens or it can be your own customized application. By far the most effective and sophisticated online help feature is to incorporate metadata into business applications. For example, when an end user runs a query and looks at the results on the screen, she can position the mouse over a column heading and, with the push of a button, trigger a small window to pop up and display the definition of that heading.

Everything that is built has to be tested. Comprehensive testing usually includes six kinds of testing activities: unit testing, integration (system) testing, regression testing, quality assurance (QA) testing, performance (stress) testing, and user acceptance testing. Because metadata repository databases and applications are much smaller than business databases and applications, performance testing is usually not necessary. If you are not building an enterprise-wide metadata repository, then chances are that QA testing will not be required either. In other cases, QA testing can be combined with user acceptance testing. In either case, the remaining four kinds of testing activities apply:

- **Unit testing**—This is performed by the developer who wrote the programming code to ensure that the code compiles without errors and functions properly.

- **Integration testing**—This test ensures that all programs in the job stream execute flawlessly and pass metadata and parameters according to specifications.

- **Regression testing**—This test is a form of integration testing. Whereas integration testing is performed on a set of new programs, regression testing is performed on a set of existing programs that have been modified or enhanced. This is applicable when the metadata repository application is expanded over time.

- **User acceptance testing**—This involves the end users who will use the metadata repository.

Deployment

Moving a metadata repository into production requires some preparation. Novice metadata administrators often underestimate the time it takes to prepare the production environment. For example, the production server platform has to be installed and tested. This includes testing the hardware components, operating system, monitoring utilities, and network connectivity. An instance of the DBMS has to be created, and parameters for it have to be set and tested under the operating system. Because metadata repository programs should reside in a version-controlled library, a library management product should be installed and tested before the programs are moved into production.

After the metadata repository is in production, some of the metadata programs must be scheduled to run automatically to capture load statistics and data quality metrics. Certain reports and queries can also be placed on the job scheduler. The help desk staff has to get prepared to mentor and support the business people with their metadata questions. They will need a reference guide to fall back on in case they get inquiries they cannot easily answer. This reference guide can also be given to business people because it contains helpful hints about where to locate specific metadata components and where to get additional help.

End users and technicians need different training on how to use the metadata repository. End users must learn how to use the access interface and the on-line help function. Technicians and "power users" must learn how to access the repository database directly. A best practice is to provide "just enough training, just in time." The first training session should be limited to a review of the metadata repository, how it is organized, and an explanation of one or two basic functions. After one or two weeks of hands-on practice while performing their job duties, the trainees should return for another training session to learn about more advanced features of the metadata repository.

MANAGED METADATA ENVIRONMENT

Managed Metadata Environment (MME) was coined by David Marco and Michael Jennings in their book *Universal Meta Data Models*. As they state in their book, the most pressing challenges that organizations face today are:

- Providing IT portfolio management

- Reducing system and data redundancy

- Preventing application failures

- Reducing IT expenditures

- Enabling knowledge management

- Adhering to regulatory requirements

- Enabling enterprise (cross-organizational) applications

MME addresses all these challenges with its six architectural components or layers:

- Metadata sourcing

- Metadata integration

- Metadata repository

- Metadata management

- Metadata marts

- Metadata delivery

One might say that an MME manages metadata as a business asset. Unfortunately, many organizations have not yet accepted the idea that *business data* should be managed as a business asset, much less metadata. For these organizations, an MME might be out of reach in the near term. However, some corporate and government organizations are moving full steam ahead in implementing the MME components.

We already discussed the metadata repository at great lengths. Now, we review the other five components.

Metadata Sourcing

The first step in an MME is to gather all the disparate metadata from its sources. As Figure 4.1 shows, metadata is collected on a multitude of media.

- **Word processing files**—These can be manuals, programs, or other less formal documents that contain data definitions, business rules, or programming specifications.

- **Spreadsheets**—These contain calculations and macros written by business analysts who have downloaded data from various operational systems.

- **CASE tools**—These contain the business metadata, such as business names, definitions, and data relationships, as well as technical metadata, such as table and column names, primary and foreign keys, and referential integrity rules.

- **DBMS dictionaries**—These are an integral part of all DBMSs. These dictionaries store the technical names for storage groups, table spaces, tables, columns, primary keys, foreign keys, and indices. They also contain the data types and lengths of all columns.

- **Developer tools**—The internal dictionaries of program generators, ETL tools, and OLAP tools store all the programming logic.

In addition to the previous metadata sources, purchased package applications, such as ERP or CRM systems, have their own internal data dictionaries that can feed into a metadata repository.

Metadata Integration

Metadata integration is the process of connecting or linking the technical and process metadata to the business metadata for each metadata component. Eventually, the usage metadata is added. This is not an easy process, and in many cases, it involves manually establishing the relationships. For example, when you extract and load the business name Interest Bearing Checking Account Monthly Average Balance from the CASE tool and the technical name INT_BRG_CHK_ACCT_MO_AVG_BAL from the DBMS dictionary, how does the metadata repository know that these two names belong to the same data element and should be connected? It doesn't. It gets even more complicated for data warehouse projects in which you have to merge data from multiple operational systems. In that case, the COBOL name on one file might be INT-CHECK-ACCOUNT-AVG-MONTHLY-AMT and on another file, it might be CA-MON-AVG-INT. There is no magic way for your metadata repository to know that all of these names are technical "aliases" for Interest Bearing Checking Account Monthly Average Balance. Unless you write a program with some parsing and pattern-matching algorithms using your official abbreviations list (if you have one) to translate name components, you have to manually connect these metadata components.

Metadata Management

Think of managing a business application and apply those activities to the metadata repository; now you have a definition for metadata management. The components will be familiar to you:

- **Archiving and purging**—These activities are as applicable to metadata as they are to business data. Define the requirements and set up triggers that will either archive or purge older or outdated metadata at an appropriate time.

- **Backup**—This activity refers to the common database backup process. If your metadata repository is relatively small, you can take periodic full backups. Otherwise, you may take occasional full backups supplemented with periodic incremental backups.

- **Enhancements**—Unless you build the entire metadata repository with all possible metadata components and functions at one time, you will be expanding and enhancing the metadata repository incrementally over time.

- **Database tuning**—This type of tuning refers to the relational metadata repository database and the multi-dimensional metadata marts, which we discuss in the next section. Both types of databases are used to access metadata. If access paths change or the amount of concurrent users grows, then the databases might have to be tuned or even redesigned.

- **Environment management**—At a minimum, you should have a development environment and a separate production environment. Preferably, you also have a test environment in which you can conduct integration, regression, QA, and user acceptance testing. These environments may or may not be configured identically, in which case you have to manage the changes and the transitions among the different environments.

- **Job scheduling**—Metadata is not a one-time deliverable. Some queries and reports are scheduled to run on a regular basis (for instance, weekly or monthly load statistics and error reports).

- **Recovery**—Hardware failures and database crashes do not just affect application databases, but they also affect the metadata repository. You have to be able to recover from such failures using a previous version of the metadata repository, and you should have procedures to handle such situations.

- **Versioning**—Metadata is not static. It does not change as frequently as business data, but it does change. Therefore, you might be required to keep several versions of metadata on the metadata repository to track the history of metadata changes. Consider the use of versioning numbers or effective and expiration dates on your metadata components to enable versioning.

Metadata Marts

Metadata reports in the past were plain, static reports of data definitions or printouts of tables and columns. With OLAP technology, multi-dimensional metadata marts are becoming popular. The metadata marts are sourced from the metadata repository for specific metric-based requirements. For example, if you have a metadata mart for data error statistics, you can report the number of data errors by error type, column name, application name, and run date. In this type of hub-and-spoke metadata repository architecture, the metadata repository is treated as the metadata "data warehouse" and the metadata marts are the reporting and querying databases. Using this type of architecture shields the end users from any disruptive maintenance or enhancements to the metadata repository.

Metadata Delivery

Metadata can be delivered in a variety of ways. We already discussed two delivery mechanisms: the end-user access interface and the metadata marts. In some cases, it might be advantageous to store some metadata components on the same row with business data on the application database. For example, you can store the metadata component Data Quality Indicator right next to the data element Original Loan Funding Amount.

Purchased package applications (ERP or CRM), messaging products (EAI or EII), and developer tools (ETL or OLAP) are not only sources of metadata, but can also be the recipients of metadata. In that case, you need to create a metadata extract file from the metadata repository, which the applications or tools can access.

Metadata can also be a deliverable to external entities, such as your suppliers, vendors, customers, partners, or government agencies. Usually, you create and transmit an extract file to them, unless you and the recipients utilize XML-enabled technologies. You can also deliver metadata to them through an extranet or your public website.

Communicating and Selling Metadata

The importance of metadata is not understood by most business executives. They have either never heard of the term or they think it is some type of system documentation that the technicians do for themselves. They are completely un-informed about the return on investment an MME or even a simple centralized metadata repository can bring to their organization. IT needs to do a much better job in communicating and selling metadata to the business people.

Metadata and data quality are inextricably connected. You do not have one without the other, and both are tied to data standardization and logical data modeling, which is still the most effective technique to discover data anomalies through the normalization rules. Regrettably, IT often does not embrace these disciplines because they can develop systems without metadata, data quality, data standardization, and logical data modeling.

CONCLUSION

A data strategy is not comprehensive or complete without a metadata solution. Even in its most rudimentary form as "documentation," metadata is an IT best practice. However, as we discussed in this chapter, metadata goes far beyond being documentation for technicians. It is a tool to manage the IT portfolio, reduce system and data redundancy, prevent application failures, reduce IT expenditures for maintenance and development, enable knowledge management, adhere to regulatory requirements, and enable the development of enterprise (cross-organizational) applications. All of these objectives contribute to an organization's bottom line by cutting costs, curtailing risks and exposures, and providing a competitive advantage.

REFERENCES

Beyer, Mark. "Metadata: The Compliance Get-Out-of-Jail-Free Card?" *Enterprise Analytics Strategies*, 26 October 2004.

Marco, David and Michael Jennings. *Universal Meta Data Models*. New York, New York: John Wiley & Sons, 2004.

Marco, David. *Building and Managing the Meta Data Repository: A Full Lifecycle Guide*. New York: John Wiley & Sons, 2000.

Moss, Larissa T. and Shaku Atre. *Business Intelligence Roadmap: The Complete Project Lifecycle for Decision-Support Applications*. Boston, MA: Addison-Wesley, 2003.

Tannenbaum, Adrienne. *Metadata Solutions; Using Metamodels, Repositories, XML, and Enterprise Portals to Generate Information on Demand*. Boston, MA: Addison-Wesley, 2002.

Data Modeling

If you are implementing a data strategy at your organization, you need to understand the significance of data modeling and how an enterprise data model is the architectural foundation for all other data management disciplines discussed in this book.

In this chapter, we discuss logical data modeling of the business and physical data modeling of databases. In the section on physical data modeling, we emphasize modeling data for data warehouse (DW) applications by comparing the pros and cons of entity-relationship modeling of business activities and associated business data (as introduced by Peter Chen) with dimensional modeling of reporting patterns and associated analytical data (as introduced by Ralph Kimball).

The significance of entity-relationship modeling is first and foremost its process-independent representation of business data, and second, its rapid adoption by database management system (DBMS) vendors as a viable form of data management. The value of entity-relationship modeling—in particular enterprise logical data modeling—has always been to establish the "single version of the truth" of one's business, or to put it in today's terminology, to see the "360-degree view" of an organization.

This has database design implications, especially for data warehouses, which are supposed to combine operational data from various operational systems into one integrated, nonredundant, 360-degree view of an organization. When a DW is implemented as a centralized enterprise database, the benefits of implementing an entity-relationship model are multifold. Data does not need to be stored redundantly in multiple databases designed to support special access or reporting needs. That means that all queries, reports, and applications can reuse the data from a single database, which eliminates the root cause for most inconsistencies among reports. Because there is only one database to maintain, fewer programs have to be written and maintained and there is no need to reconcile multiple extract transform and load (ETL) processes for multiple databases. That translates into savings on hardware (servers and storage), and better utilization of IT resources (database administrators, architects, developers, data modelers), and it frees up the business people to be more productive by not having to spend their time reconciling data discrepancies among databases.

The first half of this chapter explores the origin and significance of logical data modeling as well as the concepts and principles behind the technique. It also explains the differences between logical and physical data modeling, something that has been misunderstood by many data modeling practitioners. The second half of this chapter focuses on physical data modeling by describing the mature and proven database design options available for operational and decision-support databases, including multidimensional database design schemas.

ORIGINS OF DATA MODELING

In the early days of data processing, the entire focus of system development revolved around automating tedious, manual business processes, such as order processing or accounts receivable. Thus, the main effort during the system development life cycle (SDLC) was to produce a set of programs that automated a business process. In other words, processes were the key drivers for information systems, not data or information. The data used by those systems simply "tagged along" as a byproduct.

As the technology and the complexity of systems grew, methodologies and modeling techniques were invented to improve the quality of the deliverables and to ensure that inexperienced programmers could follow repeatable SDLC processes. Quite predictably, the first modeling techniques revolved around processes. *Data flow diagrams*, popularized by Gane-Sarson, Ed Yourdon, and Tom DeMarco, modeled the business processes. *System flow diagrams* and *structure charts*, popularized by Ed Yourdon, Larry Constantine, and Meilir Page-Jones, modeled the automated processes (program modules and system flows).

Just as process-oriented modeling techniques were becoming the standard of SDLC methodologies in the 1970s, Dr. Peter Chen broke the pattern of process-oriented system development with his invention of the *entity-relationship* (E/R) model, which soon became known as the *logical data model*. Dr. Chen's first version of the E/R model represented entities (business objects) as rectangles and relationships between entities as rhombuses (diamonds) on the relationship lines. It also graphically showed attributes (data elements) as circles attached to either entities or relationships, as shown in Figure 5.1. This notation made it possible to maintain many-to-many relationships (such as a customer with many accounts and an account with many customers) without resolving them into associative or intersection entities. (Because many-to-many relationships cannot be implemented in a relational database, an associative entity in the middle holds the foreign key combinations from both entities for each instance where the two entities are related.)

Dr. Chen's original work was later expanded by Mat Flavin and Robert Brown with E/R modeling extensions that we take for granted today; for example, classifying entities as supertypes and subtypes with data inheritance, expressing optionality (minimum cardinality) that indicates a mandatory versus optional relationship, and showing other relationship constraints, such as an "exclusive or." (An "exclusive or" means that entity A is related to either B or C, but not both.)

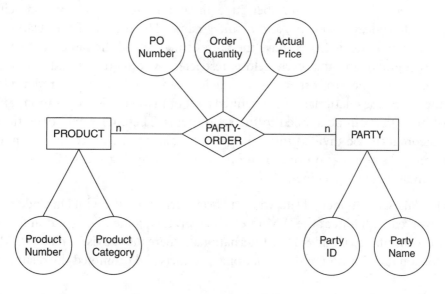

Figure 5.1: An example of an early version E/R model

SIGNIFICANCE OF DATA MODELING

E/R modeling was revolutionary in that—for the first time in data processing—data, not processes, were at the center of both business analysis and system design. The implications were enormous; data could become a reusable commodity, which meant that every unique data element was identified and inventoried once and only once. That provided the ability to track every business object using the unique data elements for any purpose. The concepts of data-driven analysis, and later of data-driven methodologies, were born as business analysts and data modeling practitioners realized that they could finally create a business model of their organization that would *logically* portray a nonredundant "single version of the truth" of their enterprise in terms of its data resources. Companies created departments called data resource management (DRM), information resource management (IRM), and data administration to manage business data as a corporate asset, just like they manage financial assets, fixed assets, real estate, and human resources.

At the same time, Dr. Edgar F. Codd, who was a researcher at IBM in the 1970s, began his work, which eventually led to the development of DB2. In his seminal article, "A Relational Model of Data for Large Shared Data Banks." Dr. Codd presented the relational model as an unordered group (or set) of items, in which each item was divided into fields with atomic values. *Atomic* refers to data elements at their lowest decomposed level. For example, an address has several atomic data elements: street number, street direction, street name, unit code, city name, state code, postal code, and country name. The theory of the relational model is that all items (rows) have the same structure and the same number of fields (columns), and that each field is restricted to contain one and only one atomic data type. In other words, fields can no longer be redefined. Furthermore, the relational model defined a set of mathematical operations and constraints that can be applied to the set of items. These relational operations can theoretically be divided into components that can be processed by independent tasks running on one or more central processing units (CPUs), and even on distributed machines.

In 1983, Christopher J. Date, who had been corresponding with Dr. Codd and later worked with him at the IBM research laboratory, joined Dr. Codd in forming the consultancy, Codd & Date International, where they advised major DBMS vendors on the direction of their relational products and promoted the relational model through conferences and seminars world-wide. In 1985, Dr. Codd published the famous *12 rules of relational databases* (actually 13 rules when counting rule zero). These rules, derived from www.itworld.com, are as follows:

Rule Zero: Any system that is advertised as, or claims to be, a relational data base management system must be able to manage databases entirely through its relational capabilities.

In other words, a relational DBMS must be able to manage databases entirely through its relational capabilities.

Rule 1, Information Rule: All information in a relational database is represented explicitly at the logical level and in exactly one way—by values in tables.

In other words, all information in a relational database (including table and column names) is represented explicitly as values in tables.

Rule 2, Guaranteed Access Rule: Each and every datum (atomic value) in a relational database is guaranteed to be logically accessible by resorting to a combination of table name, primary key value, and column name.

In other words, every value in a relational database is guaranteed to be accessible by using a combination of the table name, primary key value, and column name.

Rule 3, Systematic Treatment of Null Values: Null values (distinct from the empty character string or a string of blank characters and distinct from zero or any other number) are supported in a fully relational DBMS for representing missing information and inapplicable information in a systematic way, independent of data type.

In other words, the relational DBMS provides systematic support for the treatment of null values (unknown or inapplicable data), distinct from default values and independent of any domain.

Rule 4, Dynamic Online Catalog Based on the Relational Model: The database description is represented at the logical level in the same way as ordinary data, so that authorized users can apply the same relational language to its interrogation as they apply to the regular data.

In other words, the description of the database and its contents is represented at the logical level as tables and can therefore be queried using the database language.

Rule 5, Comprehensive Data Sublanguage: A relational system can support several languages and various modes of terminal use (for example, the fill-in-the-blanks mode). However, there must be at least one language whose statements are expressible, per some well defined syntax, as character strings and that is comprehensive in supporting all of the following items:

- Data definition

- View definition

- Data manipulation (interactive and by program)

- Integrity constraints

- Authorization

- Transaction boundaries (begin, commit, and rollback)

In other words, at least one supported language must have a well defined syntax and be comprehensive. It must support data definition, manipulation, integrity rules, authorization, and transactions.

Rule 6, View Updating Rule: All views that are theoretically updatable are also updatable by the system.

In other words, all views that are theoretically updatable can also be updated through the system.

Rule 7, High-Level Insert, Update, and Delete: The capability of handling a base relation or a derived relation as a single operand applies not only to the retrieval of data, but also to the insertion, update, and deletion of data.

In other words, the relational DBMS supports not only set-level retrievals, but also set-level inserts, updates, and deletes.

Rule 8, Physical Data Independence: Application programs and terminal activities remain logically unimpaired whenever any changes are made in either storage representations or access methods.

In other words, application programs and ad-hoc programs are logically unaffected when physical access methods or storage structures are altered.

Rule 9, Logical Data Independence: Application programs and terminal activities remain logically unimpaired when information-preserving changes of any kind that theoretically permit unimpairment are made to the database tables.

In other words, application programs and ad-hoc programs are logically unaffected, to the extent possible, when changes are made to the table structures.

Rule 10, Integrity Independence: Integrity constraints specific to a particular relational database must be definable in the relational data sublanguage and storable in the catalog, not in the application programs.

In other words, the database language must be capable of defining integrity rules. They must be stored in the online catalog, and they cannot be bypassed.

Rule 11, Distribution Independence: A relational DBMS has distribution independence.

In other words, application programs and ad-hoc requests are logically unaffected when data is first distributed or when it is redistributed.

Rule 12, Nonsubversion Rule: If a relational system has a low-level (single-record-at-a-time) language, that low level cannot be used to subvert or bypass the integrity rules and constraints expressed in the higher-level relational language (multiple-records-at-a-time).

In other words, it must not be possible to bypass the integrity rules defined through the database language by using lower-level languages.

LOGICAL DATA MODELING CONCEPTS

The power of relational database management systems (RDBMSs) is inextricably tied to the concepts of Peter Chen's original E/R model, that is, to the logical data model. At its core is the notion of separating data from processes (both business and system processes) for update (operational) as well as access (decision support) purposes. The logical data model achieves this separation from a business perspective, and the physical data model implements this separation from the database perspective.

Process-*Independence*

Separating data from processes during logical data modeling means disregarding access paths, programming languages, SQL versions, query and reporting tools, online analytical processing (OLAP) tools, and RDBMS products. All these process-dependent variables are completely immaterial during business analysis (logical data modeling), which focuses only on *what* data comprises the organization. The processes come into play later during database design (physical data modeling), which addresses *how* data will be used and, therefore, how data should be stored.

Business-Focused Data Analysis

Logical data modeling facilitates business-focused data analysis, which is quite different from the usual kind of analysis we perform during a SDLC, which is *system* analysis. An old—but very appropriate—term for activities performed during system analysis is "external design" because the thought processes applied during system analysis are geared toward producing design alternatives for a system. In fact, every project in which requirement definitions for a specific application are followed by design activities omits business-focused data analysis and performs only system analysis—at best.

Whereas system analysis activities produce preliminary design alternatives, business-focused data analysis activities are geared toward understanding the enterprise-wide usage of business data and uncovering existing defects in the data (for example, business rule violations or referential integrity violations), irrespective of any database design or implementation method. Business-focused data analysis uses rules of normalization to build a nonredundant and fully integrated data model, which reflects the 360-degree view of a business or its "single version of the truth." *Normalization* is the process of removing data redundancy and update dependency by separating data according to the six normalization rules: First Normal Form (1NF), Second Normal Form (2NF), Third Normal Form (3NF), Boyce Codd Normal Form (BCNF), Fourth Normal Form (4NF), and Fifth Normal Form (5NF). The normalization rules are explained in more detail in the "Normalization Rules" box that follows.

NORMALIZATION RULES

Following are descriptions of the normalization rules:

1. 1NF, or First Normal Form, states that you have no data redundancy caused by repeating groups. For example, a PRODUCT table with *repeating supplier data* would not be in 1NF unless the supplier data was moved into a separate SUPPLIER table in which each supplier is uniquely stored.

2. 2NF, or Second Normal Form, states that you have no data redundancy caused by partial key dependence. For example, a SUPPLIER PARTS table with *repeating part descriptions* caused by the same part being available through multiple suppliers would not be in 2NF unless the part descriptions were moved into a separate PART table in which each part is uniquely stored.

3. 3NF, or Third Normal Form, states that you have no data redundancy caused by non-key relationships in the data. For example, a PART table with *repeating category descriptions* that are related to category codes (and not directly to parts) would not be in 3NF unless the category descriptions were moved into a separate CATEGORY table in which each category is uniquely stored.

4. BCNF, or Boyce-Codd Normal Form, is an expansion of 3NF except that the reason for redundancy is an alternate candidate key. For example, a CUSTOMER RELATIONSHIP table with the *repeating* columns Bank Branch Number and Account Executive ID would not be in BCNF unless the column Bank Branch Number were moved into a separate BRANCH table where each branch is uniquely stored for each account executive.

5. 4NF, or Fourth Normal Form, states that you have no data redundancy if you isolate N-ary relationships (more than two entities participating in the same relationship) into multiple binary *independent* relationships. For example, let's assume you want to track the programming languages your programmers know (such as COBOL, C++, or JAVA) and the platforms they can work on (such as AS400, UNIX, and LINUX). A PROGRAMMER SKILL table with *repeating programming languages* and *platforms* would not be in 4NF unless the programming languages for each programmer and the platforms for each programmer were split into two separate tables: PROGRAMMER LANGUAGE and PROGRAMMER PLATFORM.

6. 5NF, or Fifth Normal Form, states that you have no data redundancy if you isolate N-ary relationships into multiple binary *dependent* relationships. For example, let's expand the example of 4NF with the requirement to track which platforms support which programming languages, so that you would know what programmers you could assign to projects that require certain programming language skills on a certain platform.

A PROGRAMMER SKILL table with *repeating programming languages* and *platforms* would not be in 5NF unless the programming languages for each programmer and the platforms for each programmer *and* the programming languages on each platform were split into three separate tables: PROGRAMMER LANGUAGE, PROGRAMMER PLATFORM, and PLATFORM LANGUAGE.

Data Integration (Single Version of Truth)

Data integration enforces entity and attribute uniqueness. Unique, non-redundant attributes are the building blocks of the "single version of the truth" that enable you to reuse the same data without the need to duplicate it and without the additional development and maintenance costs of managing the duplications. Data integration requires several actions during logical data modeling:

1. Examine the definition, the semantic intent, the attributes, and the domain values of each logical entity to find potential duplicates of business objects that would otherwise not be discovered because the objects are known under different names in the systems.

2. Ensure that each entity instance has one and only one unique identifier (primary key), which, in turn, is never reassigned to a new entity instance, even after the old instance expires and is deleted from the database.

3. Use the six normalization rules to put "one fact in one place," that is, one *attribute* in one, and only one, owning entity. This means that an attribute can be assigned to only one entity as either an identifier of that entity or as a descriptive attribute of that and no other entity. This modeling activity ensures that each attribute is captured once, and only once, and that it remains unique within the data universe of the organization. Hence, the "single version of the truth."

4. The last and most important activity of integration is to capture the business actions (or business transactions) that connect the business objects in the real world. These business actions are shown as data relationships among the entities. It is paramount to capture them from a logical business perspective (not from a reporting pattern or data access perspective) because these relationships are the basis for all potential access patterns, known and unknown, now and in the future.

Data Quality

Because the activities of logical data modeling are solely business-focused analysis activities, they include the validation of the logical data model components (such as entities, attributes, relationships, definitions, domains, business rules, and so on) against the existing operational data in the source files and source databases. The validation activities include asking probing questions, applying normalization rules to put "one fact in one place," and scrutinizing definitions, domains, and semantic meanings of all entities and all attributes to ensure their uniqueness.

Performing this type of data archeology during business-focused data analysis inadvertently exposes data quality problems that would otherwise never have been detected during database design activities because database designers do not have the time or the responsibility to perform such validation activities while they are trying to design an efficiently performing database. Therefore, logical data modeling directly contributes to improving data quality.

ENTERPRISE LOGICAL DATA MODEL

The benefits of logical data modeling are more completely derived from building the 360-degree view of a business, not from designing a database for a specific business function or a specific reporting pattern. However, the difficulty in building the 360-degree view of a business is that the current data chaos in most organizations is so immense that it can take significant time and effort to rationalize the existing data into an integrated, nonredundant enterprise logical data model. Because of this difficulty, there are conflicting opinions about how to best approach building the enterprise logical data model.

Big-Bang Versus Incremental

Occasionally, one hears debates about whether to build the enterprise logical data model in one big-bang effort or in small increments. Back in the early 1980s, organizations that embarked on logical data modeling followed the best practices of that time and attempted to model the entire enterprise view all at once. The business people who participated in the modeling sessions gained invaluable insights into the functions and data of the organization, but they had little to show for their efforts besides a lot of E/R diagrams decorating their cubicle walls. The reason was that developing the enterprise logical data model was never part of any system development project because the big-bang approach took too long and would have delayed the implementation of new systems. By the time the enterprise logical data model was completed, the systems had already been developed independently and without adherence to the model.

Big-Bang Pros and Cons

Advocates of the big-bang approach still argue that the benefits of big-bang enterprise logical data modeling outweigh its shortcomings. They point out that unless all major business objects (entities) and their relationships are identified upfront, the enterprise logical data model will contain errors and will need to be reworked. They also declare that unless all the attributes pass all of the normalization rules, some of the attributes are guaranteed to be misplaced and will need to be moved. In addition, they say that unless all the definitions, domains, and business rules are defined for all the attributes, the enterprise logical data model cannot be considered complete or accurate. They favor the big-bang approach because if an incomplete enterprise logical data model—fraught with all those errors—were to be used to design one or more application databases, those databases would have to be redesigned as the errors are discovered, which would have a domino effect on all the programs accessing those databases. Although there is some truth to all of these points, the arguments against a big-bang approach far outweigh the risks.

There are two practical arguments against the big-bang approach. First, it takes much too long to find and resolve all of the conflicting data views and data rules that currently exist among business people, not to mention finding and resolving all of the data redundancies and data inconsistencies that currently exist among systems. Second, it requires too many participants from too many business areas (various data owners, data stewards, subject matter experts, information consumers, and so on) to be involved in all the logical data modeling sessions. The big-bang approach requires that all individuals be involved upfront, or the enterprise logical data model cannot be considered complete or validated; however, this is a physical impracticality. The coordination of people's availability and meeting rooms alone can be a major challenge, not to mention the facilitation effort to keep these meetings productive and moving forward.

Incremental Pros and Cons

The arguments against an incremental approach to building the enterprise logical data model are the same arguments used to defend the benefits of the big-bang approach. Building the enterprise logical data model incrementally means to build a project-specific, fully normalized, fully attributed, fully defined, and fully documented logical data model during the SDLC of each project, but to limit the logical data modeling activities to only those data elements that are in the scope of that project.

Assuming that no prior enterprise logical data model exists, the first project-specific logical data model is the first increment or iteration of the enterprise logical data model. The second project-specific logical data model, which is also limited to the data elements that are in the scope of the second project, is then merged with the first one to produce the second increment or iteration of the enterprise logical data model. Any discrepancies, ambiguities, or inconsistencies between the two models are presented to the participants of both projects to be resolved. This process is then repeated with all subsequent projects, as illustrated in Figure 5.2. This way, over time, an enterprise logical data model can be achieved with incremental value obtained along the way.

 Note: To avoid excessive rework, the normalization rules must be followed without exception. This is the only way to ensure that the disjointed pieces of the evolving enterprise logical data model will fit seamlessly as they are assembled from the various project-specific logical data models over time.

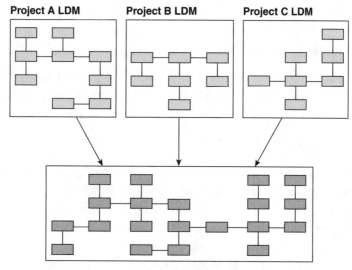

Figure 5.2: Incremental development of enterprise logical data model

The benefits of incrementally building the enterprise logical data model can be reaped immediately:

- The additional effort and time it takes to produce a project-specific logical data model is miniscule in comparison to a big-bang effort. This approach involves fewer participants at one time because of the reduced project scope. The validation time is also shortened due to the reduced number of participants.

- The project-specific logical data model can be used as a baseline for database design, regardless of whether the database will be an E/R schema or a star/snowflake schema (see the section on physical data modeling in this chapter).

- Business rules and metadata can be collected, validated, refined, and revised slowly over time, which comfortably accommodates the rate of change in business policies in most organizations.

- Errors, misunderstandings, omissions, hidden obstacles, and other unavoidable issues can be resolved incrementally, which gives the organization time to mature into a learning organization. A learning organization is an organization that has increased its capacity to rapidly adapt to changes.

Top-Down versus Bottom-Up

Another debate that often occurs is the topic of top-down versus bottom-up logical data modeling. This is an ill-conceived debate because *both* techniques must be applied to ensure a robust and realistic logical data model.

Top-Down Logical Data Modeling

Top-down logical data modeling refers to the technique of facilitating fact-finding discussions among participants from various business areas who own, originate, or use the data. The logical data modeler, who is usually the facilitator in these discovery sessions, helps the participants to identify the major business objects, the data relationships among them, the unique identifiers of those objects, the most significant and obvious attributes of those objects, and the main business rules for those attributes.

This fact-finding activity produces a "straw-man" (first-cut) logical data model. The logical data modeler and one of the participants then go through several iterations of revising and fleshing out the details of the logical data model, and then writing the definitions for the entities and the attributes. Throughout this process, they periodically call back the other participants to validate their work using follow-up discovery sessions. When the logical data model is deemed to be finished, the forward-engineering function of the computer-aided software engineering (CASE) or data modeling tool can be used to produce the first-cut physical data model that the DBA can then use to start his database design activities.

Using the top-down data modeling technique produces a relatively valid logical data model in a relatively short time. However, using this technique alone has several inadequacies:

- The logical data model will most likely not be complete because it is impossible to think of all the details during discovery sessions without performing some amount of bottom-up analysis of the operational source files, databases, and programs. This type of analysis often reveals additional attributes, relationships, business rules, and in some cases, even additional entities.

- The logical data model will most likely not reflect the correct representation of all the data because it was based on the participants' understanding of their business or their industry and on the business rules they thought "should" govern the data. Analyzing the existing source files and databases often reveals that some of the stated business rules are either not enforced or they are incorrect because they are not reflected in the source data.

- Discovery sessions are extremely effective for finding and resolving many high-level issues with diverse participants in a short time, but they are not helpful when performing detailed analysis and research. On the contrary, the more people who try to analyze the same thing, the longer it takes. In addition, participants get anxious and feel they are wasting time when the research activities bog down in laborious details.

So the bottom line is that top-down logical data modeling goes only so far before it has to be augmented with bottom-up logical data modeling.

Bottom-Up Logical Data Modeling

Bottom-up logical data modeling refers to the painstaking task of normalizing existing process-oriented (denormalized) data structures into a "best-guess" logical data model. The steps include:

1. Review record layouts and data definition language (DDL) to find potentially embedded entities.

2. Trace through primary and foreign keys to locate inferred entities and their potential relationships. (A *foreign key* is a physical implementation of a logical data relationship between two entities. The relationship is physically implemented by copying the primary key of one table into the related table.)

3. Painstakingly apply the normalization rules to each data element.

4. Convert technical column and table names to fully qualified business names and assign prime, qualifier, and class word components. An example of a standardized business name for a data element is Monthly Checking Account Balance. The main component (prime word) is "Account," which is further qualified by the word "Checking" to indicate what type of account. The class word indicating the type of data value contained in this data element is "Balance," which is further qualified by the word "Monthly" to indicate the type of balance. This is an industry standard naming convention.

This process is sometimes referred to as *reverse engineering*, which is a common feature in CASE and data modeling tools. However, the reverse-engineering capabilities of these tools cover only a small part of the process in bottom-up logical data modeling—and then only if the existing data structure is a relational database. These tools produce a *physical* data model of the underlying database by tracing through the primary and foreign key relationships among tables in the database (Step 2) and then simply calling the tables "entities" and showing the traced key relationships as data relationships among entities. They do not perform any analysis, normalization, or business name qualification. In some cases (for example, in the case of a 3NF E/R-based database implementation), such a physical data model can be a useful starting point to approximate or "best-guess" the logical entities. The logical data modeler (usually the data administrator) can use those inferred potential entities to continue the normalization process. However, without further normalization, a reverse-engineered physical data model is never equivalent to a true bottom-up logical data model. And it is doubtful that tools will ever be able to mimic the human reasoning and judgment processes that are intrinsic to bottom-up logical data modeling.

As just described, using the bottom-up data modeling technique produces a relatively complete logical data model. However, there are also several inadequacies using this technique alone:

- The bottom-up approach to produce a "best-guess" logical data model cannot be trusted until it is meticulously reviewed and validated by all end users who own, originate, or use the data.

- The logical data model is immediately large and complex because it includes all the details from the existing source files and databases from the start. This makes it overwhelming for some end users to review the logical data model and some even refuse to participate in any review sessions. This immediate complexity is also problematic for some less experienced logical data modelers who can easily get lost in the ambiguities and open questions during the iterative refinement process.

- The logical data model most likely does not reflect the correct representation of all the data because it is based on the built-in structural constraints of the existing files and databases and on the programmed-in business rules of the existing applications. When people are asked to validate these derived logical data models, they frequently point out incorrect or missing business rules, data relationships, attributes, and even entities.

So, the bottom line is that bottom-up logical data modeling goes only so far before it has to be augmented with facilitated top-down validation. As you can see, both the bottom-up and top-down approaches bring solid benefits, but each is somewhat incomplete without the other.

PHYSICAL DATA MODELING CONCEPTS

Physical data modeling is synonymous with the term logical database design. It is a graphic representation of the proposed tables, relationships among tables, primary and foreign keys, and columns.

Process-Dependence

Unlike logical data modeling, which is process-*independent*, the physical data model must be process-*dependent* and take into consideration the access paths, programming languages, SQL versions, query and reporting tools, online analytical processing (OLAP) tools, and RDBMS products. If you review the definitions for these process-dependent variables, it is easy to understand their influence on database design:

- Access paths must be determined, analyzed, and applied during database design when the physical data model is created to determine how data will be stored in the database. For efficiency reasons, some entities can be collapsed (denormalized) to avoid excessive database joins.

- Programming languages, such as COBOL, C++, or Java, have their own idiosyncratic rules about making SQL calls to relational databases. These rules have to be understood and considered during database design.

- Query and reporting tools translate the abstract user instructions (metadata) into a form of SQL, which then executes against the database. Some query and reporting tools produce rather inefficient SQL code and database administrators might have to replace the tool-generated SQL code with their own more efficient pass-through queries.

- OLAP tools typically provide multidimensional functionalities, such as slicing and dicing and pivoting query results that require the underlying database to be designed in a multidimensional schema. Furthermore, some OLAP tools have a specific preference for either star schemas or snowflake schemas and other OLAP tools even provide their own proprietary DBMS engine. Using the wrong database design can prevent the OLAP tool from functioning properly—or at all.

- RDBMS products compete with each other through their unique functional extensions (SQL) and optimization capabilities. Therefore, the most perfect design for one RDBMS is not necessarily the best design for another. For example, when migrating from Oracle to Teradata, the existing database designs should be reviewed and adjusted, or even redesigned, to take advantage of the different optimization capabilities of the new product.

Database Design

Physical data modeling facilitates logical database design with the primary focus on performance. Thus, database designers (usually database administrators or database-savvy developers) must consider and balance all application-specific, process-dependent variables. They must also have a good understanding of how the RDBMS product-specific optimizer will react to these variables, so that they can apply the minimum amount of denormalization to achieve the maximum amount of performance.

PHYSICAL DATA MODELING TECHNIQUES

A number of different techniques are applied during physical data modeling, including denormalization, surrogate keys, indexing, partitioning, database views, and dimensionality. Some of the physical data modeling factors discussed in this section include those unique to DW applications. Each factor requires us to define guidelines that lead to intelligent design decisions.

To illustrate the physical data modeling techniques, we use the fully normalized logical data model for a dessert application for a large restaurant chain, as shown in Figure 5.3. All desserts (banana split, brownie sundae, and so on) are described and priced in the DESSERT entity. A DESSERT can belong to one or more CATEGORIES and a CATEGORY can contain many DESSERTS. For example, the banana split can belong to the frozen and indulgent categories, and the frozen category can also contain the brownie sundae. A DESSERT can be offered in many RESTAURANTS and a RESTAURANT can offer many DESSERTS. In addition, DAILY ORDERS are kept for each DESSERT by day and RESTAURANT. A REGION can contain many RESTAURANTS (for example, the Northeast contains 50 restaurants), but a RESTAURANT can reside in a single REGION only.

Denormalization

Denormalization is the process of selectively violating normalization rules and reintroducing data redundancy into the model. This extra redundancy can reduce data retrieval time, which is the primary reason for denormalizing. You can also denormalize to create a more user-friendly model. For example, it might be quicker to retrieve and easier for end users to understand if all time data elements existed in a single table instead of ten normalized tables.

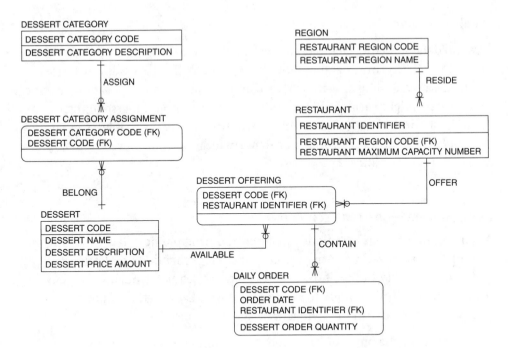

Figure 5.3: Dessert logical data model

Tables 5.1 and 5.2, as well as Figure 5.4, illustrate two examples of denormalization. DESSERT CATEGORY and DESSERT CATEGORY ASSIGNMENT are no longer separate tables and now exist only as three sets of data elements in DESSERT. This type of denormalization is called an array. An *array* is a fairly severe form of denormalization because it is a repeating group, and therefore, it violates 1NF. A few rows in the table might be as follows in Table 5.1:

Table 5.1: Denormalized Dessert Table

Code	Name	Desc	Price	Cat 1 Code	Cat 1 Desc	Cat 2 Code	Cat 2 Desc	Cat 3 Code	Cat 3 Desc
1	Banana Split	Several bananas, and so on	$4.95	1	Frozen	2	Indulgent		
2	Brownie Sundae	Large piece of brownie, and so on	$3.95	5	Cake	1	Frozen	2	Indulgent
3	Low-Fat Yogurt	Healthy choice, and so on	$2.95	3	Healthy Choice	1	Frozen		

Note that it can be quicker to retrieve certain kinds of information from this denormalized structure; for example, if the end user wants to view all of the desserts priced over $4.00 along with each of their categories. Note also that denormalization can make other types of reporting more difficult, such as viewing all frozen desserts. Looking for frozen desserts in this denormalized structure requires searching through each of the three category data elements.

Finally, notice that REGION has been denormalized into RESTAURANT in Table 5.2.

Table 5.2: Denormalized Restaurant Table

Restaurant ID	Maximum Capacity	Region Code	Region Name
456	20	NE	Northeast
1234	150	NE	Northeast
789	60	SW	Southwest

This is the most popular denormalization technique. The parent entity goes away and the parent data elements and relationships are now a part of the child. There are several other ways to denormalize as well, but they all share the characteristics shown in these two examples, namely that there is extra redundancy, but the tradeoff can be faster retrieval and more user-friendly structures. Still, you need to be selective about where you introduce denormalization, as this extra redundancy comes with a price. It can:

- **Cause update, delete, and insert performance to suffer**—When you repeat a data element in two or more tables, you can usually retrieve the values within this data element much quicker. However, if you have to change the value in this data element, you need to change it in every table in which it resides.

- **Take up more space**—Repeating the Region Name for each restaurant means more space is used. In a table with a small number of records, this extra storage space is not substantial. However, in tables with millions of rows, every character can require megabytes of additional space.

- **Introduce data quality problems**—By having the same data element multiple times in the design, you substantially increase opportunities for data quality issues when value changes occur. Also, denormalizing reduces the number of relationships and therefore reduces the amount of referential integrity.

- **Stunt the growth of the application**—When you denormalize, it can become harder to enhance structures to meet new requirements because before you add data elements or relationships, you need to understand all of the hidden rules on the physical data model that were shown on the logical data model.

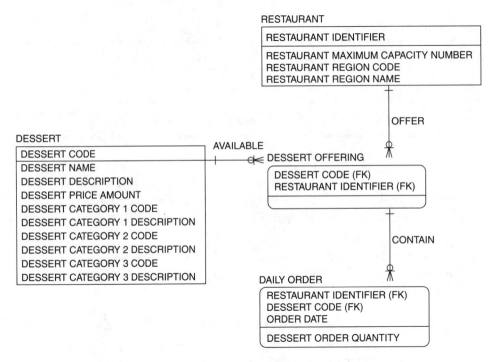

Figure 5.4: Dessert relational physical data model

Surrogate Keys

A *surrogate key* is an artificial unique identifier for a table. Characteristics of a surrogate key include that it is an integer, which has no meaning based on its value. That is, you cannot look at a Month Identifier of "1" and assume that it is January. It is usually a system-generated counter. Surrogate keys are in almost all cases not visible to the end users; instead, they stay "behind the scenes" to help maintain uniqueness.

Surrogate keys provide for a number of benefits, the two most important being integration and efficiency. For example, a DW will more than likely be sourced from more than one operational system, and therefore, there is a good chance that a fair amount of integration will be necessary. Surrogate keys can be defined as unique across source systems, so that a Robert Jones from system XYZ and a Renee Jane from system ABC might both be identified in their respective systems as RJ, but when they are loaded into the DW, they are each assigned a unique, non-overlapping key. Surrogate keys are also integers, and therefore, they take up less space and provide quicker joins than other formats or composite keys. (A composite key is a primary key made up of multiple columns.) In Figure 5.4, an example of a surrogate key is Restaurant Identifier.

Indexing

An *index* is a pointer to the real thing you are looking for. An often-used analogy is when you visit your library and find the book you need in the card catalog. The card catalog points you to where the actual book is on the shelf, which is much quicker than looking through each book in the library until you find the one you need. Indexing works the same way for finding data. The index points to the actual place on the disk where the data is stored, making retrieval much quicker.

In applications in which there is a lot of retrieval in the form of reporting and queries, indexing is essential. Indexes work best on data elements that are often retrieved and rarely updated. Indexes also provide the most value, as you might expect, for tables with a lot of rows, such as CUSTOMER and ORDER. Indexing is specific to the underlying RDBMS and you might find that what works well on one RDBMS falls short on another.

Partitioning

Partitioning is when a table is broken up by rows, columns, or both. If a table is broken up by columns, it is called *vertical partitioning*. If a table is broken up by rows, it is called *horizontal partitioning*.

In Figure 5.4, if DAILY ORDER gets too large (too many rows) to be an efficient querying table, you might want to use horizontal partitioning to break out the rows by year. (Be sure to define "efficient." RDBMS optimizers handle the data retrieval as efficiently as possible, but the response times might not be desirable.) Horizontal partitioning by year would be efficient if most of the queries do not cross years, but would be inefficient if queries were executed, such as, "Show me all of the days over the last 5 years when we sold more than ten banana splits in a given restaurant."

An example of vertical partitioning is storing Dessert Price Amount in its own table because it might change much more frequently than the rest of the dessert data elements. Partitioning, as with indexes, is RDBMS-specific and you should consult the vendor's database documentation to learn the guidelines on when to partition.

Database Views

The key point with database views is that at times they can offer all the same benefits as denormalization *without the drawbacks associated with data redundancy*. For example, a view can provide user-friendly structures without sacrificing referential integrity. A view keeps the underlying model intact, and at the same time, presents a denormalized or summarized view of the world to the end users. There are different types of views. Views that are generated when accessed might not match the performance of an actual denormalized table, but this depends on the type of RDBMS, number of rows, and so on. However, some types of views, such as materialized views or snapshots, can match and even sometimes beat retrieval speed from actual tables because they are generated at some predetermined time and stored in a system cache.

Figure 5.5 shows two views. The view built on RESTAURANT and REGION allows for the region information to be presented in the same structure as restaurant information, which saves the end user and report tool the job of locating and performing the join across these two tables. In CATEGORY_SALES_BY_DAY_VIEW, we built a summary on top of the underlying tables without increasing space requirements.

DIMENSIONALITY

Databases that are solely designed for reporting, such as DW databases, must take dimensionality into consideration. Therefore, DW physical data models are commonly referred to as either "relational" (meaning mostly normalized data structures as reflected in operational business activities) or "dimensional" (meaning mostly denormalized data structures as reflected in decision-support reporting patterns). The book, *Mastering Data Warehouse Design*, has a great definition of a relational model: "The relational model is a form of data model in which data is packaged according to business rules and data relationships, regardless of how the data will be used in processes, in as non-redundant a fashion as possible. Normalization rules are used to create this form of model."

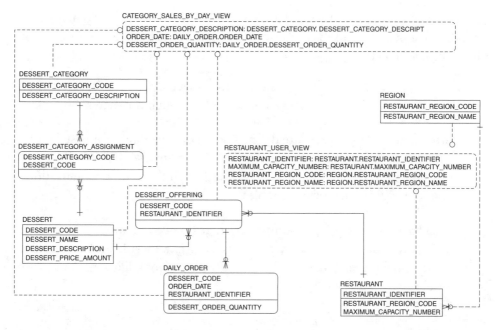

Figure 5.5: Dessert relational physical data model with views

 Note: In the purest sense, these labels are not accurate because both types of physical data models ("dimensional" and "relational") are drawn as entity-relationship diagrams, both can contain normalized as well as denormalized data structures (tables), and both are implemented on relational databases.

From the same book: "A dimensional model is a form of data modeling that packages data according to specific business queries and reporting processes. The goals are business user understandability and multidimensional query performance." Note that there is nothing in this dimensional definition about business rules and normalization. How the data will be used and how it will perform are contextual and physical concerns; therefore, dimensionality is a physical data modeling technique.

A dimensional design is a seemingly simple structure where all the elements viewed on reports or in queries appear in a central table (called a *meter* or fact table), and all the ways of reporting on the data appear in dimensional structures by subject area. Each subject area is called a *dimension*. There are two major rules in a dimensional structure that make its appearance completely different from the relational structure:

- You can never have relationships between subject areas. That is, all relationships between dimensions must appear only through the meter.

- Within a dimension, tables are defined based on levels and not based on normalization. So for example, in the TIME dimension there could be separate tables for YEAR and MONTH, even though there are normalization violations within each of these tables.

Going back to our dessert example, let's say you need to answer the business question, "How many desserts do we sell by restaurant, month, and dessert category?" The initial dimensional model might therefore look like what appears in Figure 5.6.

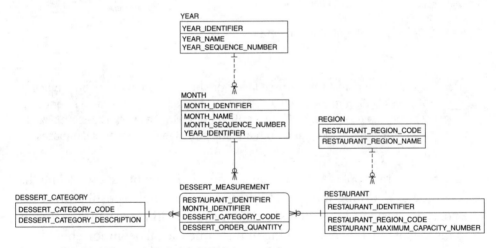

Figure 5.6: Initial dimensional physical data model

The dimensional model is the first step in a physical design. The next step is to change this model further into a Star schema, Snowflake, or Starflake.

Star Schema

A *star schema* is when each set of tables that make up a dimension is folded into a single table. We use the phrase "folded" instead of "denormalized" because a dimensional model is never normalized to begin with, but instead separated into different tables by level as mentioned previously.

The meter is in the center of the model and each of the dimensions relates to the meter at the lowest level of detail. So for example in Figure 5.7, the meter DESSERT MEASUREMENT relates to the MONTH dimension at the month level. If 15 desserts were ordered in January, 2003, the end user or reporting tool can then query as to how many desserts were ordered in all of 2003. A star schema is relatively easy to create and implement, and it visually appears elegant and simplistic to both IT and end users. For these reasons, it is often used in many situations in which it is not the optimal design choice. We discuss guidelines shortly, but in a single sentence, a star schema is most useful when the dimensions have relatively few rows, the meter contains only metric facts (see Guideline 8), and there is a short-term, specific purpose for the database.

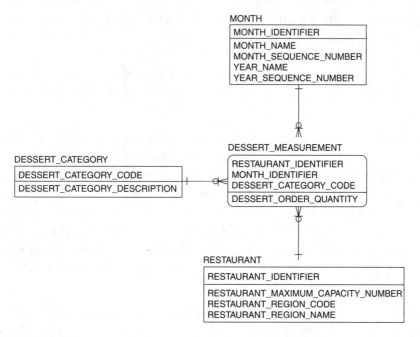

Figure 5.7: Star schema

Snowflake

A *snowflake* is when the initial dimensional model is implemented without folding up any tables. Therefore, in most cases, the snowflake design looks exactly as shown in Figure 5.6. Tables are not folded up for a variety of reasons, the most common being that the rates at which data values change might vary across hierarchy levels.

Starflake

A *starflake* is a combination of both the snowflake and star schema, hence its name. Certain dimensions have all their levels folded into a single table, whereas other dimensions have their hierarchy levels remain in separate tables. Applying guidelines at a subject area level instead of at a model level can easily lead to a starflake. For example, some dimensions might experience varying rates of change while others remain relatively static.

FACTORS THAT INFLUENCE THE PHYSICAL DATA MODEL

Choosing the "right" physical data model for your database depends on a number of factors in your environment. For example, if you design operational OLTP databases or decision-support databases that need to be around for a long time, such as an enterprise DW, it is in your best interest to choose the relational physical data model. However, if you design decision-support databases that will be replaced in the near term or that exist only to answer a few key business questions, such as data marts, you should choose the dimensional physical data model.

One of the ways decision-support applications differ from operational applications is that a substantial number of data access requirements are not known until after the decision-support applications go live. For example, if you build an order-processing application, you most likely know the functions of such an application. It needs to process orders, track shipments, and so on. However, if you are building a profitability data mart, you might have some reports and queries that make up the initial requirements, but you can be sure that shortly after the end users have the reports and query responses in their hands, new follow-up questions and reports will arise.

Following are additional guidelines for deciding whether the relational or dimensional physical data model is the most appropriate for your decision-support database.

Guideline 1: High Degree of Normalization for Robustness

A robust model calls for a high degree of normalization. Most DW applications need a robust model.

A robust model is one that can gracefully handle changes to data requirements. Examples of changes include:

• A new source system is added or an existing source system is replaced.

• The Week is now required in the TIME subject area, which currently just contains Day, Month, and Year.

• Several new types of customer identifiers need to be accommodated.

A model that is normalized can more easily adjust to the first two of these changes because the business rules in the form of relationships are visible and it is therefore more evident to see what adjustments might be necessary. Part of making a model robust also comes from applying logical data modeling techniques outside of normalization, such as abstraction (for example, supertypes and subtypes), which is outside the scope of this book, but allows for more gracefully accommodating the third change.

Guideline 2: Denormalization for Short-Term Solutions

A short-term solution can be fairly denormalized.

The more short term and specific the business needs are, the less important it is to think of the future, and therefore the less denormalization will impact your design. If you build a data mart that addresses a specific set of business questions, you will find yourself applying a larger number of physical data modeling techniques, the primary ones being denormalization and views.

Guideline 3: Usage of Views on Powerful Servers

If you have a powerful server, think twice about denormalizing your physical data model, with the exception of the use of views for user friendliness and security.

The more powerful the server, the quicker joins can be performed across tables, the faster data can be entered and retrieved, the more normalized your physical data model can remain, and therefore, the closer your physical data model can resemble your logical data model. If there is no apparent performance difference whether one or ten tables are joined to retrieve information, the advantage to keeping the data in ten tables is that you maintain data integrity and you minimize redundancy.

Guideline 4: Usage of Views on Powerful RDBMS Software

If you have powerful RDBMS software, think twice about denormalizing your physical data model, with the exception of the use of views for user friendliness and security.

Your RDBMS software has a direct impact on how much denormalization is introduced into your design. This is because as you denormalize, you reintroduce redundancy into your design and reduce table joins to produce query results and reports. If your underlying RDBMS can join across tables with lightning speed, there is no need to denormalize. For example, if you use Teradata, denormalization should be substituted by views wherever possible. On the other hand, if you use Microsoft Access, you need to denormalize much more frequently to compensate for the RDBMS software.

Guideline 5: Cultural Influence on Database Design

A quiet force at work is the culture in your company. Funding and rewarding quick wins more than likely leads to standalone dimensional models, whereas funding and rewarding long-term benefits leads to a well-integrated environment that includes the relational model.

If you work in an organization that emphasizes documentation and long-term benefits over short-term wins, you might find yourself designing a fairly robust architecture, including a normalized relational DW and a series of well designed data marts with excellent documentation. On the other hand, if you work in an organization where the funding and focus is department-specific, you will probably find yourself designing a large number of stovepipe (stand-alone) dimensional data marts that are not integrated and are designed to answer specific questions from specific departments, not for the organization as a whole. If your organization tends to outsource the design and development of applications, you will probably find a model designed to meet more immediate needs, but it will lack in long-term benefits and usefulness. You will also probably find below-average documentation, little or no standardization on definitions, and inconsistent modeling practices because of too many "hands in the soup."

Guideline 6: Modeling Expertise Affects Database Design

Strong modelers in general tend to produce normalized designs with views, selectively add denormalization, or selectively choose the dimensional route. Strong report writers can leverage reporting tools to provide user-friendly structures to the business.

For example, your model might contain complex materialized views over normalized structures or several strategically placed summary tables. Likewise, if your report writers are skilled and know the subject matter well, you might have a fairly normalized looking design underneath sophisticated reporting views and queries.

Guideline 7: User-Friendly Structures

Design your model with the end user in mind. This translates into user-friendly structures, including selectively denormalized tables and, or views.

You also need to consider the technical skills of the end users. If they are comfortable navigating normalized structures (and most are not!), then you can provide them with a subset of the normalized model and they can have at it. If they know and want to see only spreadsheets and pie charts, you might find yourself denormalizing or adding views to the model. For an operational application, such as order processing, the end users generally have the same level of technical expertise and needs for information. However, for a single DW application, there can be several end users who have the technical ability to join tables and require full access to all underlying tables. There can also be a large number of end users who need to receive and view reports and a few senior managers who require a dashboard to monitor key performance indicators. This requires a number of different types of structures to accommodate the different skill levels.

Guideline 8: Metric Facts Determine Database Design

If your application uses metric facts, you will have a dimensional physical data model. If your application does not use metric facts, your physical data model will be relational.

Identifying whether you have metric facts or not is a major question that determines the basic physical characteristic of your model, that is, whether it should be dimensional or relational. What is a metric fact? To informally summarize the definition of *fact* from the Data Warehousing Institute, it is a data element that the user wants to see in queries, reports, dashboards, and so on. A *metric fact* is a fact that can be mathematically manipulated. This is as opposed to a *qualifier*, which is what the users want to see it by. So for instance, going back to our dessert example, let's say your DW application would like to answer the following two questions:

- How many desserts do we sell by restaurant, month, and dessert category?

- What is the name of our most popular dessert by restaurant, month, and dessert category?

Our facts in these two questions are the number of desserts and dessert name. Our qualifiers are the restaurant, month, and dessert categories. Because a metric fact is a fact that can be mathematically manipulated, the number of desserts is a metric fact because it can be summed up to year or region. Dessert name, however, cannot be mathematically manipulated—you would never want to see the sum of dessert names, as it would make no sense. When you have metric facts, dimension models work best because they allow the end user and reporting tools to easily "drill up" and "drill down" hierarchies.

Guideline 9: When to Mimic Source Database Design

If there is no loss in functionality or user-friendliness, you can choose to let your physical data model mimic the design of its source.

The "keep it simple stupid" (KISS) principle can have a large impact on your physical design. We sometimes look for easy and efficient solutions to difficult design problems. One solution, for example, might be to create a physical data model that resembles the source database. This allows for easy coding of extract/transform/load (ETL) logic as well as very fast load times and is relatively easy to support. Make sure however, that the KISS principle is not applied at the loss of some of the other guidelines in this section.

CONCLUSION

When designing databases, it is helpful to remember the principles of logical data modeling because they carry over into database design (physical data modeling). This is especially important when designing DW databases because they are as much about bringing order to data chaos as they are about functional decision-support capabilities. It is important to use a data-driven approach that focuses on reusability of data rather than building silo solutions that contribute to uncontrolled and costly data and program redundancies.

Data reusability requires a "single version of the truth" about the organization, which can be achieved through a combination of top-down plus bottom-up data modeling using the six normalization rules to place each unique atomic data element into its owning entity once, and only once. It is important to remember that the "single version of the truth"—or enterprise logical data model—is not and should not be built all at once (that would take too long), but that it evolves over time as the project-specific logical data models are merged, one-by-one, a project at a time.

A physical data model represents the data requirements from the logical data model. It is specific for a given environment, such as a database or application. A number of different techniques can be deployed to create the most appropriate physical data model, including denormalization, surrogate keys, indexing, partitioning, views, and dimensionality.

You need to be careful about where you deploy these techniques, as undoing the work of normalization can come with a huge price. Therefore, you need to carefully understand the factors at work in your environment and define guidelines that lead you to make intelligent design decisions.

REFERENCES

Adelman, Sid and Larissa Terpeluk Moss. *Data Warehouse Project Management.* Boston, MA: Addison-Wesley, 2000.

Codd, Edgar F., Dr. "A Relational Model of Data for Large Shared Data Banks," *Communications of the ACM.* Volume 13, Number 6, 1970.

Hoberman, Steve. *Data Modeler's Workbench: Tools and Techniques for Analysis and Design.* New York: John Wiley & Sons, 2001.

Kimball, Ralph. "A Dimensional Modeling Manifesto," *DBMS Magazine*, August 1997.

—"Bringing Up Supermarts," *DBMS Magazine*, January 1998.

—"Is ER Modeling Hazardous to DSS?" *DBMS Magazine*, October 1995.

—"The Matrix," *Intelligent Enterprise*, December 1999.

—"There Are No Guarantees," *Intelligent Enterprise*, August 2000.

Imhoff, Claudia, Nicholas Galemmo, and Jonathan Geiger. *Mastering Data Warehouse Design.* New York: John Wiley & Sons, 2003.

Inmon, Bill. "The Problem With Dimensional Modeling," *DM Review*, May 2000.

—"Data Mart Does Not Equal Data Warehouse," *DM Review*, May 1998.

Moss, Larissa and Shaku Atre. *Business Intelligence Roadmap.* Boston, MA: Addison-Wesley, 2003.

Moss, Larissa and Steve Hoberman. "The Importance of Data Modeling as a Foundation for Business Insight." Teradata.com, 2004.

CHAPTER 6

Organizational Roles and Responsibilities

"A basic rule of organization is to build the fewest possible management levels and forge the shortest possible change of command."

—Peter F. Drucker

No effective data strategy will ever be developed without a primary responsibility assigned at a high enough level so that the rest of the organization will take the effort seriously and cooperate to make it a success. First of all, the chief information officer (CIO) and the chief technology officer (CTO) (or higher) must make it clear that creating and implementing a data strategy is critical to the success of the organization, that it will be established, and that it is not just an "initiative of the moment" that will soon be scrapped along with all the others. The CIO should describe the reasons for the data strategy to all the stakeholders and, if possible, solicit buy in from them. The obvious choice for heading up the data strategy is the CTO. The CTO does not typically have day-to-day responsibility for running the IT organization. Instead, the CTO evaluates technical alternatives and sets technical direction for IT. The CTO's performance plan should include developing, maintaining, and enforcing the data strategy. We need to be careful about the title of CTO and know where he or she reports, which must be to the CIO, who has overall responsibility for all IT operations. If the CTO does not report to the CIO, his or her position in the organization is too low to have the influence and power required to make the project successful.

BUILDING THE TEAMS WHO CREATE AND MAINTAIN THE STRATEGY

Creating a strategy takes more time and effort than it takes to maintain it. At a minimum, while the data strategy is being developed, a full-time person (let's call him or her the data strategist) should be dedicated to this effort. The role for the data strategist is described later in this chapter. The data strategy team consists of the following individuals:

• Database administrator

• Data administrator

• CTO

• Technical strategist

The ideal candidates from each group are the managers. There will be many times and prolonged periods of time when individuals from each group will work with the data strategist, but the managers of each group should be present at the weekly meetings, so that timely decisions can be made and important developments relevant to the data strategy will always be in front of the group. A consultant who specializes in data strategy can also be part of the team. The consultant can bring in ideas and knowledge of what other organizations have done, where they have succeeded, and where they have failed. The consultant can validate the data strategy as it's being developed and keep the team from going down the wrong road.

It's imperative that the team meets regularly, at least once a week, to discuss status, issues, decisions that need to be made, and how to communicate the data strategy. A sample agenda for these regular meetings is included at the end of this chapter.

RESISTANCE TO CHANGE

As you build up your data strategy team, be aware that you might encounter resistance. People often feel threatened when they see changes to the status quo.

Existing Organization

The folks in IT don't like change if they believe it will diminish the power of the IT group. This is particularly true for managers. Managers put forward countless reasons why the organization should stay as is, especially if a change can decrease the number of employees they control because managers often equate headcount to power in the organization.

If the technicians are comfortable with the roles and the functions they perform, they do not want those designated functions to change. Few people welcome the new challenge.

Resistance to Standards

IT personnel have always been reluctant to accept standards. Although they might give lip service to standards, they are usually loathe to embrace them and usually express concern that conforming to standards will jeopardize the project's schedule. Business people (the "users") often resist change, especially when it involves lost autonomy due to standardization. They want things "their way" and feel they are entitled to get their way because they are paying for the systems.

"Reasons" for Resistance

There is no end to the reasons you will hear for why a data strategy should not be implemented. Some might seem legitimate, but as each is examined, the reasoning falls apart. The following are some of the more common reasons:

- This is just the most current initiative. We all pretend like it will happen and waste lots of time, but in the end, nothing good comes of it.

- If we have to follow the standards imposed by the data strategy, it will cause our project schedule to slip.

- The powers that be in the IT organization will quietly sabotage the effort.

- The business will never stand for being shackled by a data strategy.

Dealing with this resistance is where social sensitivity, leadership, and power come into play. Social sensitivity is the ability to read the players and respond appropriately to their concerns. Leadership and power can quickly overcome most resistance to change and allow you to establish an environment and convince management to properly support the data strategy.

OPTIMAL ORGANIZATIONAL STRUCTURES

When people spend a percentage of their time on one project and another percentage of their time on another project, the actual amount of work accomplished does not add up to 100 percent. A certain amount of effort is always lost when moving from one train of thought to another. With a dedicated team, the members are more available for interaction and communication. A team that has only a portion of its time dedicated to the project experiences delays and wasted time. For example, waiting to hold a meeting or make a decision because a part-time member is not available will cause a delay. A dedicated team is far more effective and efficient.

Appropriate staff levels are a function of:

• The number and size of the databases

• The number of source systems

• The complexity and quality of source systems

• The number of users

• Users' need for support

• Speed of implementation

• Severity of SLAs (performance, availability, and data quality)

• The speed of response to user requests

• Skill levels

• Experience

• Knowledge of the environment

• How well the staff is managed

• The skill and administration requirements of the end-user tools

• The productivity of the tools

The decisions on how to best staff IT comes down to the status of your systems, people, and your level of service.

Distributed Organizations

Distributed organizations are always more difficult to manage because they are less productive, they cause scheduling problems, communication is not as clear, team camaraderie suffers, and disputes arise that are difficult to resolve. If at all possible, the team should reside in the same city. It's better if they are located in the same building, even better if they are on the same floor, and best when they are adjacent to each other.

Outsourced Personnel

IT jobs are being outsourced for many reasons including scarce availability of skills, the desire to staff a position only for the time required to complete a particular task or project, the difficulty and expense of recruiting, and the push to save money. In particular, offshore work is being performed for significantly less than possible in Western industrialized countries.

The time zone differences between offshore and local work locations are usually dealt with by having the offshore workers available during the organization's local business hours. However, a few problems are still associated with offshore work:

- Face-to-face communication is usually superior to communication via the phone or e-mail.

- The native language of the offshore organization might not be the native language of the sponsor.

- There can be serious security issues related to transferring sensitive data to another country because most other nations generally have different security and privacy laws.

- Concerns about the quality of the written code.

- Concerns about supervision and project management.

- No knowledge is transferred to the home organization.

- Concerns about loss and theft of intellectual property. Certain roles lend themselves more readily to offshore work. In data warehouse activities, extract/transform/load processes, and certain types of data cleansing are good candidates for offshore work.

Even if the outsourced work is performed locally or even if it is performed on site, there can be problems with the work not being performed by full-time employees (FTEs):

- Contractors and consultants have a learning curve to understand the organization, how things work, who to go to when information is needed, and so on.

- When the contractors and consultants leave, they take the knowledge of the organization with them. This knowledge is then lost.

- Consultants and contractors generally do not have the same sense of loyalty to the organization as regular employees do, which could result in the contractors and consultants leaving the project prematurely. Consultants and contractors typically have less at stake in the success of projects and the success of the organization than FTEs.

- Security issues can restrict the ability of contractors and consultants to access necessary data and resources.

TRAINING

Personnel responsible for aspects of data need experience and training in data strategy, such as data modeling, data architecture, database management system (DBMS)-specific training (DB2, Oracle, Teradata, and SQL Server), performance, and security. The timing, choice of classes, mindset of those attending the class, and decisions about who to send to the classes determines your coefficient for the effectiveness of training. Experience comes through practice, learning from mistakes (being allowed to make mistakes), and using mentors and consultants to provide feedback on data-related activities.

Who Should Attend

Let's be clear, you have a limited budget for training and the time away from the office probably means that others have to pick up the slack or some portions of your projects will be delayed. Classes should never be seen as means to reward; they should be used only to train your people on skills they need to carry out their jobs. Although some of your people might whine about not getting the opportunity to attend classes, they become dangerously angry when they perceive that a favored employee attends a class that has little relevance to that employee's work.

If your people can acquire the skills in a more effective way, such as reading, working with the product, or learning from a colleague or consultant, and if these means are more cost effective, it might make sense to forgo the class. However, if you do so, be sure to give the employee the time and the means to acquire the skill; don't assume she can pick it up in her spare time.

Send everyone who needs the skills. Don't expect a student to teach the class to the rest of the staff upon her return. She will not be proficient enough and will waste everyone's time. The trained employee can give a short review of the class and its relevance for others who might want to attend. Consider staggering the training and not sending everyone to be trained at the same time.

Mindset

Students are often sent off to class without a clear understanding of what they should learn. Spend some time with the potential student explaining your intentions for what she should learn, the expected level of expertise she should return with, and most importantly, what you expect her to do with the newly acquired skills. The student should be familiar with the product as much as possible ahead of time. For example, if the class is on DB2 fundamentals and the student is being groomed to become an apprentice database administrator (DBA), the student should spend some time with the current DB2 DBAs to find out what to do. The student should be told that upon returning she is responsible for the monitoring and recovery aspects of the supplier database. In addition, the experienced DBAs might suggest focus areas and something to the effect of, "Be sure to learn about the following capability; it's the most important."

Choice of Class

There might be many or a few choices for classes for a specific set of skills. The vendor might teach the class or training might be performed by a third-party organization. Be sure you send your students to the right level of course. Don't expect novices to to skip introductory classes. Advanced sessions will "go over their heads." Carefully review the course outline to be sure it covers what you need and does not waste time on areas that you have no interest in or are not relevant to your environment; for example, training on SQL Server if you are a UNIX shop.

Find out who is teaching the class. The abilities of instructors vary and this is a major determinant in the effectiveness of the training. Talk to the instructor if you have any questions about the curriculum. Get a few references from people who have taken the class. Ask about the instructors, value of the course, who should attend, prerequisites, what to look for, what might have been done differently, and how to prepare for the class.

Timing

Just-in-time training is the most effective. Schedule the class so that the student can be assigned to exercise newfound skills immediately upon return from the class. If 6 months goes by before she can work with the tool, she will lose much of what she learned.

ROLES AND RESPONSIBILITIES

A data strategy requires assigning specific roles and responsibilities. Some of the roles are probably already in place but the organization might not have assigned and authorized all the requiring responsibilities, and some of these roles (such as the data strategist and data quality steward) might be new. In addition, consultants and contractors can fill in the gaps and provide important direction to a data strategy initiative, but only if they are properly positioned.

Data Strategist

The data strategist is responsible for creating and maintaining the data strategy. This includes fully understanding the strategic goals of the organization. If the CEO plans to change directions, this should not be a surprise to the data strategist. For example, if a company has a strategic plan to squeeze costs from its supply chain, the data strategy must ensure that complete, accurate, and integrated data, as well as the necessary processes, will be available to support the plan. The data strategies develop the umbrella policies for standardization and integration of data and streamlining of business processes.

The data strategist must know (or learn) the existing environment including the important internal databases, the external data that will be integrated, and the data quality characteristics. The data strategist must be aware of the data volumes expected in the next five years. For example, if the amount of data in a health care organization is expected to increase fourfold, that information must be considered as platforms are evaluated. If the number of users is expected to double, this affects the requirements for hardware and network components as well as for training and support.

The data strategist must be aware of changes in the business that will require more complex transactions and queries. He or she must also be aware of governmental factors including regulations and governmental reporting requirements. The data strategist must know about the requirements of service level agreements (SLAs) for both performance and availability and be sure that the data strategy supports those SLAs (it's also likely that the data strategist would have input into creating those SLAs.) And finally, the data strategist must be wired into the politics of the organization so that his or her proposals will be pragmatic and accepted by management and staff.

Database Administrator

The database administrator (DBA) is responsible for the physical aspects of the databases. This includes database design, performance, backup, and recovery. Before starting, DBAs must understand the users' basic requirements and how the operational and decision support databases will be accessed and updated, as well as how data will be created and deleted. Some changes to the design and configuration of the system are more easily made than others. The more that is known initially, the less disruptive and costly the changes will be.

Data warehouse DBAs are usually more closely involved with the users than the DBAs responsible for operational (OLTP) systems. Data warehouse DBAs constantly monitor and tune the data warehouse databases by adding indexes and summary tables. They also monitor the SQL generated from the queries to help improve individual query performance.

DBAs typically use a data modeling tool to create the database design. They create both the logical database design, which is called a physical data model, and the physical database design, which is expressed in the data definition language (DDL) for partitioning tables, dataset placement, indices, and so on. The DBA should work closely with the data administrator, who should use the same data modeling tool for the logical data model. The advantage is that the mapping between the logical and physical data models can be done on the same data modeling tool and exported to the central repository without having to write additional programs. Database administrators then create the DDL or use the data modeling tool to create the DDL to build the databases. Database administration always has an eye to performance. Performance dictates design and the creation of keys and indexes.

If a distributed database environment is being considered, a good rule of thumb to remember is that a distributed database is three to four times more complex than a centralized one. This does not mean databases should not be distributed. In fact, there are excellent reasons for distribution, but cost, complexity, increased administration, and availability risk must be factored into any distribution decision.

DBAs are sometimes responsible for capacity planning and always responsible for physical design for good performance and for monitoring response time and resources used (such as CPU and disk I/O). They are also responsible for evaluating performance problems, tuning the databases, and reviewing the complicated SQL statements written by both application developers and power users using business intelligence tools.

Data Administrator

The roles and benefits of the data administrator (sometimes called the data architect) have not been well understood by most organizations and as a result, the role of data administrator was relegated to writing documentation that was rarely used. Although a few organizations have succeeded in the past, we now see many more organizations that want to integrate data from multiple systems as well as integrate internal data with external data. A prime example for this integration is the customer who is typically known to multiple systems and multiple databases. A banking customer might have a checking account, a savings account, a safe-deposit box, a credit card with the bank, and a home loan. A healthcare customer (sometimes known as a patient) might have data stored when hospitalized, during laboratory work, when receiving and filling a prescription, when being diagnosed, when medical procedures are performed, or when she is billed. It has become apparent that the primary roles of the data administrator are important to any successful data integration.

Data administrators model the business data according to the business rules and policies governing data relationships. They also document and maintain the mapping between the logical data model and the physical database design models as well as between the source data and the data warehouse target data. They understand the source files and know the appropriate source files for extraction. They establish and maintain the naming standards. They communicate the availability of data and, when appropriate, suggest that departments share data. The data administrator is generally responsible for administering the tool used in data modeling and administering the tool libraries, although in some organizations, this is the responsibility of the application development team.

Metadata Administrator

The metadata administrator is responsible for administering the metadata repository. Metadata comes from a number of sources: modeling tools, extract/transform/load (ETL) tools, query tools, results from reengineering the source file data definitions, and direct entry into a metadata repository tool. The metadata repository can potentially be updated as well as accessed from sources such as ETL tools, online analytical processing (OLAP) tools, and data mining tools. Tight controls are necessary to minimize corruption of the metadata. The metadata administrator is responsible for controlling entries, updates, and deletes.

Data Quality Steward

Don't assume that just because the organization has a data quality steward, no one else has responsibility for data quality. Data quality is everyone's job, but it is the *only* job of the data quality steward. Although information about data quality problems often originates in IT, it most often comes from the users. The data quality steward is responsible for finding and reporting problems relating to data quality, tracking these problems, and assuring that the resolution is assigned to a responsible party. Some of the discovered problems must be reported to data administration, where the data exceptions can be properly incorporated into the logical data model. The data quality steward can be involved in writing the programming specifications for the transformation logic that needs to occur during the data warehouse ETL process.

Not all data quality problems can be resolved nor should they be. It might cost more to fix the problem than it's worth. The data quality steward, along with other interested parties including the data originators and the information consumers, should determine the criticality of the problem. Analytical requirements can determine the quality requirements. The cost to fix the problem should be estimated and then the priority should be assigned.

The data quality steward should be proactive in trying to find problems before they surface. Data quality analysis tools or simple queries can identify many of the problems.

The most important role for the data quality steward is evaluating and improving the processes that contribute to data quality: specifically data entry, data edits, and the ETL process. By improving the processes, the quality of data is sure to improve. The data quality steward might also seek out cleaner sources of data, including data from external vendors, to replace those that have proven troublesome.

Data quality is a critical success factor for any system. We often hear that users are reluctant to accept the results of reports due to conflicting reports as well as the perception (often true) that the data is dirty, invalid, incomplete, redundant, untimely, poorly sourced, and so on. Data quality profiling identifies dirty data. It accomplishes three objectives:

- It makes the users more comfortable with the quality of the data because the problems are found and can be fixed.

- It allows the organization to understand the status of the quality of the data and then to triage the activity required to cleanse the data; that is, to take the next step to determine the value of cleansing (not all data can or should be cleansed).

- It alerts the users to problems with data, which should minimize the number of misinformed decisions based on dirty data.

  Specifically, the data quality steward is responsible for:

- Profiling data (in other words, delivering a report card of the quality of data)

- Helping to identify critical and important data elements

- Helping to determine the effort required to address the critical and important data elements

- Analyzing the return on investment (ROI) of addressing data quality problems as well as the return on assets (ROA) realized from the reusability of clean data

- Identifying the root causes of data quality problems (such as insufficient program edits, defective program logic, insufficient incentives for data quality data entry, insufficient time for data entry, poor data quality training, no data verification process, no domain definitions, or no common metadata)

- Performing ETL activity to cleanse the data, verify quality, and certify the ETL process

- Establishing procedures to continually monitor data quality

- Establishing standards that impact data quality

Consultants and Contractors

Consultants can be major players in developing a data strategy. They assess the situation, give advice, help plan the implementation, and sometimes provide the complete implementation. They have varying degrees of influence which, when overly powerful, can often create problems with the existing IT staff. This can be demoralizing to the existing employees because they are unable to significantly influence the process and direction of projects. In addition, consultants have been known to misrepresent their ability to rescue a data strategy project from impending failure.

On the other hand, consultants and contractors can make a significant contribution to a project involving significant database activity—the question is how best to use them and their expertise. Organizations also need to know how to make the best use of a budget for consultants and contractors.

When consultants and contractors are allowed to do all the work on a data strategy project, they end up being the only ones who know the underlying reasons for the decisions that comprise the data strategy. If they leave, the organization is left with employees who have not been allowed to participate in the process, learn the options, and debate different data strategies. The documentation is rarely adequate to help employees fully understand the data strategy. Contracts often include a section covering knowledge transfer to the full-time employees, but consultants often ignore these clauses. Inadequate schedules can become a reason for bypassing the knowledge transfer part of the agreement.

Consultants should be brought in to help (*help*, not to do all the work themselves) build an architecture, help establish data standards if none exist, recommend methodologies, help develop a project plan and a project agreement, and help the client select software.

Contractors should be brought in when the organization lacks specific skills that are necessary for the successful completion of the data strategy project. In the process, the contractors should teach those skills to client personnel assigned to the data strategy project. The project manager should make sure client personnel are in place to learn the skills.

Security Officer

Security is becoming more and more important as people outside the organization are being given access to reports, results sets, and even the ability to query the organization's data warehouse. Access is given to suppliers in an effort to improve their ability to supply quality parts in a timely fashion. Access is given to commercial customers to tie them as closely as possible to the organization's products and services. With access allowed outside the organization, security must be exact and uncompromising.

The European Union (EU) has mandated strict security and privacy standards that have also been adopted by a number of countries outside the EU including New Zealand, Australia, and a number of countries in South America. Global companies headquartered in the United States are finding it advantageous to adopt EU standards so they can support global enterprises without having to follow a myriad of security and privacy standards and to make it easier to market, communicate, and deal with other countries on a truly global basis.

Many department heads are concerned about anyone looking at their data. If department heads have the authority to restrict access, the security officer must set up the procedures to implement the restriction and make the department heads feel comfortable that they retain control of the access. This type of control is especially important for data that has been classified as private, even within the company. Examples include personnel records, sensitive client data, and patient data.

Data can be secured at different levels of granularity. For example, data might be available at the summary level but not at the atomic or detailed level. Or, data can be partitioned across multiple servers with restricted access to the server with the sensitive data.

The security officer should work closely with those administering security (web administrator, DBA, query tool administrator, repository administrator, data modeling tool administrator, and ETL tool administrator) to understand the capabilities of the products and determine the optimal approach to establishing security. This includes exposures, difficulties in administration (we don't want to make this a bureaucratic nightmare), and the productivity of administration.

The primary role of the security officer is to identify exposures and recommend actions to plug security holes. Another important responsibility of the security officer is to understand the interaction between the security features in the tools and the relational database management system (RDBMS). There have been cases reported where the security feature of one tool negated that of another.

Sharing Data

Although we would all like access to all the data in the organization, this is not possible. Besides the organization's privacy policies and the governmental security restrictions already mentioned in this chapter, data is not shared for a more insidious reason—department heads' jealously want data restricted. They want the restrictions for a number of reasons including:

- They don't want other department heads (who they compete with) to use shared data to criticize their performance.

- They don't want their own management to micromanage them.

- They want enough time to be able to develop an appropriate explanation (read *spin*) when their performance numbers are less than stellar.

The end result is that data is shared only when department heads are forced to do so and even then, sharing is done reluctantly and with the possibility of information sabotage. This raises the whole issue of data ownership. Does the data belong to the department heads or does it belong to the whole organization? Ideally, it belongs to the whole enterprise, but this is often not the way it is seen by the department heads. The mandate to share data should be a strategic goal. Data standardization and the mandate to reuse data forces the sharing issue. It is a critical success factor to any data strategy because constantly and inconsistently replicating data takes too long to reconcile and keeping data consistent across systems requires writing programs, which takes too long and is too costly.

Strategic Data Architect

The strategic data architect develops the architecture for the operational and decision support environments. This includes the software, utilities, tools, interfaces, and how they work together and feed each other.

The architect determines whether or not an enterprise data warehouse is to be used and how it would feed the data marts. If an operational data store (ODS) is to be used, he specifies how and by whom the ODS would be accessed and how it would feed the enterprise data warehouse or the data marts. The architect is heavily involved in understanding and determining data sources. The architecture painstakingly details how the data marts will be integrated and reconciled and specifies if the data warehouse will be two or three tiers.

Technical Services

Technical services, sometimes called system administration, is responsible for establishing the data warehouse technical architecture. This includes decisions about the hardware, the network, the operating system, and the DBMS. Technical services should develop capacity plans and make plans that allow the system to scale to a much bigger size than originally planned. Technical services should monitor transaction volumes and response time, batch processing, ETL, and query performance at a high level. For example, technical services does not need to know detailed measurements, such as the average response time for a transaction, but it does need to know the overall response time and whether it's degrading. Technical services is also responsible for keeping track of increased resource usage. This gives them time to plan for an upgrade long before performance becomes unacceptable. Technical services also develops disaster contingency plans in line with the criticality of the systems.

DATA OWNERSHIP

Of course the organization owns the data, but specific responsibilities for the data must be assigned. The data owners can be the originators of data or they can be the primary users of the data. Someone, some department, or some line of business must make the decisions discussed in the following sections.

Domains

The domains (valid values) for the data need to be determined. The data owners are in the best position to establish and then document (as metadata in the metadata repository) the domains for each data element. The domains can then be used to establish edits for entering data, as well as for merging and integrating data from other sources. If an external file to be integrated contains an address with a state code of "ZA," the program that uses the state code domain would identify ZA as an invalid value and either reject the entry, leave the state code blank, or look at the zip code, city name, or telephone area code and assign AZ to the entry.

Security and Privacy

Someone has to determine what data can be accessed and when it can be accessed. That someone is the data owner. In a health care organization, federal HIPAA regulations are explicit and those regulations need to be codified into rules and procedures. For example, disclosure of laboratory results must be limited to the patient, the attending physicians, and a limited set of personnel who administer the patient's chart. The health insurance company administering the claim needs tight restrictions on who can see the diagnosis that initiated the laboratory procedure. A bank must closely restrict access to loan application data that contains net worth, debts, and current salary.

Financial data for publicly traded companies is extremely time sensitive. Improper access to financial results resulting in foreknowledge of unexpected profits or loses can result in charges of insider trading (you go to the big house for this mistake) and a black eye for the company. Releasing financial information that might not need to be publicly disclosed (for example, the company paying for the CEO's mistress's apartment) can be a public relations nightmare for the company and somewhat embarrassing to the CEO himself.

Availability Requirements

The data owner is the one who can best determine the scheduled hours and days the data needs to be available in operational systems. The information consumers are the ones who give availability requirements for decision support systems. Some systems require the application and the underlying data to be available 24 hours per day and 7 days a week. Centralized global systems often have this requirement as well as systems, such as airline and hotel reservation systems. 24/7 systems are costly to architect and support, and the decision to build such as system should have cost justification.

Within the scheduled hours and days of availability, service level agreements (SLAs) target the percentage of time the system and the underlying data needs to be available. This is always described as a percentage. Many online systems, such as airline reservation and scheduling systems, require a high percentage of availability, such as 99.99 percent. These SLAs can be achieved only with redundant hardware, robust software, smart designers and architects, and diligent and motivated administrators—all of which cost much more than SLAs that are less demanding.

Timeliness and Periodicity Requirements

Timeliness relates to the elapsed time to access data following an end of a period, such as the end of day or the end of the week. For example, data might be available by 6:00 A.M. following daily updates or by 5:00 A.M. on Mondays following weekly updates that take place over a weekend. The data owner knows how timely the data needs to be accessed for an operational system. Information consumers have timeliness requirements for decision support systems. Please note that timeliness is gated by the availability of the source data. If source data is not available until the tenth of the month, anything earlier than the tenth is not possible.

Periodicity relates mostly to decision support systems (data warehouse) and designates how frequently data needs to be updated. The periodicity could be quarterly, monthly, weekly, daily, or near real-time. The required periodicity is a function of the nature of the application, whether the application is tactical or strategic (tactical requires more frequent updates), and how clean the data needs to be. It's more difficult, but not impossible, to cleanse and validate data when it's being updated in near real-time. The volumes and the method of updating the data (for example, load versus update) might also affect how frequently the data is refreshed.

Real-Time Versus Near Real-Time

Real-time means an almost instantaneous update of the data with each transaction applied to the database without being batched. Real-time applications are appropriate for money transfers and airline reservations. You don't want to schedule two people sitting in the same seat and you absolutely don't want to leave any empty seats. Near real-time does not have to be instantaneous, so the transactions are batched. The delay of submitting the batch and thereby updating the database can be several seconds, minutes, or even hours; again it depends on the application.

Performance Requirements

The data owner is able to designate response time requirements for the operational systems. Information consumers have response time requirements for decision support systems. Response time affects the productivity of the user. If it takes too long for the system to respond, the user tends to lose focus, not to mention the lost time waiting for the response. Long response time can also affect the satisfaction of a customer waiting for an answer from the customer service rep. "The system is a little slow today" is the all too common refrain. When response time is slow, some users have the tendency to abuse the system by hitting the Enter key more than once. This can exacerbate an already bogged down system.

Performance requirements are usually codified in an SLA for response time. For example, "95 percent of the transactions completed in two seconds or less." The more demanding the SLA, the more costly the system in terms of hardware and the greater the requirement for smart, experienced personnel who are strongly motivated to meet the SLAs. The staff involved with supporting the SLAs must be part of the initial design and active in monitoring and tuning for performance.

Data Quality Requirements

Not all data has the same requirement for quality. The data owners, in cooperation with the information consumers, are responsible for identifying each data element as critical, important, or insignificant. This then determines where the effort should be spent to establish edits, apply business rules, and change data entry procedures and incentives. Data entry staff should be motivated and rewarded to enter data accurately, not rapidly at the expense of data quality.

Business Rules

The data owner has the responsibility to establish business rules that are enshrined in edits, validation code, data cleansing code, and RDBMS specifications and documented as metadata in the metadata repository. Edits disallow entries such as a health insurance claim for a hysterectomy performed on an insured male. Validation and data cleansing code correct improper or missing data such as a correcting and incorrect zip code (after validating the rest of the address) or assigning "Male" to a missing gender entry if the person's first name is "Harold." The RDBMS specifications include referential integrity rules, unique designations, mandatory fields, and so on.

Another example of business rules is one that specifies that a claimant is no longer eligible for medical claims coverage following the divorce from an insured spouse.

INFORMATION STEWARDSHIP

Much of this material in this section is taken from *Corporate Data Stewardship Function* by Michael Scofield. The roles and responsibilities of information stewards as presented here overlaps with some of the roles and responsibilities of the data quality steward, data administrator, and data owners. However, it's presented as a whole for situations where the data quality steward, data administration, and data ownership are not well defined and an organization wants to promote information stewardship.

Information stewards normally come from the business areas, not from IT. Nevertheless, there must be a close relationship with IT. Information stewards are responsible only for the data in their own specific business area. Line-of-business managers need to identify a primary and a secondary information steward in each department for each major operational business area. For example, in a school district, stewards need to be assigned for the following:

• Test scores (assessment data)

• Facilities

• Suspensions

- HR, personnel, and payroll

- Teacher qualifications

- Migrant status

- Student, roster, and academic records

- Curriculum content

- Financial management

- Budget

Organizations need information stewards when:

- No one has responsibility for monitoring the quality of the data. Data quality problems result in the need to retroactively reconcile inconsistent data, which is much more expensive than to address data quality proactively.

- No one has the responsibility to determine the quality requirements for the data (not all data has the same data quality requirements).

- No one has the responsibility for defining the business rules that often results in corrupted data.

- Data is easily misinterpreted because the real meaning of the data has not been defined nor is it readily available.

- Sensitive data (such as bank balances, salary information, student test scores, or student suspension data) can be exposed because it's not clear who establishes security specifications or administers security for each area of responsibility.

- There is little coordination among the information subject areas, which causes a need for extensive interfaces to be written to be able to integrate information and get an overall perspective of how the organization functions.

- Relationships between systems are difficult to establish, which means that data cannot be easily integrated. For example, classroom utilization is difficult to manage if there is no integration between facilities data and course data. Identifying profitable customers is impossible if a bank cannot pull together data from checking, savings, credit cards, and mortgage loans.

- Reconciliation of inconsistent data between systems that house redundant data is labor-intensive, wasteful, and challenging.

- Standards directing how data should be captured, created, transformed, stored, validated, and maintained are either absent or have not been enforced, which results in wasted effort, duplication of effort, and systems that require significant maintenance.

Without information stewards, it is difficult to implement critical portions of an overall strategic IT implementation plan. The activities and deliverables of the stewards support the functional needs of the plan. They assist in providing and supporting the underlying data required for the plan to succeed.

For each area of responsibility, the information steward can address the following questions:

- What kinds of data do we need?

- When is it needed (how current does the data need to be)?

- What is its quality requirement?

- How should it be transformed and integrated?

- What is the required timing of transformation, load, and delivery of the data?

- What business rules apply to the data and to its usage?

- What are the valid values of the data?

- What are the security requirements of the data (who can access it, when, and at what level of detail)?

Roles and responsibilities include:

- Establish business operational definitions for the data.

- Responsible for the content of the metadata associated with his or her area.

- Determine security requirements for the data.

- Determine currency requirements for the data.

- Provide feedback to data origination on the quality of the data captured.

- Monitor quality of data, completeness, and currency of the data.

- Anticipate new data needs and watch for new operational and decision support data needs.

- Evaluate changes in data behavior (data quality as well as how data is captured and used) and notify data users who need to be alerted.

- Act as a reviewer for new reporting systems to help ensure data integration involving his or her area of data responsibility.

- Receive data requirements for new systems and participate in creating the new systems.

- Participate in the data merging function of acquired external data (A.C. Nielson, governmental data, divorces, census, and so on).

- Participate in data warehouse projects evaluating data needs and consult on potential sources of data.

- Establish policies and guidelines for correction of data in the database found to be in error. This includes determining which data requires cleansing and which data can be left as is.

- Reconcile data from disparate systems.

Other general roles and responsibilities include:

- Act as a reviewer for applications in data sourcing and integration

- Monitor and be aware of overall organization strategy, legal requirements, and governmental reporting requirements.

- Ensure that all data needs for accomplishing the operational goals are anticipated.

- Work with other information stewards to ensure consistency, avoid redundancy, and provide integrated data (for example, an integrated view of the customer).

Steward Deliverables

Information stewards are responsible for the following deliverables:

- Security specifications for data

- Data definitions for the data

- Control of the business rules for their area

- Valid value specifications

- Data quality requirements

- Report status of their data

Key Skills and Competencies

Stewards should have the following skills and competencies:

- Understanding of metadata (contextual information about data and processes) and its form and usage

- Ability to interpret data behavior in ways understandable to IT and the operational business areas

- Ability to communicate to all users of his or her data about the meaning of the data, its life cycle, the sources used for data warehouse applications, the quality of the data, and the methods of integration

Time Commitment

Initially, because of the major activities, the information steward should be dedicated full time to the project. After the definitions are created, the security is defined, the valid values are determined, and the rest of the key items are completed, the time commitment should be reduced based on the requirements for maintenance.

The information stewards should meet periodically as a group, as well as with the data quality stewards, the data administrators, and the data strategist, to collaborate on standards and make decisions regarding information steward issues. In addition, information stewards should be encouraged to connect when data needs to be shared between departments.

WORST PRACTICES

The best practices are described throughout this chapter. Now it's time to identify the worst.

- Let each department head, including IT (the DBA manager and the DA manager), determine her own data responsibilities; those functions that are not adopted don't get done.

- Allow overlapping responsibilities. Doing so results in energy expended on turf battles and not on delivering real capability to the organization.

- Not educating management on the value of data.

- Not assigning responsibility for data quality.

ASSESS YOUR ORGANIZATION EXERCISE

This assessment will help determine how ready your organization is to go forward with its own data strategy initiative.

1. Does management understand the value of data?

    a. Management values data as an asset and recognizes its critical role to the success of the organization.

    b. Management has a vague notion of the importance of data and will assign resources if pushed.

    c. Management's only commitment to data is the effort it takes to complain about it being wrong, late, impossible to understand, and in the wrong color.

2. What is the prime objective of those responsible for data entry?

    a. The data must be entered correctly the first time. The department has strong incentives for accurately capturing data.

b. The data should be entered correctly, but not at the expense of doing it slowly.

c. Get it in and off our desks. We are measured by how many documents we enter each day.

3. Have the roles associated with data been well defined?

a. Each of the roles in this chapter have been defined, assigned, and there is no disagreement about overlapping roles.

b. Most of the roles are assigned, but some functions are still not carried out and there are some overlapping roles.

c. We really don't know who is doing what except for the weekly battles over competing functions, or nothing is being done to ensure data quality.

4. Has data ownership been established?

a. Each operational business area has a recognized data owner and that owner is the undisputed czar of his or her own data.

b. The organization recognizes the value of data ownership and some line of business managers are functioning as data owners, but they have no information stewards.

c. The mantra is that data is a corporate asset and everyone should be responsible for the data. However, nobody is responsible for the data, and data is still treated as an inconsequential by-product of systems.

5. How readily is the organization willing to change to be able to adopt a data strategy?

a. This is a flexible organization whose culture allows it to adopt new ideas and make procedural and organizational changes.

b. The organization is reluctantly willing to make changes when the benefits can be shown beyond doubt.

c. Most of those in power are either waiting to retire, are terrified by change, and will accept something new only when their cold dead hands relinquish their quill pens.

AGENDA FOR WEEKLY DATA STRATEGY TEAM MEETING

These meetings should be scheduled for no more than 1 hour and less if there is not much to cover or report on. The meetings should always start on time, always end on time, and no time should be spent filling in anyone who comes late. An agenda for the meeting should always be provided ahead of time. The meeting should always be recorded by a scribe and the minutes distributed the same day to all the attendees as well as anyone else interested in the project. Donuts encourage the sugar freaks to come early. Keep the meeting on track, don't let the discussion degenerate into topics that are not on the agenda, and know what topics should be tabled, assigned, and left to another meeting. The attendees should know that the meeting will be crisp, constructive, and will not waste time.

The following is an outline you can follow to produce your agenda for each meeting:

1. Discussion of agenda (does anything need to be added?)

2. Questions and discussion from the last meeting (based on minutes of the meeting)

3. Status (where you are, what's been accomplished, and what's been decided)

4. Reports from people with to-do lists

5. Topics for discussion (this section gets fleshed out)

6. Decisions that need to be made and sign-offs that are needed from other managers

7. Assignment of to-do list items with timeframes (when they are due)

8. Agenda topics for next week's meeting

9. Adjournment

 Note: Much of the material in the previous section was derived from Michael Scofield's "Corporate Data Stewardship Function."

CONCLUSION

The success of a data strategy rests on the shoulders of those who execute it. This means that the roles and responsibilities must be completely understood by senior management, the roles and responsibilities must be carefully and fully assigned, and the roles must be supported and maintained in perpetuity—or as long as the organization wishes to remain in business. The organization must examine its existing skill sets, understand the availability of resources and assignments, and establish the proper organizational structure to support the data strategy. The organization must also develop a training plan and a succession plan. Finally, the organization must understand how best to use consulting and contracting resources.

Performance

Some of the ideas in this chapter were derived from the Teradata white paper titled "Measuring Data Warehouse Return on Investment," by Sid Adelman.

The goal of this chapter is to put data performance in perspective. It is not an in-depth guide on how to design or tune. (*High Performance Client Server,* by Chris Loosley and Frank Douglas is an excellent book on this subject). It does, however, identify each of the key components of performance, address the critical success factors, and highlight the steps an organization must take to ensure systems meet performance expectations.

It is important to make a distinction between the decision support environment or data warehouse and the operational or online transaction processing (OLTP) environment. The performance characteristics of these processes, the workloads, the volumes, the variability in the resources used, and performance service-level expectations are different. This chapter refers to processes in the decision support environment, those associated with ad-hoc requests as *queries,* and the processes of repeatable online transactions as *transactions.*

When discussing performance, it is critical to understand the scope of the discussion. If terms are not specifically defined, the discussions are meaningless. Performance can describe any and all of the following:

• Response time for an online transaction

• Response time for a web transaction

- The number of transactions per second that the system can process

- Response time for a query

- The number of concurrent users that can run query jobs

- Elapsed time to run a batch job

- Elapsed time and resources used to perform the extract/transform/load (ETL) process associated with a data warehouse

- Elapsed time to run a utility (load, backup, recovery, reorganization, and so on)

- CPU and disk utilization for any of the previously listed items

The five parts for delivering good performance are: computer hardware, database, operating system, application, and communications. If any of these components do not work well, are improperly tuned, or are undersized, the overall performance is substandard. The database design may be excellent, but if the application code is poorly written, response time suffers. Some designers over engineer one or more of these components—most often the computer hardware or the communication system—hoping that they can compensate for poor database design, bad application code, or an undefined and unknown performance problem. They will not be able to compensate.

If an organization starts off with guiding principles for performance, the decision process will be consistent. Following is an example set of performance-guiding principles:

Principle 1: The most critical component to achieving good performance is properly setting user expectations.

Principle 2: Good performance is achieved only by diligent attention and concern for good performance, and this requires assignment of management responsibility for overall performance and coordination with others whose jobs can impact performance. It also requires assigning technical people, usually DBAs, to monitor performance and tune the database management system, the databases, and the applications.

Principle 3: No system of any significant size or importance should be implemented without first understanding how it performs.

Principle 4: Performance is never optimal on the first implementation. There is always a requirement and an opportunity to improve.

Principle 5: Performance should always be identified as a critical success factor in any important system.

Principle 6: If monetary performance objectives are attached to satisfying performance SLAs, then those SLAs are much more likely to be achieved. A bank rewarded the managers responsible for performance and availability SLAs with significant bonuses each month when the SLAs were met.

Principle 7: Consistent and exceptionally good performance can be achieved only by spending money on hardware, performance software, and skilled technical staff.

Principle 8: Low-tech solutions are often the cheapest and easiest. As an example, an old technique to minimize unused standard reports and to save the machine resource used to produce those reports is to stop distributing the reports and reinstate them only when there are complaints.

Principle 9: A database must be designed for either OLTP or DSS. Trying to develop a compromise design satisfies no one.

There are four major components to performance:

- Capacity planning

- Designing, coding, and implementing

- Monitoring

- Tuning

Each of these components is discussed in this chapter.

PERFORMANCE REQUIREMENTS

The classic approach to defining performance requirements is to ask the users of the system (the business) for their performance requirements. The method of asking the questions and the subsequent negotiations are critical to truly understanding those requirements. If there is no difference in price between the very fast and the moderate response time option, they will invariably choose *very fast*.

The users generally have some implicit performance expectations. These expectations are usually derived from previous experience or, more often, from their current experience with their own PCs running PC applications. PC response time is usually good and almost impossible to match with any system that requires interaction with another computer across a network, whether through a LAN or a remote link. User expectations cannot be overlooked. They must be explored in detail and do not accept "as fast as possible." This fuzzy metric will continue to elude you.

Excellent performance is *not* free. It costs more to deliver subsecond response time than it costs to provide a 3-second response time. When business users are told that the subsecond response time option will cost them an additional $2,000,000, they might opt for the 3-second option. Business users can be given more than one option to allow them an opportunity to weigh price and performance benefits.

In the examples given in Table 7.1, the business user is provided the type of information needed to make an intelligent decision. This process can be used only if IT is willing to follow these negotiations with service level agreements (SLAs) between IT and the business users. IT can provide price/performance options only if IT fully understands what it is capable of delivering and knows the costs of these options.

Table 7.1: Price/Performance Options

The following are examples of options that can be proposed to a client to decide what performance they are willing to purchase:

For System: _____	
Option 1: 90 percent of the transactions in less than 1 second	$3,000,000
Option 2: 90 percent of the transactions in less than 2 seconds	$2,500,000
Option 3: 90 percent of the transactions in less than 4 second	$2,000,000
Option 4: 90 percent of the transactions in less than 7 second	$1,900,000

SERVICE LEVEL AGREEMENTS

Your users expect some level of service and most scope agreements include SLAs. There always is a tradeoff. SLAs that are demanding will cost more and will take more IT effort. Whoever is responsible for establishing the SLAs must be aware of the costs, the time, and the effort.

Response Time

Operational or Online Transaction Processing (OLTP) transactions are usually well defined in terms of what database will be accessed, what create, access, update, and delete functions will be executed, and even the number of CPU cycles used. SLAs are usually established for the high volume of OLTP transactions. It is important to remember that network time can be the majority of the elapsed time as observed by the user.

Because data warehouse queries can be extremely variable in the resources they use (the query may access ten rows or ten million rows, or join two tables with ten million rows each), response time SLAs should be established for specific, identified, and known queries. If an upper limit is given for response time, it should be done so for 95 percent of the queries. For example, 95 percent of the queries should come back in 10 seconds or less. There always will be one or two queries that take multiple minutes, not seconds—remember *The Query that Ate Cleveland.*

SLAs are written agreements between the business—the folks that will be using the system—and IT—the people who are responsible for building and providing the infrastructure. The SLAs will identify your goals and the metrics will tell you if the goals have been met. Metrics supporting the SLAs may include:

- Availability

- Response time

- Response to problems

SLAs let you know which of the performance requirements are met. SLAs also serve to hold user expectations in check.

SLAs are usually negotiated at a system level, which means that all the transactions or applications in the system have the same SLA. We know that not all transactions have the same performance requirements, but having a common SLA is easier than looking at each transaction or class of transaction.

Without SLAs, IT is not able to defend itself against charges of poor performance. After the business users have agreed to the SLAs, the results are objective. Was the SLA achieved?

A more demanding performance SLA should cost the business department more money. By charging for better performance, the business user is less likely to demand superior performance if that performance is not warranted.

Following are examples of performance SLAs.

Online Transactions

System 1: Transaction X: 95 percent of the transactions in less than 5 seconds.

System 2: With the exception of transactions D and H, 90 percent of the transactions in less than 3 seconds.

Transactions D and H: 70 percent of the transactions in less than 20 seconds.

Data Warehouse Canned Queries

Query Z: 80 percent of the queries in less than 1 minute.

Query W: Due to the extreme variability of the access in this query, no SLA can be established.

CAPACITY PLANNING: PERFORMANCE MODELING

No system of any size should be implemented without first having a rough idea of how well it will perform. See the cases at the end of this chapter for an example of what happens when this principle is ignored. It is expensive to make changes late in the development life cycle. Many of the problems that would eventually be experienced can be predicted early in the cycle by design reviews, performance modeling, and benchmarking.

Effective performance modeling requires vital information such as the following:

- The number and complexity of transactions anticipated

- The number and complexity of queries anticipated

- The number of concurrent users

- The location of the users

- The location (distribution) of the data

Performance can be anticipated in a number of ways. The techniques used will be determined by the importance of the system, the performance requirements, the size of the system, and the organization's interests and skills in performance. The following techniques can be used:

- If an application package is being implemented, the experience of other organizations can be used to extrapolate. This is the least expensive approach.

- Reviewing the design of the system, the database, and the application. An outline of a design review is included in this chapter.

- Using an analytical (performance modeling) tool to predict performance.

- Simulating the system.

- Benchmarking the system. This involves writing code, executing the code in an environment similar to the target production environment, and measuring the results.

Performance modeling facilitates evaluating multiple courses of action without the cost and disruption of actually implementing the options. Modeling is generally performed during the initial design but also can be effectively used when evaluating multiple tuning alternatives, such as the impact of different types of disks. Modeling is not a free activity and will require the involvement of a skilled performance person.

Modeling can provide important information without causing the organization to expend the money and human resources to experiment with options, such as adding more line capacity or installing a faster CPU that may not significantly improve performance.

IT is constantly changing, but one thing that does not change is the misguided assumption that the *new change* will not measurably affect the performance of the existing system. This change can be a new release of the DBMS, a new release of the application software, a hardware change, or an additional workload on the hardware. What often happens is that the change causes poor performance in the existing operational systems. Because the effect was not anticipated, IT must go into a traditional dance to fix the problem. It is far better and much less disruptive if the impact of the change is anticipated. Although modeling will not catch all problems, it should anticipate the majority of problems and thus shield the changes from the users. Modeling can improve the reputation of IT and help it meet the performance SLAs by minimizing the number of performance problems caused by system changes.

CAPACITY PLANNING: BENCHMARKS

Benchmarks are an effective means to determine how much hardware will be needed to handle your planned workload. A benchmark can help avoid catastrophic mistakes such as terrible response time or a limit on the number of concurrent users. A benchmark will help avoid surprises, such as the inability to load data in the available time window.

Why Pursue a Benchmark?

Benchmarks are expensive, take time and effort from personnel important to the organization, and can delay the start of a project. A benchmark can even result in lost momentum on a project. The effort and activity required by a benchmark can be profitably spent on other endeavors, so do not start one unless you must. However, you must benchmark if:

- You expect your system to grow beyond a level that might cause performance problems. The level can include growth in data volume, number of concurrent users, complexity and size of the workload, or situations in which batch processes have problems, such as short windows for load or update.

- You established mandatory criteria for product selection that includes the ability to handle your proposed volumes with specified SLAs. Mandatory means that if the product does not satisfy that criteria, it will not be chosen regardless of functionality or any other satisfying criteria.

- Your growth can increase the cost of the system so much that the project loses its cost justification.

- You have no guarantees of how you will grow and expand (a merger may be in the offing), but you want to ensure the system you choose will scale.

- Management is leaning toward a solution with questionable capabilities. They do not believe or understand your concerns and the only way to convince them of the problems is by insisting on a benchmark.

- Management questions the proposed configuration's capability to support the expected workload.

- Management believes a modest (and insufficient) configuration will do the job.

- You want to determine which vendor's product(s) will best support your requirements.

- You have already purchased and are running with a vendor's product, but a major new application is on the drawing board and you want to determine its impact.

- The more cautious people in the organization want to over configure to ensure adequate performance. This over configuration is expensive and you do not want to buy more hardware than necessary.

- You might be concerned that vendors have low-balled the proposed hardware to be price competitive and expect you to buy more hardware when additional computer resources are needed.

You might need to benchmark with more than one vendor. The best approach is to benchmark with your first choice vendor. If that first benchmark does not support your SLAs, your performance requirements, and your goals for the proposed system, then benchmark with your second choice vendor. If the first benchmark satisfies your measures of success, no additional benchmarks are necessary. If the boss already has decided on a course of action, and you believe it will scale to your intended data volume and user activity, then do not waste your time on a benchmark.

Benchmark Team

The benchmark team should include an architect, one or more DBAs, business users, operational managers (administration, facilities, computer room manager), and technical personnel. If the benchmark includes the use of an ETL or BI tool, bring someone with an architectural understanding of the tool. Do not expect the vendor to have that expertise. The team might also include an independent consultant who can keep the team on track. Interested executives, perhaps the CIO, might want to come for the last day or two of the benchmark. The team should also include vendor nonadvocates, but these opponents should have an open mind to the results of the benchmark.

Benefits of a Good Benchmark: Goals and Objectives

There are significant benefits to a proper benchmark, and it is important that you establish measurable goals and objectives. The following is a set of such goals and objectives:

- Assure management that you are doing the right thing.

- Validate a platform choice and a configuration that will support your future requirements.

- Determine hardware and software costs.

- Provide insights into the effort and resources needed to build and maintain your system.

- Determine if your configuration will support your SLAs for availability and performance.

- Support your estimates on when additional hardware will be necessary to increase data volumes and to grow the number of concurrent users.

- Validate the vendor's hardware and software proposal.

- Provide insights into the vendor's capabilities and level of support.

Problems with "Standard" Benchmarks

Standard benchmarks were established so that competing vendors would have an identical workload and identical rules by which to play, but there are a number of problems associated with the standard benchmarks.

- They do not tell you how much effort it takes to implement these systems.

- They do not tell you how much effort it takes to administer your proposed configuration.

- They do not give you any information about recovery time. This should be part of the benchmark if you are proposing an availability SLA.

- You do not learn anything about the software and how it functions.

And most importantly, these benchmarks tell you nothing about the impact of your specific workload, including any problems that result, and if your availability and response time SLAs are met. They do not provide enough information to justify spending (wasting) 18 months and $10,000,000 on a solution that will not support your workload. You will not be able to answer the question, "Yes, but will it work for us?" Consider the impact of responding with, "It should" compared to, "It will."

The Cost of Running a Benchmark

Benchmarks are never cheap. The vendor may even charge you for running the benchmark. You will also want to include the costs of travel. The time and effort to prepare and run the benchmark is always significant. We have found that it can take four- to eight-person weeks to prepare for the benchmark and an additional 3 days to 2 weeks to perform the benchmark. The people involved will be valuable and highly paid resources. Their internal, fully burdened costs should be considered. This internal cost can range from $400/day to $1200/day. You also may want to include a consultant on the project. A consultant's charges range from $2000/day to $4000/day. The consultants would be involved in all aspects of the benchmark. If you plan to use a consultant, estimate the same number of billed days for the consultant as for one of your internal people who is most heavily involved in the project.

Identifying and Securing Data

It is important that the data used in the benchmark represents the true characteristics of your data including the outliers, the skewed data, and the aberrant data clusters (your data will not be evenly distributed). You will want to bring in the representative volumes of data for your environment today, as well as what you expect to have in 5 years. This always is a difficult activity. Allow enough time for this task and assign it to people who are very familiar with the data, know how to extract it, and also know how to validate that the data represents your intended environment.

Establishing Benchmark Criteria and Methodology

Planning for the benchmark is critical to its success. This also means you must have a reasonably complete understanding of what the proposed system will do, the volumes, the architecture, the hardware, and the software. You should know what constitutes success and by what metrics the system will be measured.

Data Volume

OLTP systems typically grow with the size of the customer base, with greater acceptance of company services, and with additional services. Data warehouse installations grow from 20 percent to 50 percent (and sometimes much more) each year. The growth will be in additional historical data, more atomic data, more granular periodicity (loading daily versus monthly), new subject areas, additional external data, and new columns to be added to existing databases. You want a solution that will support that growth. Your benchmark should go beyond where you are today to where you expect to be in 3–5 years. You do not want to have to limit your expansion or, worst of all, convert to a new system that will support your growth.

System Configuration

The benchmark should be run on the configuration proposed by the vendor. If the benchmark is conducted on a larger configuration, you will not be able to verify performance on the configuration you buy.

Actual Test Data, Actual Queries

Your test data should be real detail data with all the columns in the records represented. The data should cover multiple subject areas, such as Customer, Product, and Supplier. Be sure the benchmark has a good representation of your workload. For example, if 60 percent of your queries are simple, 30 percent are of medium complexity, and 10 percent are complex, be sure your workload mix has the same percentages. Also include the query that has never been completed and the query that was considered too ugly to even launch. Be sure to test summarization queries, especially if you are using some of the new features of the DBMS, such as materialized tables and views.

Establishing Clear Success Criteria

Before you embark on a benchmark journey, you need to establish clear success criteria. You do not want to complete the benchmark and then realize there were some questions that were never answered. The following are some success criteria you should consider. Choose those most appropriate to your benchmark and add any not represented here:

• Online transactions run successfully.

• Queries and reports run successfully.

- Batch processes run successfully.

- The ETL process runs successfully. The number of rows read and loaded are reconciled.

- ETL load times are acceptable (you specify what is acceptable).

- Query response times are acceptable (you specify what is acceptable).

- Concurrent activities run with the proposed configuration.

- Effort to administer is understood and not out of the range of expectations.

- Measurement and metrics return important information on how the system will perform.

- The results of the benchmark are complete enough to satisfy stakeholders.

- The benchmark produces lessons learned that will speed implementation and minimize dead-end techniques and solutions.

- The team gains significant knowledge and that knowledge is documented.

- The costs of the system are better understood.

- The relationship with the vendor is solidified.

Availability

There are three dimensions to availability, but only two are relevant to the benchmark:

- Scheduled hours—For example, the system might be scheduled for access 18 hours a day and 6 days a week. This dimension is relevant if a batch process, such as a load, impacts the scheduled hours.

- Availability during scheduled hours and days—For example, during scheduled hours, the SLA for availability is 99 percent. This cannot be determined in the benchmark, but it can be inferred by checking references. Be sure to ask the references what availability they have been experiencing.

• Time to recover—You need to test what happens when there are failures (not *if* there are failures). The benchmark should include demonstrating recovery processes when there are hardware failures (disk and CPU), operating system problems, database corruption, query failure, and so on. In the case of a system failure, how long does it take to recover before users regain access to the system? The benchmark should provide information on performance degradation during recovery, including response time and number of concurrent users. Tell the vendor what you want to fail by giving them a few scenarios. Vendors can initiate hardware failures as part of the benchmark.

Load Time

If the proposed architecture precludes access during load, the time to load is important in determining scheduled availability and should be a critical success factor for the benchmark results. If the queries can be run during the load, the impact of the load on the concurrent usage and query response time should be measured.

Evaluating and Measuring Results

Be sure you know beforehand what you are testing. You need to monitor, measure, and document the following:

• Batch processes

• ETL process:

  – Time and effort to transform the data.

  – Time and effort to create indexes.

  – Time and effort to load the full set of data.

  – Database tuning.

  – Problems experienced.

• Queries:

  – Response times.

  – Number of concurrent users.

  – Workload mix.

  – Machine resources used.

  – Problems experienced.

• System availability during the benchmark:

  – What was the recovery process?

  – Do the queries have to be resubmitted and how were they resubmitted?

  – What recovery techniques were used?

  – Query performance during recovery.

  – Does a load recovery cause any aberrations in the database, such as loss of referential integrity?

Verifying and Reconciling Results

There is an old saying, "Trust your mother, but cut the cards." You may feel your first choice vendor has the same level of integrity as your sainted mother, but if you are going to benchmark on their system, you want to be able to verify the results. You will want to be there when the benchmark is run. You will want to participate in reviewing the measurements (load times, response time, resource usage, and so on). You also might want to have an independent consultant participate in the benchmark and have that consultant verify the key measurements and validate any conclusions from the measurements.

Validating results also means that the number of rows returned is the correct number compared to your expected number. You will not be able to validate all the results, but sample and verify the most critical queries.

Communicating Results Effectively

You will want to fully document the results of the benchmark, including the hardware configuration, the software employed, the time to perform the batch processes, the metrics coming from the measurement tools, the response times of the test queries, the time and effort to administer, and any other factors that you needed to test and verify. These results should be included in a document. We all know that a word is worth .001 pictures, so in addition to the raw numbers and your conclusions, use charts and graphs to show the results. The presentations should always be given by your staff, not by the vendor.

You might think of a benchmark as an insurance policy. You are ensuring that the system you buy will perform as expected, that you will be able to handle the volumes of data for your target environment, and that you will be able to support a complex workload with a large number of concurrent users with acceptable response times. You are ensuring that your SLAs are satisfied and that the system will be able to scale. The time and effort expended on a benchmark should be well spent, so be sure to do it right and to make sure the vendors play fair.

APPLICATION PACKAGES: ENTERPRISE RESOURCE PLANNING (ERPs)

Application packages, commercial off-the-shelf (COTS), and ERPs can satisfy many of the most difficult and programmer-intensive activities of IT. Therefore, organizations are more often making the choice to buy rather than build new applications. These packages come with either a required DBMS (it can run only on SQL Server), or a choice of DBMSs (it can run on DB2 or Oracle) that can work with their package. In the case of application packages, the business people usually make the choice, and they pay little attention to any underlying requirement for the platform and DBMS to support the package. The various DBMSs perform differently and the COTS and ERPs will have different performance characteristics depending on which DBMS is used. The COTS and ERP vendors write code that is generalized and geared to work with a variety of DBMSs, but the code is not written to maximize performance with any one DBMS. It is up to IT to be sure the application will work well within the organization and that the DBMS is properly configured to assure adequate performance. There are two issues that IT must address:

- Does the package require a DBMS that is not an organization standard? If this is the dilemma faced by IT, clearly IT came too late to the party. IT should have been involved early in the selection process and should have established that one of the mandatory requirements for any application package was that it conformed to the organization's standard for DBMSs. For example, if the standard was DB2 for operational systems, an application package that required Oracle should have been dropped from the list and never considered. This requirement for the package to conform to the DBMS standard can become an extremely contentious problem between the business and IT. The business should be made aware of the problems of selecting an application package with a nonconforming DBMS including the costs and the need to increase the DBA staff.

- The package vendors typically focus on the function in their systems and pay less attention to the performance. Many do not even stress test their system, so any performance due diligence becomes the responsibility of the purchaser. If your data volumes are small, if your performance SLAs are not demanding, and if you expect a small number of concurrent users, the performance capabilities of the packages should not be much of an issue. However, if your performance requirements are demanding, you will need to validate the performance capabilities of the application package. The easiest and cheapest way to validate is to include questions about performance in the list of questions when the reference checks are conducted. When you ask the vendor for references, be sure to ask for one or two that run on your intended platform (operating system and DBMS) and have data that is at least as large as you expect to be and at least your number of users. Following is a list of sample questions:

How long does it take to perform specific operations, such as load, update, and refresh times, response time for queries, number of concurrent users, and workloads?

What is the size of your entire database?

What is the largest table? (They may give you the size in gigabytes or by number of rows. If they give one answer, ask for the other as well.)

How many concurrent users do you have?

Do you measure performance (resource usage and response time), and if so, how do you do it?

Do you have performance SLAs? What are they and are these SLAs met with the application package in question?

What performance problems have there been with this application package?

Who in your organization (role) is responsible for anticipating performance problems, monitoring problems, and tuning databases and application code?

How much time do these people spend on performance related tasks?

DESIGNING, CODING, AND IMPLEMENTING

Designing, coding, and implementing are critical components of the performance picture. Any of these can be the weak link that can result in disastrous performance. Above all, the designers, coders, and implementers must know the characteristics of the data and must know how the data will be created, transformed, accessed, updated, and deleted. See Table 7.2 for data characteristics.

Table 7.2: Data Characteristics

Characteristic	Description
Size	Number of rows, number of columns, and number of bytes.
Volatility	How much of the data will be updated and how frequently?
Data Quality	How clean and complete is the data?
Security Constraints	Limitations on access, update, creation, and deletion.
Expected Access	Number of concurrent users and workload.
Availability Requirements	Percentage of time the system should be running during scheduled hours.
Historical	Number of months and years of data stored in the database.
Scheduled Availability	Hours/day, days/week.
Timeliness	How soon does the data need to be available after a time point (end of month)?
Periodicity	Update frequency (real time, daily, weekly, monthly, and so on).

Designing

Designing the overall architecture of the system encompasses the hardware, software, and the database design. The architecture includes decisions on operating systems, DBMSs, distributed data, major security implementations, utilities, data marts, enterprise data warehouse, operational data stores where number crunching takes place, and many more. If a performance-critical system is not being designed or reviewed by one who understands performance, the system is doomed. If the architecture of a house is not properly conceived, or if the structural engineer is new to the job, any earthquake over 5.0 can bring it down. Time wisely spent in the design will minimize the need for subsequent monitoring and tuning and will result in a much better system.

The logical design of the data does not consider the performance ramifications, whereas the physical design of the databases is very much a function of performance requirements and the requirements of the business application. The design of the database is critical. Relational databases are more easily changed than the older hierarchical or network databases and flat files. However, this should not be an excuse to use quick and dirty database designs because these quick and dirty designs often survive as long as the systems they support. These databases will not perform well, will cause manageability problems, availability problems, and will not support the applications as well as a good database design. There is a strong case to be made for allowing only DBAs who were trained on the DBMS to design databases. Following is a checklist of the information DBAs need as they design, configure, monitor, and maintain the databases and as they support the user community:

Environment: Hardware architecture, network topology, and global/local environment.

Application: The DBA should have a feel for the application, what it is doing, OLTP versus DSS, timeliness requirements, and an understanding of the business requirements.

Data: The DBA needs to know the characteristics of the data including volumes, volatility, create, update, access, and delete activity.

Users: Data entry, analysts, OLTP users, casual, and power.

Security requirements: Security and privacy issues, how the data is to be secured, and who makes these decisions.

Performance requirements: SLAs for response time.

Access requirements: Number of accesses, creates, updates, and deletes.

Schedule: 24 x 7, 18 x 6.

Availability: 99.99 percent, 98 percent.

Coding

Poor application code has often been the villain in a system with bad performance. Programmers are typically measured on the functional capabilities of their programs and on meeting time schedules, but rarely are they measured on the quality or the performance of their deliverables. Programmers often take a programming shortcut that does deliver the function, but they do so at the expense of retrieving a row that already has been retrieved or causing an additional and unneeded sort. The programmers cannot be blamed because they are rarely told that performance is important.

Sometimes, inefficient programming is not apparent and it is not manifested in bad performance that can be seen by the user, but it does remain an eternal burden on the machine resources.

If code generators are being used, programmers have less control of the code generated. In the past, code generators often created inefficient code. This is less so today, but the code generated by these products should be analyzed and measured by the DBA to validate their performance characteristics.

Implementation

Implementation, sometimes called promotion, is the process of bringing the system into production. This involves a number of decisions such as the size, number, and assignment of buffer pools, position of the DBMS in the dispatching order, and many other factors that will contribute to both good and bad performance. These decisions must be made by personnel who understand performance and who care about and are given strong incentives to maximize the performance characteristics of the system.

An important part of implementing is stress testing systems that have large databases. Stress testing can identify problem areas prior to the system going into production, and can give the developers the opportunity to fix these problems before they impact users. The stress test can minimize the disruption to the user that is normally associated with the introduction of a new system.

After stress testing, time must be allotted to tune and improve the system's performance. Improvements can be realized if the schedule and personnel allocation are in place. It is important not to compromise adequate testing with the justification of a tight schedule.

Design Reviews

Design reviews can spot poor database designs, inefficient code, and deficiencies in the implementation process. They can also uncover an architecture that will not properly support the system or its eventual and planned expansion.

One goal of the design review is to validate the design, process, and implementation of the system. Another goal is to anticipate any problems and suggest corrective action prior the system being delivered to the end users. The reviewers will be looking for opportunities to improve the performance and robustness of the system. They will be looking for anything that might inhibit successful implementation. An important rule for the design reviews is that there should be no attempt to assign blame to any previous actions or decisions.

A design review is just one step in a continuing process of actions and steps to improve the system being reviewed. Most large systems are implemented in multiple phases, the first phase having less functionality and volume than later phases. The review would focus on the phase under discussion, but also should try to understand and support the larger volumes and additional functions that would be expected in subsequent phases.

The time allotted for a design review is rarely adequate; therefore, it is important to prioritize which topics should be covered. The participants should assign each item under discussion to a category, as follows:

A: Definitely to be covered in the design review.

B: To be covered in the design review if time permits.

C: This item will be postponed and considered for a future review.

D: This item has been covered or is not an issue.

E: This item is irrelevant for this project.

The notes from the review should be distributed to all participants. The notes should include all critical information, definition clarification, assumptions, decisions made, and the reasoning behind those decisions.

The design review should generate the following documentation:

• Decisions and agreements made during the session.

• Responsibilities, tasks, and additional research required. Not everything will be finalized in the design review.

• Schedules: when the assigned activities will be completed and when project milestones will be achieved.

• Items to be resolved by people outside of the review. There will usually be management decisions that must be addressed that may include cost and performance tradeoffs.

• Notes on the topics discussed, the analysis, and the decisions made along with assignment, schedules, and other relevant information.

• Suggestions for subsequent reviews.

The design review can look at the following:

1. The volume of processing:

   • Transactions

   • Queries

   • Batch processing: extract, load, or update including any problems with the window in which the batch processing runs.

  - Backup and recovery

  - Database reorganization

2. Phases of implementation.

3. Where is the system now in the development process? If it is an ERP, what are its performance characteristics?

4. Who are the users? What are their characteristics (operational [transaction], knowledge workers, power users, report generators, executives, casual users, and so on)?

5. Query and reporting tools.

6. Milestones, dates, schedules.

7. Goals for performance and availability. What SLAs are in place?

8. Hours of operation (24 x 7 or 18 x 6).

9. How is performance measured? What tools are being used?

10. How is availability measured? What is the impact of outages?

11. Development methodology, especially data modeling.

12. Hardware environment:

    - CPU including any existing capacity problems.

    - Disk configuration including any existing disk contention problems.

13. Testing environment:

    - Functional testing

    - Performance (stress) testing

    - System testing

14. Integration issues with any other systems including feeds coming in and output to other systems.

15. What software is being used?

    - Operating system

    - Database

- ETL tools

- Query and reporting tools

- Utilities and measurement tools

16. Skills and training:

- Skills inventory

- Skill requirements

- Training and support for end users

- Training and support for IT

17. How timely does the data have to be (daily, every 30 minutes, and so on)?

18. Attachment facilities (MQ, CICS, TSO/batch, and so on).

19. Are existing shortcuts going to be a problem in the future (for instance, incorporating standards at a later date)?

20. Guidelines for cost versus performance decisions. Cost may supersede excellent response time requirements.

21. Data quality issues.

22. Data distribution issues.

Not all databases and tables within those databases need to be reviewed. Any of the following characteristics indicate that these tables should be reviewed:

- Large tables

- Tables that are frequently accessed

- Mission critical data

- Tables that are on a critical path

- Tables that have any special characteristics that could make them a potential problem, such as dirty data

- Heavily denormalized tables with redundant data

Tables

Participants in the reviews will need information on the following:

- Physical data models.

- Have the tables been normalized? How far? To the third normal form?

- Have the tables been denormalized? Should they be?

- Data Definition Language (DDL).

- Volumes:

  - Number of rows

  - Number of columns

  - Characteristics of the columns (variable length or large objects)

- Growth rate

- Indices:

  - On which columns and how is this determined?

  - Primary keys (clustered) and how is this determined?

  - Unique keys.

  - Types of indexes to use (b-tree, bitmap, and so on).

  - Use of multiple indices.

  - Local indices.

  - Global indices.

  - When are the indices created? At load time or later and why?

- Referential integrity:

  - Is it being used?

  - Should you let the DBMS perform RI or should it be in the program?

  - Should the RI be performed by both the DBMS and the program?

- Compression:

    - Is it being used?

    - How was this determined?

    - What are the plans for compression?

    - Is compression in the program, in the DBMS, or is there a hardware assist?

- Partitioning:

    - On which columns and how is this determined?

    - Vertical.

    - Horizontal.

    - Is it being used?

    - How was this determined?

    - What is the partitioning based on?

    - How is partitioning being used to archive old data?

    - What sort of parallelism is being used?

- Volatile columns.

- Segmented table spaces.

- Storage groups.

- Small tables, lookup tables, control variable tables, and reference tables.

- Special characteristics of the tables.

- Repeatable read and cursor stability.

- Storage media (DASD, CD/DVD, and tape).

Queries and Reports

Not all the reports and certainly not all the queries will be known at the time of the design review. Those that are known should be included. Fill in the rest with educated estimates and guesses.

- Anticipated access:
    - Number of queries during peak periods.
    - Types of queries.
    - Expected number of rows to be returned.
    - Which columns in the heavily accessed tables are being frequently accessed?
    - Access paths.
    - Will access be made through indices?
    - DBMS functions (SQL), such as SUM, AVG, COUNT, and others.
    - Commonly used predicates in the WHERE clause.
    - Sorts (explicit or implied [GROUP BY]).
    - Business Intelligence (BI), front-end query tools, and homegrown front ends.
    - JOINS and UNIONS.
- SQL code accessing the tables.
- STATIC and DYNAMIC opportunities and requirements.
- Are views being used? How are these determined? Are materialized tables or views being used?
- Role of the work stations in performing various functions.

Reporting

The following questions should generate thought about how reporting should be implemented:

- Reporting software:
    - Thin/thick client.
    - Ease of use.
    - Who is responsible for creating the reports?
    - Report libraries—how are they controlled and managed?
    - How will the reports be delivered (hard copy, email, or the Web)?

Testing

Participants will need information on the following:

- What has been tested?

- Was there a test plan? Did it have representative test cases?

- Have the results of the tests been documented (please provide)?

- Has performance been monitored? For which functions (please provide results)?

- What is the plan for continuing testing? What else is needed?

- What additional testing, such as a system test or stress test, is required?

- Test to reflect the complete daily cycle with normal volume.

Operations

Participants will need information on the following:

- Anticipated peak periods.

- Anticipated peak volumes.

- Initial load times.

- Extract and load process:
    - How long does it take?
    - How will this change as volume grows?

- What system parameters were chosen, and what defaults were taken? Have these parameters been analyzed?

- Backup and recovery process:
    - How long will it take to recover the databases?
    - Will there be an order to the recovery process to recover the most important databases first? What are the dependencies among tables?
    - What are the backup and recovery options?

- Reorganization:
    - How often are database reorganizations needed?
    - Are there plans for archiving/discarding old data?
    - How long does reorganization take?

- What is the process for purging old data? Will it be archived (partition roller)?

- Process of allocating disks.

- Process for data set placement.

- Support software or productivity tools, such as Computer Associates and BMC.

- Plans to monitor and report on performance.

- Plans to monitor and report on availability.

- Chargeback information.

Organization

Who is responsible for the following?

- Establishing standards.

- Creating views.

- Determining what data should be in the databases.

- Establishing security.

- Dataset and disk placement.

- Performance:
    - Performance modeling or benchmarking (capacity planning and anticipating performance).
    - Designing for performance.

- Monitoring performance.

- Tuning.

- Coordinating with other groups to improve performance (for instance, disk farm and networking).

- Training end users and IT.

- Help desk.

- Logical data models.

- Physical data models.

- Database tables.

- Reviewing database access (SQL) paths.

- Providing feedback to users and senior management.

Communication

The means of communication can have a significant impact on the performance of the system:

- Gateway.

- Network topology.

SETTING USER EXPECTATIONS

The most important component of performance is properly setting business user expectations. In some cases, a query may generate a scan of a one million row table. Returning the resulting set will take time. If the users are expecting unrealistic response times, they will never be happy. They should know before the system goes into development about the broad range of response times.

Demonstrations of the system and the training classes often set unrealistic performance expectations. Demonstrations and classes usually use small databases. The person giving the demonstration often does not have access to the full database. She just wants to demonstrate a system function quickly and show the system in its best light. Those running the class workshops also do not have access to the full database, and they want the students to have good response times in the workshops (they have many other concerns besides the performance of the class exercises). Unfortunately, the demos and the class exercises give the future users unrealistic performance expectations. The classes must properly set performance expectations, especially the variability of query performance.

SLAs can document what the user expects and provide a goal for IT. SLAs for online transactions should contain two components: the percentage of transactions and the response time for this percentage. As an example, an SLA for an online banking transaction might be 90 percent of the transactions that will be returned in 4 seconds or less. It is important that the SLA not specify 100 percent of the transactions because that SLA will never be achieved. There always will be an aberrant condition that will cause some transactions to take more than four seconds.

If your organization charges back the cost of IT to the business users, it is important that the business user get a bill in line with what they expect to pay. The resources used for transactions can be anticipated or predicted from experience. Queries are less predictable, so there must be some way to let a business user know that the query they are about to launch will exhaust this year's budget. Many relational databases have governors to prevent such a query. In addition, some databases, as well as BI tools, give an indication of the expected resource expenditure prior to running the query. This lets the business user abort the query and prevents an unexpectedly large bill and a very unhappy business user.

A common mislabeling of performance is associated with outages. Some users erroneously label any outage as bad performance. While the experience is bad for the user, the problem is unavailability not poor performance. Users should understand the distinction and assign their dissatisfaction with the correct label. Both availability and performance should be covered in the user training.

MONITORING (MEASUREMENT)

Running a system without the advantage of metrics is like trying to navigate a ship without a chart, compass, sextant, or now GPS. Without metrics, we have no way of knowing if we have delivered a system that anyone considers to be successful. We have no idea about response time, machine utilization, availability, user satisfaction, or the quality of the data. When performance gets bad (at some time, it will get bad), you will have no way of knowing what caused the performance problem or where to direct your efforts. More importantly, it will be difficult to anticipate the problem and to take corrective action before the user is impacted.

Conformance to Measures of Success

Most projects have explicit or implicit measures of success. The measurements of a system will determine if it was or was not a success. Measurements can be objective and subjective. An objective measurement is a count generated by a program (for example, the number of records with data domain violations). A subjective measurement is a survey of opinion, such as user query response time satisfaction.

Types of Metrics

There are a number of metrics that are relevant for understanding performance. These include:

- **Usage**—Usage tells you if the system is being used, to what extent, and by whom. For example, you may have a goal of 90 percent of the trained users using the system. Your metrics may show that your goal was met when 92 percent of the users, who were trained on the tools, ran a query or report during the previous month.

  Metrics on usage are often an eye opener when you discover large numbers of intended users are not using the system or use it only sporadically. This type of information can point to deficiencies in training, in poor targeting of intended users, lack of predefined queries and reports, inadequate support, or lack of emphasis by management.

- **Response time**—Performance is usually reflected in response time. A response time SLA is appropriate for operational systems. Although we do not recommend a SLA for ad-hoc query response time, it is important to measure how long a user has to wait for an answer. It is usually too late once the users start calling or screaming that response time is terrible—the damage already has been done to the reputation of the system. You will want to know what percentage of the queries, for example, ran longer than 10 minutes, how long they actually ran, and you will want to know which departments experienced the long run times.

Measurements sometimes uncover poor performing queries that are the result of users not understanding the ramifications of some of their actions. The appropriate response could be more comprehensive training that focuses on the dos and don'ts of writing queries. If a column is frequently being summarized, then the response could be a summary table. As it becomes apparent that a column is accessed frequently, or that tables are being joined on a specific key, then the DBA can build an index for those fields.

ETL performance is particularly important for large and very large databases. The elapsed time required to perform the processes of transformation, cleansing, aggregations, and loads can sometimes exceed the window for the ETL process. The metrics on each of these processes can help determine the source of the problem and help direct where to focus the resources.

- **Resource utilization**—This would include the number of machine cycles, memory usage, and accesses to the disk. The information about the percentage of disk utilization should result in a better distribution and partitioning of the data on the array of disks, or it should point out the necessity of purchasing additional disk drives or controllers.

- **User Satisfaction**—Satisfaction surveys tell us how well the system meets user expectations. Satisfaction surveys should be taken two to four times per year and the results of those surveys should promote action to improve the areas where the users are unhappy. Sometimes these surveys uncover misunderstandings in the way the system was intended to be used. Satisfaction surveys typically include questions on the use of the operational system, on the access and analysis (BI) tool, data quality, availability, response time, and support. The success of the system as perceived by upper management will be based primarily on the users' assessment of these factors. By giving the users some high-level information on response time, they may be inclined to more favorably modify their responses on the user satisfaction survey.

- **Dormant data**—Dormant data is data that is never accessed. Loading this unused data night after night is expensive, consumes disk space, and may reduce the likelihood that the system will be available to the users by 8:00 AM when they were expecting it. Dormant data is a total waste to the organization and is the albatross that will weigh down the budget, extend batch and ETL time, and tax the skills of the DBA staff.

Dormant data exists either because the requirements gathering process was lax, or because the users were unable to sufficiently articulate their requirements, resulting in loading useless data for fear that the users may possibly need it. Dormant data remains because there may be no tools in place to even let the DBAs know that the data is not being accessed.

Responsibility for Measurement

It is not always clear who should be responsible for measurement. Some organizations have groups dedicated to performance and these are the folks who normally have the primary responsibility. Depending on the specific measurement, the responsibility may fall to the DBA group, the Architecture Group, or to Capacity Planning. Measurement is usually not a full-time job, but it is a job that cannot be forgotten or denied. If there are performance problems or availability problems, immediate awareness is paramount so that the responsible persons can be alerted and effective actions can be taken. This means that the responsibility for performance needs to be a management assignment. When there are problems, there needs to be one manager who takes responsibility for addressing the problem even though the cause was outside his or her area.

Because performance is affected by a number of departments (technical services, DBA, and application developers), monitoring should not be the sole province of just one department. The information should be shared and should be the common source of performance information for all interested groups. Weekly meetings, especially in the initial stages of a project, should be mandatory to address performance and other problems.

Means to Measure

A number of the database-related products have built-in capability to capture and report on the system. These metrics can be accessed and delivered in a form that is meaningful to the technical people, to the users, and to management. In addition, there are add-on products that supplement information on how the system is performing. Quite often, organizations have these means of measuring but are either unaware of the product feature's existence, or no one has been assigned to execute the measurements and then take action on the results.

Use of Measurements

We need to measure because large systems *always* have performance problems, and initially, systems should be considered a work in progress. No major system has been implemented without the need to make changes and enhancements.

There is always an opportunity to enhance performance and, in fact, without enhancement, most systems would rarely meet any specified measure of success. The process should be to measure, identify problems and opportunities, and take appropriate action to solve the problems and exploit the opportunities.

"What is unmetered is always over consumed. By metering things carefully, demand is self-correcting. I call it the 'Conservation of IT principle,'" said Kathleen Melymuka at Computer World (December 22, 2003) when she quoted Roger Gray, CIO of Pacific Gas and Electric.

Metering, or measuring, is required if the organization is planning to charge back the costs of operation to those departments that use the system. Charge backs are rarely welcomed because no one wants additional costs assigned to their department, but for those organizations that do charge back, the use of metrics is critical to an equitable distribution of costs. This becomes even more important when money is transferred from one organization to another, such as organizations with subsidiaries that sell to and buy products from each other.

Return on Investment (ROI)

As part of cost justification, an organization might have estimated its benefits but post-implementation, it is important to measure just what those benefits actually were. This measurement is crucial to determine the ROI from the project and also to help with future goal-setting, benefits estimates, and proposed expansions or enhancements. The measurement can highlight areas where benefits were overestimated and also uncover benefits that were serendipitous and unanticipated. It would be unusual if the resulting benefits were as predicted. It is important to review the benefits to determine the accuracy of the predictions. Armed with the results of the review, more accurate predictions can be made in each category and the prediction process can be improved with more accurate benefits projected for future projects. More accurate benefits analysis can aid in prioritizing projects. Even if you did not estimate costs and benefits, post implementation measurement will still be beneficial. You will be able to determine if your project has a positive ROI and you will still be able to determine if any existing systems should be abandoned.

Reporting Results to Management

Management wants to know how things are going. They just spent $5,000,000 for the system and they want to know if they are getting their money's worth. Are the users utilizing the system, are they happy, and are they achieving the benefits they were expecting?

Management is usually content with monthly metric reports unless there are serious problems. In this case, management will want to be briefed more frequently on the problems, the steps that are being taken to resolve those problems, and results of the resolutions. Metrics should be reported with just the information that is of interest to each manager. A good approach is to use conventional tools accessing a small metrics data mart. Any metrics that represent problems should be highlighted or shown in red. A dashboard is appropriate for metrics of performance and availability.

Each organization should identify the metrics they will need and use as they continually work to improve their own systems. An understanding of the appropriate metrics, the responsibility for gathering the metrics, and the use of those metrics can make the difference between success and failure of the project.

TUNING

Tuning, as used in this book, refers to any system changes in conjunction with the known applications that can improve the performance of the system. This includes changes to the hardware, operating system, communications links, DBMS (including using DBMS options), and the application programs. None of these should be off limits if the goal is to achieve a desired level of performance. However, tuning does not usually fix a system that has been poorly designed or one that has horribly inefficient application code.

Tuning is not a free activity and the resources employed in the tuning process most often carry a price tag. If disk wait time is high because of heavy disk usage, the tuning effort might indicate the need for additional disks and their associated cost. Tuning requires DBAs who are knowledgeable about performance, the data, the application programs, and the workload characteristics of the system.

Information on what and how to tune can come from the performance modeling effort, from simulations and benchmarks, and most importantly, from the performance monitors. DBMSs are different and the hints and tips to improve performance provided by one DBMS vendor might not be appropriate for another DBMS. A DBA who is familiar with the performance characteristics of DB2 can mistakenly assume that applying a technique used in the past with DB2 will work equally well with Oracle.

Tuning Options

Tuning a database is a function of the DBMS and the options available for that specific DBMS. The operating system also will be a major factor in the sorts or tuning possibilities available. The following are some of the tuning options, although not all of these are appropriate or even relevant for specific DBMSs:

- Establishing smart primary keys. Smart keys allow the DBMS to optimize access.

- Creating new indexes. This option can significantly improve transaction and query response time, but it degrades load time.

- Removing indexes. This can improve the time to create, update, and delete data from a database. Look for duplicate indexes or indexes that are inefficient or have insufficient value on access.

- Creating summary tables. If queries are frequently performing the same summary function, summary tables will improve response time and minimize machine resource requirements. These summary tables will have to be built and this will lengthen load times

- Buffer pool (database buffer cache) tuning. The proper grouping of indexes and critical tables (those with high activity) into multiple buffer pools and the sizing of the buffer pools.

- Caching. By forcing some data into memory, fewer I/Os will be required.

- Data partitioning. This allows for multiple parallel subprocesses to execute concurrently significantly improving response or throughput time.

- Data set placement. An optimal placement of data will evenly distribute I/O requests so that there will be fewer instances of some disks having light activity while others become a bottleneck.

- DBMS parameters. This is DBMS-specific.

- Optimizer tweaking (hints). For example, Oracle allows hints that will change the way the optimizer works.

- Governors. This capability would be used to limit resource use for a profligate query. In practice, this capability is not often implemented because it is difficult to know if a long running query is doing what it is supposed to be doing, and out of the fear of aborting a report requested by the CEO.

- Data compression. Certain data and certain activities lend themselves to data compression. If data is to be read sequentially, compressed data should result in better buffer pool performance and many fewer I/Os.

- Eliminating referential integrity (RI) on the load. *Note: This is highly controversial.* Does all data need to have RI? Perhaps not. Enforcing RI is expensive and will lengthen load times but it should be enforced when warranted. When it is not warranted, consider eliminating it.

- Archiving old data that is not frequently accessed.

- Optimizing column length. Some columns might be sized for data that was never captured.

- Optimizing and standardizing on decode and reference tables. This can either mean having one set of tables or distributing them to minimize contention.

- Removing or optimizing triggers and stored procedures when they impact performance.

Optimal performance is best obtained when all the involved departments (database, applications, operating system, and network) contribute and communicate with each other. This is most often achieved when these groups have a common stake in good performance and are working toward a common goal.

Reporting Performance Results

Organizations report performance results for a variety of reasons including:

- To report on SLAs

- To provide information to IT so they can correct performance problems

- To let the business users know what a good job IT is doing

The third point is part of the internal selling job in which IT is constantly selling its capabilities and demonstrating results to the business users. Some IT organizations give bonuses to managers when SLAs are met. In these cases, it is extremely important that the SLAs were set properly and that the measurements are correct and properly reported.

Selling Management on Performance

The cases at the end of this chapter present a convincing argument on the importance of managing performance. All these are true cases but they have been somewhat disguised to keep our lawyers' ulcers in check. Keep your own set of clippings from the trade press, especially for your industry.

The major points to management for the existence of a group dedicated to performance, and the software and hardware to support them are:

- Avoidance of potential disasters associated with systems that do not perform. See Case Study #4 in the "Case Studies" section that follows this section.

- Ability to configure the hardware without a significant amount of over configuration insurance needed because it is not known how much machine resource is required.

- Ability to spend money on the components that will contribute to improved performance, and not on those that will provide little, if any, benefit.

- Ability to justify where the money is being spent.

- Knowledge that the right things are being done.

CASE STUDIES

Case 1: A large retailer developed an online system and chose to use a DBMS that had only been used in small to medium systems. The retail online system was expecting over fifty transactions per second. The DBMS had certain architectural constraints that limited the maximum number of transactions to less than twenty five per second. The architects of the retail system knew of these constraints but believed they could be overcome by modifications to the DBMS. The modifications were not as effective as anticipated. After 2 years, the system was abandoned.

Lesson 1: If you are the project manager, beware of any unproven solutions because they may kill your project.

Case 2: A large bank chose proprietary hardware to support an online system that had a response time requirement of 90 percent of the transactions in 5 seconds or less. Performance was tested one transaction at a time. The tests met the performance response time requirement.

The bank never performed stress tests where they would drive the system at a level matching their peak rate. When the system went into production, response time was unacceptable with 90 percent of the transactions responding in 43 seconds. The proprietary hardware could not be expanded to improve performance and the system was terminated.

Lesson 1: Stress tests, performance modeling, or performance simulations are critical for high volume systems.

Lesson 2: Stress tests should be run as early in the development cycle as possible.

Lesson 3: Beware of extrapolations from small volume tests to peak volumes.

Case 3: An insurance company had established SLAs for both performance and availability. One key system was closely watched by upper management and when the SLAs were not met, the responsible manager was called to task. This system was scheduled to be up from 6:00 AM to 7:00 PM for a total of 13 hours, Monday through Friday. The measure of availability was represented as a percentage and was calculated as follows: total number of minutes the system was available divided by the number of minutes in 13 hours.

On one occasion, the system was unavailable for 15 minutes. The manager in charge instructed the operators to leave the system up until 7:10 PM that evening. This had the effect of adding an additional 10 minutes to the numerator in the availability equation. This resulted in a higher availability percentage and it met the availability SLA.

This slight of hand was eventually discovered. It hurt the credibility of the manager, and it severely damaged the credibility of IT. When last heard from, the manager had been demoted and is currently selling aluminum siding.

Lesson: Never cook the books because you will be discovered and your reputation will never recover. Measurements must be as accurate as you can possibly make them, even if it shows you or your department in a negative light.

Case 4: A large bank with a large Automatic Teller Machine (ATM) system had the misfortune to experience severe performance problems the week before Christmas. A slow news day and an ATM in the lobby of the city's main newspaper resulted in a front page article on the failure of the bank's system. The CIO was counseled to not have this problem recur.

A performance and compensation plan was established for all the managers who could, in any way, affect the performance and availability of the ATMs. Very tight and closely monitored SLAs were established. The plan compensated managers for meeting the objectives regardless of which department contributed to improvements or caused problems. This approach resulted in the managers working closely, and working to anticipate and correct problems, rather than the traditional time and energy spent on fixing blame.

The response time of this system was consistently better than the other five largest banks in the state against which it was measured.

Lesson: If the key players have a significant stake in good performance, they will all pull together, anticipate problems before they occur, resolve problems more quickly, and deliver superior performance.

Case 5: The Department of Motor Vehicles launched a major conversion of its vehicle registration system using a well known DBMS and its 4GL. The functional tests went well and the system was promoted into production. Unfortunately, the DMV never fully tested the system with the volumes the DMV was to experience. The 4GL was not a high performance system and had never achieved the targeted volumes with any other installed user. Bottlenecks were soon encountered, response time became excessive, and registrations could not be processed.

The DMV was unable to keep up with vehicle registration. As a result, there were many cars on the road with expired license plates. The Highway Patrol was advised not to ticket expired license plates since the owners may have paid for but not received their updated tags.

Lesson: Any new technology should be evaluated for performance as well as functional capabilities, and the system should be stress tested before going into production.

Case 6: A large European bank had a very impressive set of screens displaying all facets of the performance characteristics of the system. A consultant asked the manager of the group how he knew when he had a performance problem. The manager pointed to a phone and said, "It rings."

Lesson: A high-tech and expensive solution might not be the most appropriate way to monitor performance problems.

PERFORMANCE TASKS

You will need your own plan that includes whatever portions of performance you want to implement (modeling, measuring, tuning, and so on). The plan should include the organizational issues, roles, responsibilities, and the costs.

- Assemble a team to deal with the performance requirements of the system.

- Understand the performance requirements of the system including volumes and SLAs.

- Understand the characteristics of the data.

- Understand the environmental factors including CPU, network, and requirements for distribution.

- Understand any constraints including costs, schedules, and skills.

- Develop a technical architecture including the DBMS, hardware, and disk configurations.

- Choose the DBMS if it has not already been chosen. You may want to benchmark against more than one DBMS contender.

- Model the performance of the system using analytical or simulation techniques.

- Choose additional utilities and software, including monitoring tools, BI tools, and ETL tools, among others.

- Design a prototype database.

- Review the design.

- Promote the application into a test system.

- Stress test.

- Monitor and measure everything.

- Review results of measurements and tune the databases and, or applications as appropriate.

- Continue to measure.

WATCH OUT FOR PRECISE METRICS

On a geology field trip, we were told by our leader that the rocks under our feet were 3 billion and 27 years old. When we asked how he could be so precise, he responded that when he was a student, 27 years ago, he was told by his professor that these same rocks were 3 billion years old.

When a vendor is incredibly precise with the results of a benchmark, stress test, or customer experience, take the results with a grain of salt.

CONCLUSION

Performance, or more accurately, poor performance will be the death-knell of a system, both operational and decision support. The underlying DBMS, the database design, and the way the data is accessed, updated, loaded, and deleted have profound impacts on performance. The performance implications of the data must be clearly defined and those responsible for database performance must have the tools to forecast, measure, and know how the system will perform and allow them to monitor and report on actual performance.

REFERENCES

The Computer Measurement Group, www.cmg.org. The Computer Measurement Group, commonly called CMG, is a not-for-profit, worldwide organization of data processing professionals committed to the measurement and management of computer systems. CMG members are primarily concerned with performance evaluation of existing systems to maximize performance (response time, throughput, and so on) and with capacity management where planned enhancements to existing systems or the design of new systems are evaluated to find the necessary resources required to provide adequate performance at a reasonable cost.

Sid Adelman, "Benchmarking the Data Warehouse," www.teradata.com, 2004.

Domanski, Bernie. "Simulation versus Analytic Modeling in Large Computing Environments: Predicting the Performance Impact of Tuning Changes," A White Paper from Responsive Systems Company, 1999.

Hubel, Martin. "Tuning PeopleSoft Applications for the DB2 OS/390 Environment," 1999.

Imhoff, Claudia, Nicholas Galemmo, and Jonathan G. Geiger. *Mastering Data Warehouse Design*, New York: John Wiley and Sons, 2003.

Killelea, Patrick. *Web Performance Tuning*, 2nd Edition, Speeding up the Web, 2002.

Loosley, Chris, and Frank Douglas. *High Performance Client/Server*, New York: John Wiley and Sons, 1998.

Millsap, Cary and Jeff Holt. *Optimizing Oracle Performance*, Sebastopol, CA: O'Reilly Publishing, 2003.

Pendse, Nigel and Richard Creeth. "Responsive Systems," www.responsivesystems.com.

The OLAP Report—www.olapreport.com.

Teradata—www.teradata.com.

CHAPTER 8

Security and Privacy of Data

This chapter deals with security and privacy only as it relates to data. It does not cover the extensive concerns of security and privacy of the Web or wireless issues. It also does not deal with viruses and worms.

The attention to data security has become more and more important because employees often keep their own copies of highly sensitive data on their laptops, home computers, and even PDAs. For example, employees often download company data to their laptops or home computers to allow them to work from home. Employees can also copy extensive amounts of data to CDs and DVDs. Companies rarely have any idea who keeps this data and rarely understand the implications to security and privacy.

Fraud or misappropriation of sensitive organizational data—especially when that fraud or misappropriation is reported in the *Wall Street Journal*—is often the catalyst for organizations taking action to address their security and privacy issues. It's not just that the horse is already out of the barn; it is that quite a few other horses are ready to bolt. Management should realize the security exposures and be ready to listen and approve the money and people resources that it will take to build and support security and privacy policies.

Technology has made security and privacy even more of an issue because critical data can walk out the door on a removable disk the size of a key fob. Senior management of your organization and the board of directors want to know what you are doing to protect the security of important and sensitive data and the privacy of their customers.

DATA IDENTIFICATION FOR SECURITY AND PRIVACY

Security relates to the protection of data against unauthorized disclosure, alteration, restriction, or destruction. Privacy is the right of your customers, suppliers, and partners to be sure that the confidential information you maintain on them is controlled and protected from unauthorized access or distribution.

Table 8.1 is an example of what can be done for each database or file that has security and, or privacy sensitivity requirements. This matrix identifies data access authorization at the column level (feel free to find fault with the access designations in the example). The data owner of the Customer database would make the final decisions about which user roles can create (C), read (R), update (U), and delete (D) data. This decision occurs during a process in which an analyst and a DBA meet with the data owner and identify each cell in the matrix.

Table 8.1: Customer Database: Role-Based Access Matrix by Column

User Roles Fields/ Columns	Marketing	Managers	Administrators and Authorized Programs	Customer Support	IT Support	Other Internal Departments
Customer Number	R	R	CRUD	R	CRUD	R
Customer Name	R	R	CRUD	RU	CRUD	R
Customer Address	R	R	CRUD	RU	CRUD	
Customer Home Phone		R	CRUD	RU	CRUD	
Customer Business Phone		R	CRUD	RU	CRUD	

User Roles Fields/ Columns	Marketing	Managers	Administrators and Authorized Programs	Customer Support	IT Support	Other Internal Departments
Customer E-mail Address	R	R	CRUD	RU	CRUD	
Customer Credit Score	R	R	CRUD		CRUD	
Customer Ethnicity	R	R	CRUD		CRUD	
Customer Birth Date	R	R	CRUD		CRUD	
Customer Lifetime Value	R	R	CRUD		CRUD	
Customer Gender	R	R	CRUD		CRUD	
Customer Marital Status	R	R	CRUD	RU	CRUD	

Legend: C = Create, R = Read, U = Update, and D = Delete

User Role

Role-based security would assign privileges to create, update, delete, or read (access) specific data, based upon the user's role or position in the organization. For example, an employee in Human Resources with the responsibility for entering new employees would have the privilege to create a new employee record, but that person would not be allowed to change salary information. A manager would have access to the database and the update capability to employee data only for her department.

Table 8.2 is an example of restricting data access to user roles on a "need-to-know" basis. This matrix identifies data access authorization at the row level. Again, the data owner of the *Customer Database* would make the final decisions about which user roles can access which records or rows.

Table 8.2: Customer Database: Role-Based Access Matrix by Row

	Regional Manager	*District Manager*	*VP of Sales*
Eastern District		All Eastern District Customers	All Customers
Region 11	Region 11 Customers		
Region 12	Region 12 Customers		
Region 13	Region 13 Customers		
Southern District		All Southern District Customers	All Customers
Region 21	Region 21 Customers		
Region 22	Region 22 Customers		
Region 23	Region 23 Customers		
Western District		All Western District Customers	All Customers
Region 31	Region 31 Customers		
Region 32	Region 32 Customers		
Region 33	Region 33 Customers		
Northern District		All Northern District Customers	All Customers
Region 41	Region 41 Customers		
Region 42	Region 42 Customers		
Region 43	Region 43 Customers		

ROLES AND RESPONSIBILITIES

It's not enough to have security and privacy policies, nor is it enough to have tools to identify problems, intercept aberrant access, or identify potential exposures. Without the appropriate roles and responsibilities identified, authorized, and staffed, information about breaches and potential problems cannot be addressed in a timely manner.

Security Officer

The primary responsibility of the security officer is to establish security and privacy policies for the organization. To establish appropriate and applicable policies, the security officer needs to know the security and privacy requirements of your organization. The security officer is the driver of security activities, including identification of the gaps and exposures. The security officer needs to know what needs to be accomplished to close security gaps and mitigate the exposures. The security officer should draft the security and privacy policies and have these policies validated by internal and, or external auditors and by senior management. She should work with those who administer the security and privacy processes, such as the DBAs and system administrators, to assure that the policies are executed. The security officer should validate that the security and privacy policies of the organization are implemented, and then she should test the implemented processes. In case of a discovered policy violation, she should determine what remediation efforts should be used to correct exposures. The security officer should also determine how and where user IDs and passwords are encrypted, where they should be stored, and who should hold the keys for encrypting and decrypting. Finally, the security officer is responsible for policing and enforcing the security and privacy requirements for the data.

Data Owner

This position is variously called the data owner, data steward, or information steward. We call this role the data owner. The data owner is in the best position to understand the exposures if the data is compromised, lost, stolen, or misused. The data owner is the one who knows the value of the information and can best determine the benefits of either tight or loose security policies on the data under her control. The data owner is usually the line-of-business manager in whose department the data originates. For example, the manager responsible for purchasing owns supplier data and determines the importance of certain fields (columns) in the Supplier database. The manager responsible for insurance claims owns the Claims database and the Human Resources (HR) manager owns the Human Resource database. In cooperation with the security officer, the data owner should determine the sensitivity of the data and help establish policies for the data.

The data owner should be made aware of any access to sensitive data including who is accessing the data and for what purpose. In some cases, the data owner needs to approve unusual requests for access.

System Administrator

The system administrators (sometimes called sysadmins) are the ones who manage the computer systems. They are responsible for keeping the computers up and running; maintaining the networks; backing up and recovering computers (not the databases, which are the responsibility of the DBAs); installing and testing new software; making sure the system is not corrupted by viruses;

monitoring the system's performance; allocating new storage; and—the role that's most relevant to this chapter—creating and deleting user accounts. In creating and deleting the user accounts, the system administrator is also responsible for assigning, administering, and maintaining passwords. This maintenance includes manually changing passwords that have been forgotten or compromised.

REGULATORY COMPLIANCE

Although there are always new laws passed that affect the governance of information, there are some valuable lessons to be learned from the following laws:

- The Health Insurance Portability and Accountability Act (HIPAA) mandates that specific administrative and technological policies and procedures must be in place to ensure the security of health data that is stored electronically. It also requires that role-based security be implemented by identifying who is authorized to access patient data and for what purpose. HIPAA also makes clear the rights of patients to keep their medical information private.

- The Gramm-Leach-Bliley Act enacted in 1999 specifies that any financial institution that provides financial products or services to consumers must comply with certain privacy restrictions. If an organization provides financial products or services to individuals, and if those products or services are to be used primarily for their personal, family, or household purposes, you are dealing with consumers and must comply with this law.

- Sarbanes-Oxley requires that the CEO and the CFO verify and certify that the financial results they report are accurate and that the creation of that information has followed proper and documented internal control procedures.

- California SB 1386 Identity Protection Bill requires companies to encrypt personal data and that individuals whose identities have been compromised must be notified of the violation. All organizations that have California customers, not just California companies, must comply with SB 1386.

- The Family Educational Rights and Privacy Act (FERPA) requires that student information cannot be revealed and that aggregated student information cannot be disclosed for groups of students numbering less than ten for fear that this could lead to individual identification of the student.

- International rules, including those of the European Union and Canada, are more stringent than those in the United States. Organizations with multinational operations must either keep their domestic databases separate, or they must conform to the more demanding international rules. European Union data protection laws apply only to data that directly or indirectly can identify an individual. Such data includes a person's name, address, phone number, credit card number, and tax identification number (or equivalent). These laws do not apply to statistical data as long as that data cannot be traced back to the individuals.

AUDITING PROCEDURES

Auditing procedures should be established to detect purposeful or accidental attempts by either internal or external intruders to access secured data. Many of the DBMSs and third-party tools provide the capability to capture access requests for data including the columns, views, and tables accessed. The tools should also provide information on when the data was accessed, how often and how many times, who accessed it, how often and how many times, what access products were used (for example, a business intelligence [BI] product or SQL), and whether the access was successful. Some of these auditing tools can capture and highlight abnormal use and present aberrant access patterns to those responsible for security. These abnormal and deviant situations are often the first indication that something troublesome is happening. Active auditing utilities can impact the system's performance, and so they should be intelligently and selectively implemented.

Security Audits

A security audit should be carried out periodically to validate the organization's security and privacy policies and to verify that the implementation of those policies work and are scrupulously followed. A security audit should include reviews of the following:

- Controls relating to the use of the data.

- The assignment of user IDs, passwords, and administration. These should also be validated.

- How data flows, how it is accessed, security or privacy exposures, and so on.

- The use and implementation of the security capabilities of the DBMS.

- Processes to monitor data usage, including create, update, delete, and access.

- The policies and processes of vendors, outsourcers, business partners, and supply-chain participants.

- The security capabilities of the application packages and how they are implemented.

- The assignment and roles of the data owners, their level of involvement, and activity in categorizing their data.

- Active auditing reports.

If you outsource, ask the outsourcing organization what they do to audit their own security and privacy processes. Include your required policies and procedures in your contract with the outsourcer. Review the documented policies and procedures used by the outsourcing organization and, depending on your security and privacy requirements, require an independent audit of their processes.

External Users of Your Data

You might be selling your data and you might be providing the data to partners, suppliers, and wholesale customers as part of a supply chain program. You might be sending your data to an outsourcing organization and that organization might be offshore. Your industry might be regulated and the terms of the regulation may require you to divulge certain data to the regulators; for example, clinical pharmaceutical trial results must be provided to the Food and Drug Administration. As data leaves an organization's secure environment, the level of exposure increases significantly because of exposures in the data transmission process or the loss or misappropriation of physical files. The organization that receives the data might not have the same level of security and privacy policies, or it might have policies that aren't enforced. Any sensitive data should be encrypted before transmission. The policies of the receiving organization should be reviewed and, if the data is especially sensitive, you should conduct security and privacy audits to ensure that data is not compromised.

DESIGN SOLUTIONS

Security is always harder to retrofit than to implement at the outset. This means that security and privacy should be designed into every application that warrants the effort.

If a database contains keys that can uniquely identify a customer, a patient, or a supplier, the data is exposed to some extent, especially when these keys are required in performing joins with other tables. The solution is to use system-generated keys so that the entity remains anonymous.

Database Controls

All databases provide a certain degree of security control using VIEWs to limit what tables, what rows within those tables, and what columns within those rows a user can see. Some organizations never allow raw access to tables and allow access only through the views. The DBA can also restrict some access by establishing partitions, and she can limit access by partition. For example, partitions can be established for each country in which the organization does business. This can satisfy some country-specific laws that prohibit the mixing of data with that of other countries

Security Databases

Many organizations have specialized security databases that maintain roles, user IDs, and authorization for access. These databases are used in conjunction with the VIEW capabilities of the DBMS. The security databases must be tightly controlled and include the use of active auditing tools because these security databases also need to be monitored.

Test and Production Data

Application developers need test data. Unfortunately, creating sanitized data or data that have been made anonymous is fairly difficult. Thus, many organizations use either a sample or a complete copy of the production database. This might not present a problem at the level of an employee changing his or her salary grade in his or her test data, but it does present a privacy exposure when the test data includes other employees' salary or performance information. The exposure is obviously the discovery of a fellow employee's salary or performance ranking. If the test data includes customer numbers or credit card numbers, the exposure is a stolen or compromised customer list. If exposures exist and are deemed sensitive, you must make production data anonymous before using it in a test environment.

Data Encryption

Encryption takes some overhead and should be used only on data that is transferred from one platform to another, or it should be used only on sensitive data. Most DBMSs have encryption wizards and other encryption capabilities. Make sure you research the encryption options and understand how bulletproof those options are (because they can be broken, find out what it takes to break the codes). Understand the DBA effort involved in encrypting the data and any exposures involved with your DBMS encryption, such as the loss of some data. Also understand any performance implications of using encryption as well as any other issues, such as backup and recovery, reorganization, and archiving of encrypted data. The performance costs are related to how and where the encryption takes place. Table 8.3 gives you a rough idea of the performance impact of encryption.

Table 8.3: Performance Impact of Encryption

Encryption Site	Overhead
Hardware	3–5%
Application	10–12%
Database	~15%

Standards for Data Usage

Most organizations have customers of one stripe or another. Besides the obvious types of customers, schools have students, hospitals have patients, governmental entities have citizens, correctional organizations have prisoners, professional organizations have members, and charitable organizations have donors as well as recipients of their services. Your organization should have standards of how this customer data is stored, how it's encrypted, how it's secured, and how it's connected to various internal applications.

Some security and privacy standards might come from the legal department, whereas others might come from various business units, such as sales and marketing, and others come from compliance and risk.

IMPACT OF THE DATA WAREHOUSE

The data warehouse presents some new security challenges, especially because some portions of the data warehouse can eventually be made available to others outside the organization. The plethora of new security and privacy laws requires a more complete definition and understanding of data in the data warehouse. The new data laws require an understanding of who is using what internal data. Laws, regulations, and policies impact most departments. Data disciplines need to be treated as organizational compliance issues and not just the responsibility of an individual, department, or the security officer.

At minimum, organizational leadership must be aware of concerns relating to potential for insider trading of financial data warehouse data and any laws related to the use of tax identification numbers. Corporations must adhere to Sarbanes-Oxley requirements, which include data timeliness, retention, and other regulatory security and privacy laws. Organizations must incorporate the appropriate functions into every project to support these requirements.

Applications that use customer information—most notably customer relationship management (CRM) applications—can overstep the line into a person's private life. This has significant implications on organizations that want to optimize marketing efforts while not offending and annoying the existing customer base.

As data is examined and defined, the security and privacy requirements of the data and the regulatory sensitivity of the data should be included in the metadata. The notion of user entitlement (role-based access control) should be institutionalized to limit data access by the type of user who should be able to look only at specifically authorized data elements.

VENDOR ISSUES

The software you purchase and the external data you bring in have security and privacy implications. As you evaluate these offerings, make sure someone on the team asks appropriate questions and can evaluate the answers, capabilities, and exposures from these vendors.

Software

Most software products, application packages, and ERPs have security capabilities built in, but they vary greatly in effectiveness and how closely they match your own needs for security and privacy. As tools are evaluated, security and privacy capabilities must be researched, not just for the function they provide, but for the effort involved in administration. Some administration is labor-intensive. Because the application vendors want to be DBMS-independent, some application packages override the capabilities of the DBMS by implementing their own security and bypassing the security functions of the DBMS. This can result in a major exposure to your data.

Provide the vendor with your architecture, a description of your business, your environment (including other major software products), and your requirements for security and privacy. Ask for the following information:

- Please describe the security and privacy features of your product. Indicate where your product protects the system (front-end or back-end).

- How does your software support our security, privacy requirements, and policies?

- How does your software interface with the products we use?

- How does your product use or not use the security capabilities of the DBMS?

- If you use your own software, how do you describe the responsibilities of the person who will be administering security and privacy?

- What are the names and titles of of those who work with your security and privacy capabilities?

External Data

External data has a myriad of exposures both for your organization as well as the company that provided the external data. Most sales and marketing applications need data that goes beyond the data that is internally generated. To get a better understanding of your customers, it is helpful to have demographic data that can be purchased. The demographic data can include income, age, ethnicity, buying habits, credit information, and education. Some of this data is considered private and the use of the data can violate privacy policies, if not government regulations. The marketing department, on the other hand, might be eager to use this data because of marketing programs and sales leads. In this case, the marketing department needs to know that just because the data can be purchased doesn't mean that certain parts of it should be used.

COMMUNICATING AND SELLING SECURITY

It's important that all employees understand security rules, privacy rules, and policies and know what their responsibilities are as they relate to security. For example, Table 8.1 documents that a customer address can be read by the marketing department. A security and privacy policy would make it clear that the marketing department cannot share this customer address data outside of its department. The policy should also limit what marketing can and cannot do with the data, such as transferring the data to a desktop or laptop or conversely restricting the data to the marketing server.

Security and Privacy Indoctrination

As employees are hired, they are faced with learning so much about the organization: the physical aspects, the politics, and the job they are expected to perform. The security and privacy policies are often given little attention in the indoctrination process. In the mind of the new employee, security and privacy are just not that important for success on the job. The employee handbook describing the policies is, at best, skimmed over. Security and privacy awareness needs to become part of the corporate culture. The CEO should make statements about the need for strong security and privacy controls and the exposure to the organization if the controls are not religiously implemented. Many organizations ask employees to sign a document attesting to an understanding of the security and privacy policies and to an agreement to abide by those policies.

Monitoring Employees

Rather than waiting for an employee to violate a security policy, such as downloading customer data, your organization should let employees know that computer activities are monitored and that they will have to account for any unauthorized activities.

Training

Training should include the security and privacy policies of the organization and should stress the importance of these policies with examples of the injury that can be caused by violation of policy. Employees need to know that violating the policies will lead to termination.

Before DBAs and system administrators attend classes that contain content and software capability for security and privacy, they should be briefed on the importance of these capabilities to the organization. They should also be tasked with bringing back procedures for implementing specific security and privacy policies.

Communication

All employees should be aware of the latest threats to security and privacy. They should hear about breaches in security in other organizations, in their own organization, and in their company's industry. Pictures of violators being handcuffed or dressed in not-so-fashionable orange jumpsuits help drive home the importance of the message.

BEST PRACTICES AND WORST PRACTICES

The practices itemized in the following list, along with your own security and privacy practices, should be established as standards, included in new employee training, and highlighted in all refresher programs.

- As an organization develops its own security and privacy policies, it's best to conform to the most stringent laws, rather than trying to do the minimum.

- Include a "privacy indicator" in customer record that describes each customer's privacy preferences. This customer record must be linked to all customer usage, especially when marketing to the customer.

- If you outsource, send only the data that is absolutely needed to the outsourcing organization (even more important if it's being offshored). For example, if the outsource vendor is evaluating a customer's credit, it does not need to know the customer's name, tax identification number, address, phone, employer, or anything else that can specifically identify the customer.

- Conduct vulnerability scans to detect exposures. Monitor any unusual patterns in data access.

- Conduct security risk assessments whenever new systems are implemented or whenever existing systems are significantly modified.

- Encrypt sensitive data. This is especially important if that data is transmitted inside or outside the organization.

- Establish a standard procedure that restricts access when employees are terminated. This should be obvious, but a surprisingly high percentage of companies are slow to cut off access.

- If an outside organization, such as a governmental entity, an external auditor, or a consultant requests customer data, supplier data, or any other data that is deemed to be sensitive, the request should first go to the legal department to determine if honoring the request violates the organization's security and privacy policies. Even if the request does not violate security and privacy policies, the executive committee may want to review the request.

- If an outside entity, such as an external auditor or a consultant, requests customer data, supplier data, or any other data that is deemed to be sensitive, the request should be fully understood and the right to access the data should be given only in exceptional situations and only under a nondisclosure agreement (NDA).

- Look at the cost and benefit of protecting the data. What is the data worth? *Don't spend $1 to secure information that's worth 50 cents.*

IDENTIFY YOUR OWN SENSITIVE DATA EXERCISE

Following is a simple template to understand and document the sensitive data in your organization. The template should address one subject area at a time, such as customer, supplier, part (as in inventory), or employee.

Data in Relation to Security and Privacy

Data identification

    External

    Vendors

        Suppliers

        Governmental regulators

        Partners (including customers)

    Internal

        Employees

        Administrative staff

Alternate data identification

> Location of data (database, system, and platform)
>
> Sensitivity of data to security violations
>
> Sensitivity of data to privacy violations
>
> Vulnerability: How easily can the data be incorrectly changed?
>
> Importance of data (critical, important but not critical, not very important)

Security and privacy is also related to the operations the users may perform.

Indicate the operations each user is allowed to perform:

- Unconstrained access to all of the data, read only.

- Unconstrained access and update capability.*

- Access to summary data, but not detailed data.

- Constrained read access.

- Constrained update access.

- The user has no access or update capability at all.

* Update can further be segmented into adding, changing, and deleting a record.

CONCLUSION

The effort to create and administer security and privacy policies is not trivial. Proper implementation does nothing for the organization's bottom line. The best way to look at the work and budget required is to equate it with insurance. If you don't have proper policies and if they are not properly executed, your company is exposed for substantial fines for violating governmental regulations, suits for violating customer privacy, and terrible public relations when the media exposes slipshod ways.

Knowing how far to go with security and privacy policies is difficult. Depending on your industry and in which countries you do business, governmental regulations force you to comply at specific levels for some, but not all of your data, so don't waist money and people resources on data that does not have to be protected.

DBMS Selection

You should read this chapter if you are considering which DBMS to use for your next application. Perhaps you are considering an enterprise resource planning product (ERP), such as SAP or PeopleSoft, or whether to switch an existing DBMS, or which DBMS to choose for a decision support system, such as a data warehouse or data mart. You might be experiencing or anticipating significant growth in data volume, transaction volume, number of concurrent users for business intelligence, or some combination of the above, and you are not sure which DBMS will give you the best performance. You might have merged with another enterprise that has a different DBMS standard, and you are trying to determine if you should standardize on one DBMS as you integrate the enterprise (see Chapter 2, "Integration," for further information) or maintain more than one standard DBMS. This chapter provides guidelines for making these decisions.

EXISTING ENVIRONMENT

Every organization has an existing environment with hardware, application software, operating systems, and DBMSs. In fact, you might have multiple types of hardware and more than one DBMS within your technical architecture. Along with hardware and software, you have people with skills and experience with the DBMSs. You also have attitudes and impressions of those DBMSs and their vendors, some good and some bad. You might even be considering outsourcing all or part of your IT operation (see Chapter 6, "Organizational Roles and Responsibilities," for more details about outsourcing and related topics).

Capabilities and Functions

The DBMSs today are effective and full of exceptional capabilities. Some features are implemented better than others in each DBMS and certain DBMSs might be more appropriate for your organization and your planned use of the DBMS. The requirements for a decision support database (data warehouse or data mart) are somewhat different than the requirements of an operational (transaction) database. You will want to consider the following capabilities as you evaluate the DBMSs:

- Flexibility and ability to respond to new requirements.

- Ease of integration including heterogeneous integration (more than one DBMS) and the ability to support an enterprise view of your data.

- Ability to support large volumes of data (each organization must determine what "large" means).

- Ability to support a large number of concurrent users.

- Ability to support your users' performance expectations based on response time service level agreements (SLAs). Besides indexes and parallelism, the DBMS optimizer and the capability to tune and refine operations can have a significant impact on performance.

- Index implementation—all the vendors have support for indexes, but the way they implement the indexes is often different. This can have a major impact on your performance.

- Scalability, including the ability to make effective use of your hardware and your hardware's parallelism.

- Ability to support a multitier architecture.

- Partitioning effectiveness and the management of partitions and database clusters.

- Administrative and manageability efficiency, including self-management of memory, storage, and the backup process.

- Vendor-supplied tools and utilities, system management tools, and third-party utilities that support the DBMS.

- Interface with transaction monitors.

- Interface with business intelligence, query, and report tools.

- Support for a distributed environment.

- Support for copy management services or replication services by which you maintain more than one copy of the data.

- Security capabilities, including row-level security and data encryption.

- Ability to support your organization's planned scheduled uptime (for example, 24 x 7) and availability SLAs (for example, 99.9 percent) during scheduled hours. Planned database maintenance should not affect the availability of the data.

- Ability to support your application environment, application programs, and ERPs.

- Concurrency control that determines the integrity of the data. Each vendor has their favorite way of dealing with locks and different levels of the granularity of locks.

- Backup and recovery including the effort and time to backup and recover data in various operating modes and with different problem scenarios.

- Support for industry standards and open standards.

- Integrity enforcement capabilities and options including referential integrity, domain (valid value) verification, user-defined business rules enforced with triggers, and two-phase commit processing.

• Ability to store and manipulate complex data types and multiple data types including binary object support.

Use the selection matrix at the end of this chapter to capture the capabilities and functions that are important in your decisions.

DBMS CHOICES

Currently, five possible choices of DBMS are available:

• DB2 from IBM

• Oracle

• SQL Server from Microsoft

• Sybase

• Teradata from NCR

The first four are appropriate for operational (transactional) systems as well as for decision support systems or data warehouse systems. Teradata's niche was in decision support, but they are moving into operational systems as well.

In this chapter, we do not address MySQL, Microsoft's Access (see the sidebar on Access databases), or any of the older, less used DBMSs (Ingres, NonStop SQL, IMS, and IDMS). Informix has been purchased by IBM, and IBM does not appear to be actively marketing Informix, choosing instead to recommend DB2. Although companies can continue to use Informix, not many consider Informix for a new application or as their DBMS of choice.

ACCESS DATABASES

Many organizations have a large number of Access programs and databases being run by the business units (BUs). In some cases, these are almost stealth IT operations. Many Access programs are created by extracting data from primary and secondary source databases. Many of these are used for critical internal analysis and reporting to external agencies and many are being run without standards, proper documentation, or passing normal testing, validation, and quality control processes.

The use of Access for external reporting should be minimized. Any reporting that needs to be done out of Access should follow strict standards for quality control and validation and should be run only by personnel certified to produce these reports. Access is not an industrial strength database and its use should be strictly limited. Access developers and users should be trained on and encouraged to use metadata, follow best practices, and follow standards.

If an organization intends to wean users off of Access, they must be able to provide:

- Clean data that has been validated.

- Metadata fully describing what the data means, its source, and so on.

- Timely data.

- Guarantees on the timeliness and completeness of the loads and notification if loads fail.

- Training.

- Excellent business intelligence (BI) tools.

WHY STANDARDIZE THE DBMS?

We strongly suggest standardizing your DBMS as much as possible. The alternative to standardizing is to let any DBMS be purchased and used by various IT departments, business lines, or the user community. The cost and problems associated with lack of standardization is enormous.

Integration Problems

Having multiple DBMSs will result in problems integrating the different DBMSs. You might have a query or report that requires access to a policy record stored in DB2, a claims record stored in Oracle, and a supplier record stored in SQL Server. Although the query tools claim they can pull all this disparate data together and handle multiple DBMSs, there can be problems with incompatible keys, problems with matching the supplier stored in SQL Server with the supplier stored in the Oracle claims record, problems with how the data is stored, and, regardless of what the vendors tell you, problems with performance caused by confused optimizers that try to join all these DBMS databases. In addition, each DBMS addresses the operating system interfaces differently and some

DBMSs do not run well or at all under certain operating systems. For example, Microsoft SQL Server does not run under UNIX.

Greater Staff Expense

The need to support multiple DBMSs requires more staff and more training to support the same levels of service. Although most of the basic concepts of databases are appropriate to all DBMSs, the implementations are different, the utilities are different, the measurement tools are usually different, and the best approaches for design are often different. If a DBA department must support multiple DBMSs, the DBAs become generalists with superficial skills but without the level of depth you need for mission-critical, high performance systems. For example, if an organization has both Sybase and Teradata, the Teradata DBA will have trouble replacing a vacationing Sybase DBA.

Software Expense

The more DBMSs you must install and maintain, the higher the expense for the software. Maintenance costs for software include the cost for support—a frequently overlooked charge. If you are actively using a DBMS, if the application that uses the DBMS is mission critical, or if you are making significant changes and additions, you will want the highest level of support (*Platinum*). Some vendors charge more for premium level of support. If the application that uses a DBMS is not being changed, you might be satisfied with the lower level of support (*Rust*).

Total Cost of Ownership

When comparing different DBMSs, cost is always a factor and you will want to understand the total cost of ownership (TCO). TCO goes beyond initial implementation. Most organizations focus on the cost to implement the initial application but give little thought to ongoing expenses. Over a period of years, the continuing cost will likely exceed the cost of the initial implementation. Maintenance must be sustained every year that the system delivers service to your users. Maintenance includes the contractual maintenance cost of the software (usually 15 to 25 percent of the software retail or purchase price). New or upgraded software might be required if the system does not perform as expected or if the usage and complexity go beyond initial estimates. Technical personnel will always be required to establish and run backup and recovery procedures and monitor and tune the system's performance. With the normal turnover, there will be additional costs with the introduction of new technical staff and costs associated with their training. There will always be requirements for, and costs associated with, assimilating new data, new capabilities, and new users into any successful system.

The database does not remain static. Anticipate growing your environment. The growth will be in the number of transactions per second, the number of users (Web delivery could significantly increase the number of users), the requirement to perform more complex queries, and, or an extension to users beyond your enterprise (for example, customers and suppliers through an extranet capability). You will add new data, sometimes more than the initial implementation. The design most likely will change, and the database will need to be tuned. Additional historical data will increase CPU and disk requirements. New software will be introduced, new releases will be installed, and some interfaces will have to be rewritten. As the system grows, the hardware and network will also have to be upgraded.

Use the following template to calculate your TCO for each of the DBMSs you consider.

Expense Template

Expense	*Calculation*	*Dollars*
1. Hardware—CPU and disk		
Maintenance		
Internal support		
2. Network		
Maintenance		
Internal support		
3. DBMS		
Maintenance		
Internal support		
3. Third-party utilities		
Maintenance		
Internal support		
4. Contracting and consulting		

continues

Expense Template (continued)

Expense	Calculation	Dollars
5. Internal staff		
6. Help desk		
7. Operations and systems administration		
8. IT training		
9. User training		
Total cost		

Hardware

For the system, you need CPUs, disks, networks, and workstations. The hardware vendors can help size the machines and disks. Some hardware vendors have benchmark capabilities that will help you estimate your hardware requirements (see Chapter 7, "Performance"). Be aware that unanticipated growth of the data, increased number of users, and increased usage will explode the hardware costs. Some vendors bundle the hardware along with the DBMS, which can lower your total cost. The amount of disk space required depends on the raw data and on the number and size of the indexes required to satisfy performance requirements. It also depends on the need and usage of summary tables and on the need for workspace disk storage. The multiplier can vary up to six times the amount of raw data. The need for indexes and summary tables is highly dependent on the DBMS capabilities and your desired application functionality.

Network Usage

Introducing a new system usually requires network bandwidth, which might be in place, however, additional network capability might be required, especially as the number of users increases. The architecture of the system can have a major impact on network usage; a federated or distributed system requires more network capacity than what is required for a centralized system. For a fair cost allocation, all system use of the network should be included in the cost. The network people are usually in the best position to estimate network usage and assign costs.

DBMS

The way the DBMS is priced (such as by node or by the number of users) can influence the cost of the DBMS. Although a new DBMS might not be required, an upgrade or add-on to related software, such as utilities, might be necessary.

Many DBMSs are best served with third-party utilities for performance monitoring, security, backup and recovery, and administration. These tools can be expensive and require significant technical resources to maximize their effectiveness. Consider if the DBMS of choice has sufficient third-party relationships with these types of utility vendors.

Consultants and Contractors

Consultants are engaged to help determine requirements, help plan the project, create the scope agreement, justify the cost of the project, help select the software, and establish the initial and long-term architectures. Consultants are typically more expensive than contractors, but usually don't remain on projects as long. Contractors are brought in to supplement technical skills during and after the DBMS installation. A primary role of the contractors should be to transfer their skills to the organization's employees. The cost for contractors will depend on how deficient the organization is in the required skills, how fast the organization needs the system implemented, and how long it will take to transfer skills after the implementation is complete. Most importantly, the cost for contractors and consultants is dependent on the organization's plans for outsourcing development and maintenance of its systems. Usually, vendor-supplied consultants are the most expensive, with independent consulting firms offering similar services for a lower cost. Contractors for the most popular DBMSs are available as independents as well as from the vendors.

Internal Staff

The fully burdened rate (salary plus taxes, benefits, support costs, and so on) for the IT staff associated with the project should be included in the cost calculation. Your HR department can provide the percentage or specific additional cost beyond the salary expense, but 35 to 45 percent of the annual base salary amount is usually accepted as a reasonable burden.

Help Desk Support

Most organizations find it necessary to upgrade and train help desk personnel to achieve the desired level of customer satisfaction and support the system efforts. The help desk personnel must know the supported tools and the data, they need to be familiar with the query and report libraries, and they should know something about the users and their level of training and skills. User support is an ongoing expense. Depending on the user activity, the effectiveness of the training, the ease of use of the system, and the need for hand holding, the ratio of help desk staff to active users usually ranges from 1:20 to 1:75 for decision support systems and 1:100 and up for transaction and operational systems.

Operations and System Administration

This is a grab bag of roles and costs including monitoring the system performance, executing backups, running batch programs, establishing and administering security, managing libraries, dealing with vendors, and assigning charge backs. These categories of costs are higher in the initial implementation, but exist for the life of the system. Consultants can provide suggestions on how to estimate this cost category, but organizations similar to yours can give you the best idea of what these costs will be.

IT Training

IT training will be required for most DBMSs. Your organization might already have DBAs trained and experienced in online transaction processing (OLTP) usage, but for decision support systems, you might require specific training, such as the database design, security, data models, data placement and DBMS-specific tuning. You might have a DBA trained and experienced on one DBMS, but if she will be working with a different DBMS, that DBA should attend training on the new DBMS. IT personnel also need enough time to work with the new DBMS and with its new utilities to become proficient in their use. Sometimes, the vendor includes the cost of training in the price of the DBMS.

APPLICATION PACKAGES AND ERPs

Some application packages and ERPs require the use of a specific DBMS, but most provide a choice. For example, SAP can be implemented with Oracle, DB2, Sybase, Informix, or SQL Server. The question is, when you are installing SAP, which DBMS should you choose? If you ask most ERP vendors for a recommendation, they will usually duck the question and say they run on all of them and recommend them all. This doesn't help you. You should make the decision based on the same criteria you use to make a DBMS decision with the following additions:

• What skill set do you have in place to support the ERP?

• What is the primary DBMS used by the ERP vendor for development?

• What is the distribution of customers by DBMS? For example, it might be 30 percent Oracle and 35 percent DB2. This analysis should be extended to include the distribution by operating system; for example, for the 55 percent on UNIX, 40 percent are on Oracle, and 40 percent are on DB2.

- What is the partnership relationship between the ERP vendor and the DBMS vendor? Do the DBMS and ERP vendors communicate? Do they even like each other? How much do they test with each other's products? Does the DBMS vendor supply staff to the ERP implementation project to assist in DBMS-specific efforts? One indication of the relationship is the ERP's support on the most current version of the DBMS and the support of the DBMS for the most current version of the ERP. This gives you an idea of when they give each other prerelease software to begin testing.

- What is the cost? There might be differences in the pricing of the ERPs if they are implemented by different DBMS vendors.

CRITERIA FOR SELECTION

The criteria for evaluation are at the heart of the evaluation process. Take this list as a starter set, but create your own set of criteria based on your specific situation:

- Does the product run on our chosen operating system?

- How well does the product work with products you have already chosen?

- Is the vendor financially stable? If the vendor is publicly traded, the annual and quarterly reports are readily available. If the vendor is not publicly traded, they should provide you with financial statements.

- What is the cost of the product? Include maintenance, support, required consulting, and the total cost of ownership.

- What is the administrative effort to support the product (number of FTEs)?

- What is the learning curve? How long will it take for your personnel to effectively use the DBMS?

- Are there issues involving recruiting or training staff? If you will be hiring a DBA to support the DBMS, research the availability of skilled DBAs. Research the recommended classes from the vendor as well as from third-party sources who teach the requisite skills.

- How good is the vendor support?

• Is the vendor training adequate?

• What percentage of the market does the product (not the vendor) have?

SELECTION PROCESS

Following are guidelines for the selection process:

• Determine your high-level requirements for the DBMS. Be sure to include input from the DBA staff.

• Identify the stakeholders, the decision makers, the influencers, those with knowledge of the requirements, and those with the technical expertise to evaluate the software. Convene a small selection committee. Although you might have a large number of stakeholders and managers interested in the results, the active team should have no more than three to five people.

• Create a glossary of terms to be used by the committee and by the stakeholders. This glossary should be shared with the vendors.

• Communicate what you are doing and why you are doing it with all stakeholders, that is, all those who have a business interest in the software and those IT people who will be responsible for implementing the DBMS.

• If you plan to use consultants in the selection process, determine how you will use them and how much influence you want them to have.

• Document your architecture. This includes the hardware and operating system.

• Understand what other software you need, including utility add-ons, and select which one(s) to include in the evaluation.

• Establish the criteria for selection; solicit suggestions from stakeholders.

• Research which vendors and products you want to consider and create your short list. This is a good time to eliminate any vendors who are financially shaky or vendors with less than sterling reputations.

- Create a request for information (RFI), request for proposal (RFP), or an information package for the vendors to alert them to your requirements.

- Contact the vendors giving them your architecture; planned implementation schedule; the RFI, RFP, or information package; and your rules of engagement.

- Compile a list of references from the vendors and from other sources.

- Research the products. The Internet has some useful information. Articles reviewing the DBMSs should be reasonably current because the products change frequently. Watch out for overly flattering puff pieces supposedly written by an independent third-party or by a customer. The independent party might have a monetary interest in the success of the product and the customer's piece might have been ghost written by the vendor. The litmus test is when the article has only positive things to say about the product (they all have warts, but the vendors just can't bring themselves to approve any publication that has anything negative to say about their product).

- Call the references, document their comments, and distribute the notes to the selection committee.

- Reduce the number of DBMS choices to two.

- If appropriate, ask the vendors to demonstrate their products in an environment that is similar to your own and present their solution to your organization's requirements.

- You might want to have the vendor perform a proof-of-concept to prove the effectiveness of their DBMS with your data in your environment. You might also want to test drive the software for a few weeks.

- If performance is a consideration (which it will be for a system with large databases, a large number of users, or complex transactions and queries), ask the two vendors on the short list how they plan to demonstrate how their product can satisfy your performance requirements. This can include running benchmarks and evaluating the results.

- Solicit comments from the stakeholders using your criteria for selection and weighting.

- Negotiate price and terms with the vendors and make
  your final selection.

- Sell your decision to the interested parties in your organization.

- Sign the contract and celebrate a milestone.

REFERENCE CHECKING

Selecting software can be a chore, and the process can often delay a project. Reference checking is the least time-consuming way to learn how the DBMSs function in the real world. Most organizations acknowledge that they check references; however, the reference-checking process is often disorganized and in many cases, abandoned—sometimes because they already know which DBMS they want. Let's be clear, the selection of the right DBMS and related utilities is a critical success factor for most projects. Without proper reference checking, the organization has not performed the due diligence required for such important decisions. There is an additional benefit to reference checking: You can gather lessons learned and best practices that go beyond determining the best DBMS and related utilities.

Alternatives to Reference Checking

Reference checking is by far the most cost effective, accurate, and shortest route to evaluating DBMSs and their vendors. Let's look at the alternatives. Note that none of these are mutually exclusive with reference checking, but they might *not* be necessary if you perform extensive reference checking.

- Invite the vendors to present and demonstrate their products. The vendors will tell you all that is bright and beautiful about their DBMS and never mention the trials and tribulations always associated with any significant database implementation. You will be amazed by the speed with which the vendors are able to accomplish complex tasks (they have been practicing for months) and by the speed of response (they are accessing only 10,000 records). They will highlight all their ecstatic customer successes, but never mention the failures.

- You can bring in the DBMSs that are on the short list and exercise them in your own environment. This takes considerable effort and requires time for you to learn some database products you will never use. Some DBMSs don't manifest their defects until they have been in productive use for some time. You will not discover these deficiencies and problems in the short time you have with the product. This approach will delay the choice of the DBMS and will probably delay the entire project.

- Let the vendors exercise their DBMS in your environment. Some vendors will accept the challenge, but then you have to decide how to rank the vendors who do not want to participate. They might be afraid of failing, they might not have the personnel to enable them to participate, or they might not be hungry enough. If their participation in this bake off is a prerequisite to being considered, you might be missing the best product by insisting that all vendors test their DBMS in your environment.

Selecting and Gathering References

Your first step is to contact the vendors whose DBMSs you are evaluating to request a list of references. If the vendors are smart and well organized, they will give you their best references—the ones who will say nice things about them and their products. Therefore, recognize that you will be getting a somewhat biased view and one that is not a representative sample of their customer set. That's okay. Even with this select group, by asking the right questions, you can discover the dark side of the vendors and their products. Some vendors want to participate in the call. If they participate or even just listen to the discussion, the responses from the references will be much less candid. Decline this arrangement.

Desired Types of References

If you don't tell the vendors the types of references you want, they are likely to give you some that are of no value. Tell them what you want and what you do not want. The following are some suggestions for the types of references you want to call:

- The reference site does not have to be local (you will be using the phone, not visiting).

- The reference does not have to be in your industry, although being in your industry will enhance the importance of that reference to those reading your report. On the other hand, if the reference identifies you as a competitor, they will not be as forthcoming with information.

- The reference should have been actively and productively using the DBMS under consideration for at least 6 months. You don't want anyone in the throes of implementation and you don't want anyone who is just playing with the product.

- You want the references to be on the same platform (operating system) you intend to use. The vendors should not give you a Windows reference if you plan to use a version of UNIX.

- You want a reference that has at least as many users as you intend to have with at least your expected transaction level, degree of complexity, and usage per user, as well as a reference that has a database of at least the size you are planning. Note: This is to verify performance, not function or ease of use, so you will want at least one in this category.

- You don't want a reference that has a financial or marketing association with the vendor's organization.

- If possible, ask for references that have the same products as you have already chosen. For example, if you are a Business Objects shop, ask the vendors for references that also use Business Objects. If you have PeopleSoft, ask for references that have PeopleSoft installed and actively running.

After contacting the references supplied by the vendor, you want to find other customers who use the DBMS. If possible, connect with user groups such as the International Oracle User Group (IOUG), International DB2 User Group (IDUG), Teradata Partners, and so on. Attend the meetings and talk to some of the more vocal members at the break and after the meeting. Most of the vendors also have local user groups, which meet more frequently than the international groups. Tell the existing DBMS users that you are evaluating DBMSs and ask for their time to answer a few questions. You can interview them right there or after the meeting. Finally, ask around and locate other companies using the DBMS. It's especially useful to talk to installations with more than one DBMS as well as one with a competing DBMS. These organizations are in an especially good position to tell you how the DBMSs compare.

The Process of Reference Checking

You don't have to travel to the reference site. Hosting a visit is time-consuming and in many ways, an imposition on the reference to the point that fewer references will be willing to agree to a visit. It is far cheaper, faster, and more effective (because you can talk to more references) to use the phone. It's usually best to have the same person make all the calls. This provides a certain level of consistency to the questions asked, to the documentation, and consistency in the conclusions.

Before you call, find out a little about the company you are calling including the industry, size, and any publicly available information on what they are doing. If the vendor gives you the name and number of a reference, they have probably forewarned the reference of your impending call, however, don't make that assumption. Be sure to ask the vendor to alert the references that you will be calling. On your initial call to the references, introduce yourself, schedule a time for the conversation if your initial call is inconvenient for the reference, give a brief description of your environment and project, where you are in the selection process, and the DBMSs you are considering. Thank them in advance for their time.

Don't ask them if you can record the call—the concern about being recorded will usually reduce the candor—and certainly do not record the conversation without their knowledge or approval. Use a headset or a speaker phone (they are, however, a little impersonal), so you can have your hands free to take notes (don't even imagine you can remember all that was said). Be sure to allow time after the call to complete and correct your notes.

Questions to Ask

Before you talk with the references, you must know what you will ask. It is important to be consistent in your questioning. Be sure to ask all the important questions. Don't waste the references' time, but do start off with the easy questions. The questions will vary based on your criteria for selection. Don't ask questions if you already know the answers and ask only questions that will make a difference in your decision. Be sure to thank them for their time and ask if it would be all right to contact them again with any additional questions.

The following is a set of sample questions you can use to build your own set of questions (you will not ask all these questions):

- What hardware, operating system, and network topology do you use?

- How would you describe your architecture and infrastructure?

- If you use a variety of architectures and platforms, do you experience any differences in performance, availability, or administrative activities? Would you elaborate on these differences?

- What functions or types of applications do you perform with this DBMS?

- What are your scheduled hours of availability (for example, 24 x 7 or 18 x 6)?

- Do you have service level agreements (SLAs) that specify availability and performance? What are they? Are they enforced, and if so, what has been the experience with the SLA and the DBMS?

- Would you consider your system to be mission critical? Why or why not?

- How much downtime do you experience? Is unavailability the result of planned maintenance, unplanned maintenance, software problems, or other problems?

- As a rule, do you continue to evaluate other DBMSs? Why or why not?

- How long have you had the DBMS in production?

- How long did it take you to install the DBMS and make it useable?

- What was the composition of the DBA team that installed the DBMS including the number and skill level? Where did they spend their time? How long did it take them to become proficient in the DBMS? What positions did they hold before they were trained and how skilled were they? Did the DBAs use any other DBMS before they installed this one?

- What is the composition of the team that supports the DBMS including the number and skill level? Where do they spend their time?

- What other DBMSs did you consider? Why were those rejected?

- What were your criteria for selection?

- What was your opinion of the other DBMSs?

- What kind of problems did you have with installing the DBMS? How were those problems resolved? How much did the vendor help? Did they come onsite? Did they charge extra for their assistance?

- How easy was it to migrate to a new release? Did you ever have to go back to the previous release? If yes, why?

- What kind of problems do you have with ongoing maintenance?

- If you have multiple vendors (DBMS, utilities, or ERP vendors), how well did the products work together and how well did the vendors work with each other when there were problems? Was there finger pointing?

- Does the DBMS vendor maintain metrics on their software quality and do they share this information with you?

- What has been your experience in receiving information on quality and other issues from the vendor?

- Please comment on the DBMS vendor support and the help desk.

- Did you require consulting or contracting support for the DBMS? Was the support from the DBMS vendor or from a third-party vendor? What was the quality of their consulting staff?

- Do you have any general comments on the DBMS vendor that would be helpful in our selection process?

- What DBMS security capabilities do you use and how easy are they to administer?

- Do you measure your costs? How? What are the costs associated with this DBMS? Were the costs you experienced greater than what you had expected or greater than what was budgeted?

- If you had to start over again, what would you do differently?

- Do you know any other organizations that are using this DBMS who might be willing to discuss their experience?

- One more question, do you get any benefit out of being a reference? If so, what does the DBMS vendor give you?

RFPs FOR DBMSs

A request for quote (RFQ) or request for proposal (RFP) represents a definition of specific customer requirements as well as an invitation to the vendors to submit a proposal that addresses those requirements. Many organizations mandate an RFP when the price of the product exceeds some pre-authorized monetary maximum. A request for information (RFI) is usually less exacting, less formal, and usually asks for information that will allow an organization to go to the next step, which is usually issuing an RFP. A well written RFP can be a wonderful way of communicating what is needed and the vendor's response to an RFP is a good way of ensuring that there will be fewer misunderstandings about the capabilities of the DBMS and the vendor. However, an RFP is often time and labor consuming and the activity to produce the RFP can seriously delay the project. The goal of the RFP is to solicit accurate answers from the vendors and have an unbiased process by which the DBMS is selected. Implementing RFP best practices can expedite the process and make it easier on the issuer and evaluator of the RFP as well as make it easier on the vendors.

RFP Best Practices

Because RFPs are time consuming and labor intensive, they are generally hated by those creating them as well as by those who have to respond to them. Therefore, you want to make it easy for all concerned. The following are some best practices that should make the process less painful:

- Determine who should receive the RFP in the first place. You want to limit the list to only those who you feel truly capable of satisfying your primary requirements. This might also be a good time to eliminate any vendors who you feel are financially or ethically marginal. Note: It is unethical to distribute an RFP if you have already chosen the vendor.

- A combined vendors' teleconferencing question and answer session as part of the RFP process will answer most of the vendors' questions and should minimize the amount of time you need to spend with each vendor. It might also reduce the time you need to evaluate the written responses to the RFP.

- When writing the RFP, avoid nondecisive qualifiers (adjectives and adverbs) that can be interpreted in so many ways that it will make the evaluation process inconclusive.

- Because the RFP can contain confidential information, such as the future plans of the organization, be sure to label the RFP as confidential and ask the vendors to sign nondisclosure agreements (NDAs).

- A long and complicated RFP discourages vendors and usually lengthens the selection process. The organization should keep the RFP process as well as the RFP document as simple and short as possible. A large, complex RFP document will result in vendors either not responding, responding with questions that extend the selection process, or responding just with a boilerplate proposal that does not adequately answer the RFP. Ask the vendors to not include long, wordy marketing verbiage that challenges your ability to understand the answers. The more complex the vendors' responses to your RFP document, the longer it will take to adequately evaluate and compare the different responses.

- The RFP should include only the points the organization will use to compare the vendors. This means including only "mandatory" and "highly desirable" features, not the "nice-to-have" ones, and definitely not any "blue-sky" requirements.

- Include a section on "Vision" that includes questions about the vendors' plans for the future and their view of the industry.

- Include a section for "partners" and "alliances" to allow the vendors to expand on selected categories of products that work with their DBMS. If a product or category is essential to the use of the DBMS (for instance, query products in a decision support environment), you might want to send a short RFI to those partners and alliances whose products work closely with the DBMS in that category asking questions about how the product works with each DBMS vendor that is being considered.

- You need to have a focal point for answering vendor questions, scheduling and administering vendor meetings, keeping the vendors in line, giving all the vendors the same information, and providing a fair selection process. All questions should be submitted by email and all the vendors should get the benefit of the responses. Having a vendor conference minimizes the chances of giving some information to a vendor that is not available to the other vendors.

- If you have a consultant help develop the RFP, the consultant or the consultant's organization should *not* be allowed to bid on the engagement. If they are allowed to bid, they will most likely skew the RFP to favor them and their capabilities. If any of the other bidders know that the consultant helped write the RFP, they will believe that consultant not only has the inside track—regardless of any protestations to the contrary—but that the consultant has already won the race. Knowing this, no serious competitors would waste their time to bid.

- Organize the RFP so that different groups (for example, DBAs and those looking at the financial aspects of the response) can easily write different sections of the RFP and then review the corresponding sections of the vendors' RFP responses.

- Make the RFP as electronic as possible, ask the vendors to respond electronically if at all possible, and keep the format of the responses as standard as possible. This will expedite the evaluation process.

- Provide a timeline for the various activities associated with the RFP including the RFP issue date, the date by which vendors indicate their intent to bid, the date for question and answer session, the proposal submission deadline, and the decision date at which time both the winners and the losers will be notified. Note: The drop-dead date, after which no responses will be accepted or considered, should be fixed. Depending on the length and complexity of the RFP, three to four weeks should be enough time for the vendors to respond.

- Ask for a high-level plan of how the vendor proposes to implement their DBMS if they are selected.

- If appropriate, ask for guarantees on the ability to handle a minimum level of transactions, queries, number of concurrent users, table size, and so on.

- There should never be any reason to pay vendor expenses for the RFP.

- Provide a glossary of your terminology to minimize miscommunication.

- Give the vendors *relevant* information so they can respond appropriately.

The RFP should describe the following:

- Your environment, including the operating system(s), application packages, and ERPs that are installed and scheduled to be installed, as well as your existing DBMSs, architecture, geographical distribution of the organization, data distribution, and history of past activities.

- Objectives, problems you are trying to solve, and capabilities the DBMS will be expected to perform.

- Expectations for the DBMS, such as handling 20 transactions per second and supporting a 24 x 7 environment.

- Critical success factors that relate to the DBMS implementation.

- Vendor support requirements.

- Technical and product decisions you have already made.

- Service level agreements for general DBMS product performance and availability.

- Data, transaction, and query volumes to be supported.

- Number and characteristics of your user community.

- Security and privacy requirements to be supported.

- Future organization plans that are relevant to the RFP, for instance, DBA deployment to business units.

- Expertise you expect from the vendor.

- Participation and partnership you expect from the vendor.

- Training you expect from the vendor.

- Criteria for evaluation including which criteria are mandatory.

- Schedule for implementation including plans for phasing.

- Issues relating to your industry, organization, and so on.

- Budget—This may be considered confidential, but it would be helpful to the vendors if you can include ranges or a planned budget for the project.

RESPONSE FORMAT

If you provide a format for the RFP responses, the evaluation process will be easier, and there is less chance that the vendor will leave something out. The following is a sample format to recommend for their response:

- One- or two-page executive summary.

- Key assumptions and, or constraints about the DBMS and how it would be used in your organization.

- Response to RFP questions.

- Plan to implement the DBMS including time, effort, and resources.

- Organization (yours and the vendor's) needed to support the implementation and ongoing maintenance.

- Vendor's relationship with your industry and organization (if there has been any in the past).

- At least three references of organizations that have been actively using the vendor's product for at least 6 months. This should include a description of how they have been using the DBMS and contact information.

- Costs including discounts, maintenance costs, support costs, consulting and other implementation costs, and training costs.

EVALUATING VENDORS

Some organizations look only at the functions and capabilities of the DBMS and fail to consider the company that's selling it. You absolutely want to know about the vendors for the following reasons:

- **Support**—Without good vendor support, the DBMS will cause you trouble and you might never realize the DBMS's full capabilities. You will become frustrated and might experience significant downtime, terrible performance, or the inability to make the database work with your other software.

- **Stability**—The vendor might be out of business next year and you'll be left with a white elephant that will eventually have to be converted (an unpleasant nightmare).

- **Integrity**—The vendor might be less than totally honest about the capabilities and ease of use of their products, their comparison with the competition, or future plans.

The following is a set of general questions for the vendor:

- Where is your company headquartered?

- What is the closest office to our location?

- How many employees are in that office?

- Are you publicly traded?

- How long has the company been in existence?

- Are there any existing litigations pending against your company and what is the nature of those suits?

DEALING WITH THE VENDOR

Although the product might be the best in the field of contenders, you will have to live with the vendor (consider it a marriage). If the vendor is difficult to deal with, if their support is not outstanding, if they notoriously misrepresent their product's capabilities (you will discover their exaggerations after the system is in), if you have to spend more time with your lawyers than on implementing the system, and if the vendor takes every opportunity to jack up the price after you have committed, you will rue the day you signed with them.

There are instances of vendors cutting off support to user groups or trying to compromise the independence of those groups. The trade press often has articles that can give you some insights into the way the vendors deal with their customers and the user groups organized around the products. These articles can also indicate customer dissatisfaction with vendor support or with new pricing schemes from the vendor. User groups and their websites can give some insights into customer dissatisfaction.

You want to be sure that the vendor will live up to their commitments. You want them to accurately represent their products and you want them to treat you and their other customers fairly. Ask around, talk to their existing customers and possibly to customers who have left them. The following are some of the questions you will want to get answered. As the vendor pitches to you, many of these questions will be answered:

- Does the vendor criticize the competition and misrepresent the competitor's product capabilities?

- Does the vendor misrepresent or overly embellish their own product's capabilities?

- Is the vendor vague when answering questions? Do they avoid answering questions that could hurt them?

- Has the vendor missed dates on their prior releases?

- Did they ever promise functions that they have not been able to deliver?

- Does the vendor play games with pricing? For example, do they not disclose all the costs associated with their product, including additional required hardware or software or utilities.

- Does the vendor embellish what their customers have done with the vendor's products?

- Do you trust the vendor to do what is best for you? What does your intuition tell you?

- Has the vendor misrepresented wins, successful implementations, number of customers, finances, and so on?

- Has the vendor previously underestimated the effort to install and use their product?

- Does the vendor engage in unfair marketing practices, such as demonstrating a function they are not proposing or misrepresenting a competitor's product?

- Does the vendor disregard your requests for how you want them to market to you?

- Does the vendor bypass those designated as the evaluation team and their designated contact point in your organization?

- Has the vendor purchased companies or products and then fired the purchased company's employees, withdrawn the products, or forced customers to migrate to their own products?

- Does the vendor push their marketing reps to the point that they lie to make their numbers?

- How do the vendor's partners feel about them?

- How do the vendor's customers feel about them?

- How do the vendor's employees feel about them?

Although simply choosing the right DBMS in no way guarantees success, it's important to understand that choosing the right combination of software from the right vendor is one of the critical success factors for any project. The selection process is not an area in which most technical folks typically have strengths, so they are prone to making costly mistakes in the process and making mistakes in dealing with vendors. Most vendors are honest and have a high level of integrity. They want you to be successful and be a good reference for them, but more importantly, they want to sell their product. The combination of unsophisticated technical folks and hungry vendor reps will result in product selection mistakes. The following sections describe common issues and give suggestions on how to avoid them.

Performance

For some reason, when organizations are looking at a DBMS, they either assume the DBMS will satisfy their performance requirements or they don't even consider performance issues until it's too late—meaning after you purchased the DBMS, spent a year implementing it, and put it into production. If your system is small, (a database under 30 gigabytes with just a few concurrent users), you probably don't have much to worry about in the area of performance. However, if your database is large and you have over ten *concurrent* users (Note: From a performance standpoint, the total number of users is not relevant, but the number of concurrent users is very important), performance will be one of your critical success factors (CSFs). A critical success factor means that if you don't have it, you fail. CSFs are normally reflected in your SLAs for response time, number of concurrent users you plan to support, or time it takes to run a large batch program. In this case, you better be sure the vendor's product will perform. Ask the vendor about their largest customer for data volumes and for concurrent (not registered or assigned) users—the vendors might get paid on registered users, but this has no relevance for performance. If the vendor is vague or clueless on their performance characteristics, you will want to drill down and find out more about their ability to perform. When you are talking to references, be sure the references run on your intended platform including the operating system, data volumes, and number of concurrent users.

Vendor's Level of Service

The vendor will boast about winning the "Excellence in Service" award for three years running. They might neglect to tell you that it's an internally generated award. Excellent service is a CSF, which means that if the vendor has anything less than excellent service, you should drop the product from consideration. Consider this: When you have problems (not *if* you have problems) you will need quick and accurate solutions to those problems. Without those solutions, your initial implementation might be delayed for months, your system might be down and unavailable for days, or your response time might be so terrible that the business will be severely impacted. You want a level of service that provides timely and knowledgeable technicians with whom you can easily communicate, who understand your problem and situation, and who can quickly solve your problem.

Early Code

If some feature you want is not in the generally available release, some vendors might suggest working with a beta release so you can use the new feature. A beta product is not generally available, or even marketed, because the bugs are still being worked out and, lucky you, you get to be the pioneer and uncover those bugs. Because it's a new feature, it has probably not been exercised by many other customers, so there will be more bugs to discover. Don't choose a DBMS that does not satisfy your mandatory requirements with their current release or if those required features are available only in early code or promised in the next release.

Rules of Engagement

If you don't provide the rules, the vendor will control the process. Most vendors are anxious to sell you their products. They have been doing it for some time and have methods that can waste your time, lead to confusion, and result in hard feelings in your organization. It can even lead to the wrong decision. The following is a form letter and a suggested set of rules by which the vendors should be asked to play (taken from *Data Warehouse Project Management* by Sid Adelman and Larissa Moss).

Dear Vendor:

Your product, _____, has been selected for evaluation by our organization. To expedite the evaluation and selection process, we have a set of rules we want you to follow. Those vendors who don't abide by these rules will not make the "short list" and will be dropped from consideration. We suggest that all your representatives have a copy of these rules and review them before meeting with us.

1. Your only contact(s) in our organization is/are _____.
   This includes contacts for demos, questions, phone calls, emails, and written and printed materials. Your contact will distribute your materials to the other stakeholders as appropriate. This means you are not to contact users or anyone else in our organization without our prior written approval.

2. We are interested in hearing about your company and your product. We do not want to hear your opinion of the competition. Your view of your competitors will only confuse us. We will not disclose who your competition is to you or to any other vendor.

3. We want to hear about product features that are generally available. In your presentations, do not mix what is available today with what will be available in the future. Although information about future releases may be of interest, meetings on future releases should be scheduled separately.

4. You may never misrepresent anything to anyone in our organization—IT or end users, either by omission or commission. Don't let anyone walk away from a meeting with the wrong impression of your product.

5. When asked if your product can perform a certain function, understand that we have no interest in knowing if your product can theoretically do something, we want you to show us a proven track record. This means, we expect that you know that the function is actually being performed by one or more of your customers and that you provide us with appropriate client references.

6. We will be sending you the notes from our meetings. If anything is incorrect, confusing, or incorrectly stated, please inform _____ (your contact in our organization) immediately. If we don't hear from you, we will assume that our notes are correct and valid.

7. We will inform you of our schedule for evaluation and selection, and we will try to hold to those dates. Although we appreciate your need for meeting certain dates for recording sales, it will not impact our selection schedule.

We will not tell you who in our organization will be involved in the decision. Assume it will be those individuals who attended your presentations and demonstrations.

Sincerely,

DBMS Evaluation Team

Set the Agenda for Meetings and Presentations

Tell the vendor what you want to hear in their presentation; provide them with the agenda. Tell them what questions you want answered (this will help encourage them to bring along the right technical people). In the session, be sure your questions are answered, that the answers are clear, and that you and the other attendees understand the answers. Don't be shy about asking for clarification or repeating their answers back to them in your own words. When something smells fishy (such as, "it should work") follow through and ask them if it does work and in which customer sites it's working. Take the opportunity to verify that what the vendor is telling you is indeed correct. Tell the vendor what you want demonstrated; it's okay to ask questions during the demonstrations. It's also a good idea to give them the glossary of your terms before the meeting and ask them to use your terminology to avoid miscommunication.

This is a sample agenda for the meeting:

- Introductions including who at your organization is the focal point for future communication.

- How you plan to use the DBMS (operational, decision support, data warehouse, data mart, ERP, and so on).

• Preliminary design of your database(s), logical models, and so on.

• What other related software and platforms (hardware, operating system, related databases, development tools, end user tools) you have already chosen

• What you want to see and have demonstrated, primarily functionality.

• Questions you want answered.

• Vendor presentation.

• Vendor demonstration.

• Follow up from the vendor on unanswered questions, materials, and contacts (references).

Be sure to document the vendor's representations of their products, provide them with the minutes of their presentation, and ask them to make appropriate corrections.

Professional Employee Information

Use the following worksheet to find out about the vendor's personnel capacity:

Total Number of:	Last Year	Current Year	Next Year (Estimated)
Employees			
Developers			
Developers working on this product			
DBMS support staff			
Support staff in this country			
Systems engineers in the field			
Turnover rate or average number of years with the company			

Financial Information

Use the following worksheet to find out about the vendor's financial capacity.

Currency (Specify)	Last Year	Current Year	Next Year (Estimated)
Total software license revenue			
Software license revenue for this product			
Service revenue			
R&D expenses			

In addition, submit the following request to the vendors:

"Your financial stability is an important requirement in our selection process. If your company is publicly traded, please provide the latest annual and quarterly statement. If your company is not publicly traded, please provide your income statement and balance sheet information. We will sign nondisclosures."

Selection Matrix——Categorize Capabilities and Functions

Categorize each capability and function as "mandatory," "desirable," and "nice-to-have." "Mandatory" means that if the DBMS does not have this function, it is dropped from consideration, so be very careful what you categorize as "mandatory."

Mandatory Capabilities and Functions

Capability	Yes/No
Capability 1	
Capability 2	
Additional Capabilities	

Many organizations use a scoring and weighting table to evaluate products. You need to set the weights and not be influenced by the vendor. The vendor would love to tell you what's important and establish how the results are determined. It's acceptable to give the vendor your criteria for product selection, such as which functions you are scoring, but do not give them your weightings. Weighting factors should be on a scale of 1–10, and evaluation ratings should be on a scale of 1–5.

Sample Desirable Matrix for DBMS

Desirable Capabilities	Weighting Factor	Evaluation	Score
Capability 1	5	3	15
Capability 2	10	5	50
Other Capabilities			
Total Score for DBMS			

Nice-to-Have Capabilities and Functions

The "nice-to-have" capabilities and functions should not be used in the actual selection process, but this matrix is in place to let others know that these capabilities have been considered but have been judged as not important.

Nice-to-Have Capabilities and Functions

Capability	Yes/No
Capability 1	
Capability 2	
Additional Capabilities	

EXERCISE—HOW WELL ARE YOU USING YOUR DBMS?

In this exercise, you have a chance to rate yourselves on how well you are using your existing DBMS.

1. Currency of the release:

   a. We install new releases within 6 months after they become generally available.

   b. We install new releases 6 months to 1.5 years after the release becomes available.

   c. We install a new release only when the vendor drops support for our old release.

   d. We install beta releases.

   e. We run on an unsupported release.

2. Organization to support the DBMS:

   a. We have DBAs who are trained, experienced, and dedicated to the support of the DBMS.

   b. Our DBAs are new and have not been to any classes yet.

   c. Our DBAs work part time on the database and get called only when there are problems, such as performance, a downed database, or a corrupt database.

3. The design and architecture of the databases:

   a. Our databases have been designed and architected to support our performance and availability SLAs.

   b. Because we are always being pressured to quickly implement, we put up a design and then make changes when there are problems.

   c. We can barely keep the system up without worrying about designs or architectures.

4. DBMS standards:

   a. We standardized on a DBMS and all new applications and ERPs must conform to that standard. When older systems are rewritten, they must also follow the standard.

   b. We have a quasi-standard that is more like a guideline to recommend the use of our chosen DBMS.

   c. We don't believe in forcing standards. New projects can choose any DBMS and put it on any platform they want.

5. Organization's perception of the DBMS:

   a. The DBMS is held in high esteem; it is recognized as a critical part of what keeps this organization running.

   b. The DBMS is considered to be important.

   c. The DBMS, for all its faults, is accepted.

   d. The DBMS is at fault for every problem we have with our databases (and we have plenty).

The scoring for this exercise is simple. Give yourself 2 points for every "a," 1 point for every "b," 0 points for each "c," and minus 2 points for a "d" or an "e."

CONCLUSION

The standardization and selection of the DBMS is at the heart of a data strategy. Without a standard, your organization will waste time and money, will have trouble supporting your SLAs, and will have great difficulty attempting to integrate your critical subject areas. The selection of the DBMS should be objective, should support the overall IT strategy as well as the mission of your organization, and should not be biased by the personal relationships of executive management.

REFERENCES

Porter-Roth, Bud. *Request for Proposal: A Guide to Effective RFP Development.* Boston, MA: Addison Wesley, 2002.

Data Administration Management Association (DAMA)—www.DAMA.org

DB2 Journal—www.db2magazine.com

Oracle Magazine—www.oracle.com/oraclemagazine

Professional Association for SQL Server (PASS)—www.sqlpass.org

Teradata Magazine—www.teradatamagazine.com

SQL Server Magazine—www.sqlservermagazine.com

Sybase Magazine—www.sybase.com/about_sybase/magazine

Business Intelligence

On September 12, 2001, most U.S. organizations scrambled to assess the effects of the terrorist attacks of the day before on their businesses. It was not an easy task. The information needed was not readily available. For most, it took days to calculate the losses. For some, it took weeks. There were only a handful of organizations that were able to readily measure the total monetary damage to their businesses within hours. They utilized business intelligence (BI) tools and methodologies to perform the assessment. In addition, many experts believe that the attacks might have been preventable if the information about the 9/11 terrorists had been available to various government agencies in a timely manner. In other words, if correct BI platforms had been in place, the disaster might have been averted.

Although an important part of today's information technology practice, BI remains either unutilized or under-utilized in the vast majority of organizations worldwide. BI has seldom been fully described, and therefore, its potential capabilities remain hidden to a large percentage of business line executives and other decision makers in organizations. In our contacts with business line, corporate level, and IT executives and managers in various organizations, we have realized a need for BI methodologies, and yet, many of these people are apprehensive about utilizing this technology. Part of the apprehension is due to confusion in understanding BI and various terms associated with it.

In this chapter, we define BI, its components, and associated terms. In addition, we provide some practical uses of BI in the real world and describe emerging technologies that might be of interest to any organization. We also provide a list of myths and pitfalls associated with BI.

WHAT IS BUSINESS INTELLIGENCE?

BI is a term that is defined differently by different people. Even the authors of this book each have a different definition for the term. Larissa Moss sees BI as, "A cross-organizational discipline and an enterprise architecture for an integrated collection of operational as well as decision-support applications and databases with structured as well as unstructured data, which provide the business community easy access to business data, and it allows them to make accurate business decisions." Sid Adelman defines BI as, "The capability to perform in-depth analysis and possibly data mining of detailed business data, providing real and significant information to business users. BI usually makes use of tools designed to easily access data warehouse data." Majid Abai considers BI to be, "A platform that enables decision makers in an organization to have the latest internal and external competitive information at their finger tips in a clean, consistent, and timely manner."

The previous definitions are correct. They can, however, be simplified into one sentence: BI provides organizational decision makers a 360-degree view of their business, enabling them to make faster and more reliable decisions.

In addition to providing a 360-degree view of business, a sound BI platform enables all decision makers to have access to the same consistent set of facts, regardless of geographical or hierarchical location with the organization. Accessing a consistent set of information is a major problem experienced by a large number of organizations today. Depending on the system from which a report or analysis is generated in the organization, results might vary. As an analogy, one can compare the quality of data in an organization to the quality of water at a municipality. Residents of municipalities subscribe to an unwritten contract with their local water department to deliver clean, consistent, and timely water to residences or businesses using the municipality's piping infrastructure. This unwritten contract guarantees a certain level of quality for the water. It also guarantees that regardless of the subscriber's location in the covered area, she will receive the same quality of water consistently, irrespective of the type of faucet used. The contract also guarantees that when the faucet is opened, water will flow within an acceptable and reasonable time. Trusting this contract, residents of the municipality drink the water and use it to clean, cook, swim in, and so on. Community residents do not necessarily know or care about the various sources of water or its method of delivery to their homes. They also do not care about the processes involved in cleansing the water, as long as the quality levels in the contract are continuously met. In some cases, the residents have a need for a higher quality of water (for example, drinking water) than the contract provides, and that's when they'll add an extra filter to the building or the faucet to cleanse the water.

Data flow in the organization should be like water flowing through the municipality's water infrastructure. Consumers of information should trust the fact that data will be delivered to them in a clean, consistent, and timely manner, regardless of presentation method (faucet). Any user in any part of the organization should be able to ask the same question and get the same consistent answer. Users should not worry about data sources, transformation, and cleansing techniques. They also should not worry about delivery methods.

BI is the platform that provides such data plumbing for the organization. It also provides methods for identifying sources of information, data merge and transformation, metadata collection, and data cleansing. BI also provides the faucet for delivery and analysis of the data in the organization in the format of a presentation layer.

A Brief History

In the 1960s and 1970s, as more organizations started to utilize the computers in their day-to-day processing, the systems emphasis was on batch and online transactions processing (OLTP) applications. OLTP applications refer to types of systems that perform a specific set of operational tasks. For example, in a typical banking application, a bank teller can deposit into, withdraw from, or view the balance of a specific customer's account. As transaction data accumulated in the organizations' databases, business users realized that analyzing this data can help in making better decisions. In the late 1970's, decision-support systems were born. Within 10 years, technologists realized that by combining information from various systems, users could make even better decisions. This "data warehousing" approach provided a large central repository, and at times, many smaller repositories for analyzing specific subject matters. In addition, they devised computer algorithms that actually suggested a decision for the users and they used data to support the decision. In the same banking example, these algorithms were able to identify the risk associated with a customer applying for a new credit card. These were the early examples of a "data mining" approach. In the mid 1980s, the concept of online analytical processing (OLAP) was used. This allowed for analyzing data located in a data warehouse via various analytical tools. Throughout the 1990s, the data warehousing, OLAP, and data mining processes grew into BI approach, which now includes not only internal data, but also various external demographic and competitive data that is available for purchase.

Importance of BI

There is always the question of why BI is important. Besides better decision-making capabilities, sound analytical platforms contribute directly to the bottom line of the organization by either increasing the profits or reducing cost. BI applications provide insights into data, which allows analysts and executives to easily uncover patterns and abnormalities in the business. An IDC study suggests that organizations that have successfully implemented and utilized analytical applications have realized returns ranging from 17 percent to more than 2000 percent with a median ROI (return on investment) of 112 percent. In addition, 63 percent of the companies studied had a payback period of 2 years or less.

There are tangible and intangible benefits realized from BI implementation. The tangible benefits include improved productivity and quality; increase in revenue and profits; increase in customer base; fraud and abuse detection; and cost control for both suppliers and employees. The intangible benefits include competitive advantage due to fast, complete, and accurate information; better customer service and therefore better relationships with customers; better relationships with suppliers; and increased confidence of business decision makers in IT departments.

In a competitive market like today's market, BI has become an integral part of the IT department for all industries. In addition, many large- and medium-sized companies have hired (internal or external) analysts to review data and identify successful strategies for market growth, cost reduction, targeted marketing, customer segmentation, and so on.

Based on the Gartner Group, there are four key drivers forcing companies to seek a clearer view of the internal workings of their businesses by utilizing BI. Regulations, such as the Sarbanes-Oxley act in the U.S. and similar new regulations in other countries, force companies to be more open, timely, and accurate in external reporting. This requires an unprecedented ability to access current and detailed information from within the organization.

Unfinished ERP and CRM business is another major driver for utilizing BI. Major organizations implemented enterprise resource planning (ERP) and customer relationship management (CRM) software in the late 90s and have now started to utilize BI tools to help managers make better decisions on a variety of ERP- and CRM-related issues such as forecasting, customer segmentation, employee management, and so on. BI-related ERP and CRM will finish the job of implementing enterprise resource management software and provide a collective sigh of relief for all executives, managers, and employees who are involved in such a task.

The need for better controls and metrics is the third driver for utilizing BI in the organization. The downturn in economy has forced many organizations to review spending habits. To achieve such goals, businesses need to install precise metrics. BI enables organizations to easily capture, measure, and present the status of such metrics.

The last, but certainly not the least of BI drivers, is competitiveness. By achieving fast and accurate decisions, understanding customers, and providing better service, organizations get to compete better in the market place and capture more of the market share.

On the other hand, Gartner identifies several market inhibitors that cause organizations to reject BI. One market inhibitor is office politics. Some managers are worried that BI platforms could threaten their position in the company and reduce their domain of responsibility.

Another inhibitor for utilizing BI is short-term thinking of some executives. Such executives are interested in rapid projects that deliver small ROI without considering the holistic approach to data integration in the organization. In reality, such executives are driven by shareholders who expect immediate quarterly results, leaving no room for implementing major renovations to the organization's infrastructure that might not immediately pay dividends, but will provide long-term value for the organization and its shareholders.

Impeding views against change is another major stumbling block in implementing BI applications. A holistic approach to data requires a number of business process improvement initiatives, which makes many managers skeptical.

BI COMPONENTS

Creating a sound BI approach for an organization requires analysis of the organization's short- and long-term goals and utilization of various BI components to help reach those goals. In this section, we describe BI components and when appropriate, we provide a simple example. Please keep in mind that not all components are used in all BI projects.

Data Warehouse

A data warehouse (DW) is a central part of today's BI strategy. It is a central repository of data retrieved from various internal and external sources. Data stored in the DW has been transformed and cleansed to not only fit the organization's analytical requirements, but it has also been formatted for fast delivery. There are three types of data warehouses and in any BI project; one or more of them might be utilized:

- **Enterprise Data Warehouse (EDW)**—An EDW contains data captured from one or more operational systems that has been transformed, cleaned, integrated, and loaded into a separate database. An EDW contains data from various subject areas. This type of DW contains detailed and summarized data about business operations over a long period of time. This DW is used for making both tactical and strategic business decisions that cover multiple business areas. An example of an EDW is summarized marketing, finance, and customer data for all branches of a retail chain for the past 10–15 years. Some experts argue that there should be one and only one EDW for an enterprise. The reality is that some larger organizations maintain one EDW for each line of business, and each line is so different from another that there is no need to merge the total enterprise data warehouse into one.

- **Operational Data Store (ODS)**—An ODS contains current or almost current detailed data for regular, tactical, day-to-day analysis of business operations. As with an EDW, data in the ODS is captured from various operational systems and loaded into a separate database. But unlike an EDW, an ODS contains detailed data for a short period of time. An example of ODS is maintaining the detailed sales transactions for all branches of a retail chain for one year.

- **Data Mart (DM)**—A data mart contains a subset of corporate data that is of value to a specific business unit, department, or set of users. This data can be captured directly from operational systems or from an EDW or

ODS. Data marts usually contain summarized historical data for a specific business area of the organization. An example of a data mart is the analytical modules sold by various ERP vendors that allow users in the finance department to analyze various financial information in the organization.

Metadata Repository

A metadata repository contains information about all data objects stored in the DW. This information can be broken into four segments, which are described in the following list and in more detail in Chapter 4, "Metadata:"

- **Business Segment**—This segment describes the business definition of the data element, its business need, business rules, valid values, and its respective descriptions. In addition, the source of the data and the department in the organization responsible for maintaining it are also described in this section. This segment might even contain contact information for future questions. Business users use this segment to learn more about the data stored in the data warehouse.

- **Technical Segment**—This segment describes the technical properties of a data element, such as type, size, scale, transformation methods, volumes, growth percentages, etc. Technical users use this segment to identify the correct database information about data elements in the enterprise.

- **Process Segment**—This segment describes the processes performed on the data element, such as extract and transformation methods, data cleansing and data filtering logic, and algorithms for data derivation, aggregation, and summarization. It also includes reconciliation totals, load statistics, and error statistics and descriptions. Both business and technical users use this segment to validate and reconcile the ongoing data loads.

- **Usage Segment**—This segment describes the utilization of the data element, the user ids of people accessing the data, the programs manipulating or reporting the data, statistics on the most and least accessed data, and so on. Technical users use this segment to keep the DW databases and BI applications tuned properly.

Data Transformation and Cleansing

A decision is only as good as the data supporting it. Therefore, data transformation and cleansing is an important component of a sound BI platform. As data is captured from the source systems, it must be transformed to conform to the system's definitions as described in the metadata repository. In a large number of situations, data retrieved from the source systems is either dirty or not as clean as required and needs to be cleansed to reach the data quality levels desired by the users of the BI application. The level of cleansing varies for each project and even in various subject areas within the project. Data cleansing can be easy; for example, it might be a matter of identifying the correct zip code for an address. It can also be a complex effort, such as matching a large number of customer records from several customer databases, identifying them as the same customer (based on various criteria), and storing only one record in the target database. Although data cleansing has been a highly visible topic in DW, it is also applicable to operational systems. In Chapter 3, "Data Quality," we describe the activities for data cleansing and launching data quality initiatives.

OLAP and Analytics

The cornerstone of a successful BI application is its capability to provide business users fast and easy access to data for analysis. Online analytical processing (OLAP) tools are one of the most important and widely used components of BI. Larissa Moss and Shaku Atre define OLAP as, "online analytical processing technology that creates new business information through a robust set of business transformation and calculations executed upon existing data." In addition, unlike the traditional reporting tools that provide a snapshot of data in the database, OLAP tools allow users to answer "what, why, and what-if" questions. In "what, why, and what-if" questions, we ask for more than the snapshot of a situation. We attempt to define what the trends are, why the sales are down, and if spending 10 percent more on advertising is worth it. There are various flavors of OLAP tools in the market, such as Relational OLAP (ROLAP), Multidimensional OLAP (MOLAP), and Hybrid OLAP (HOLAP), which is a combination of ROLAP and MOLAP. The major difference between the flavors of OLAP tools is that in MOLAP, data is predefined (aggregated, calculated, and summarized) for various conditions, whereas in a ROLAP, data is typically aggregated at the time of request. In addition, MOLAP data is typically stored in a proprietary database, whereas a ROLAP tool accesses any relational DBMS, such as DB2, Oracle, SQL Server, and so on.

The importance of OLAP tools as major components in the BI platform is evident, as it provides business analysts with the flexibility to view data at any level of summarization and for the view of any level of user in the organization. In addition, they allow business analysts to perform the analysis without the intervention of the IT department or the need for a sophisticated report writer.

Data Presentation and Visualization

You've heard the saying, "A picture is worth a thousand words." This is especially true in BI analytics. Visualization is the graphical presentation of data, with the goal of providing the viewer with a qualitative understanding of its contents. Presenting data in a graphical format allows users to perform analysis and understand results faster, better, and more accurately. There is, however, a difference between data presentation and data visualization techniques. Data presentation techniques provide a simple graphical view of the data (such as graphs in Microsoft Excel) without any computerized analysis. On the other hand, data visualization products do more than simply plot the data. They provide decision analysis components (what-if capabilities, parametric graphics, and so on) that support users in making decisions.

IMPORTANT BI TOOLS AND PROCESSES

In addition to the basic components of BI, there are other important tools and processes that enhance the power of a sound BI platform. In this section, we describe these tools and processes and how they are widely used in various industries today.

Data Mining

The explosive growth of data in corporations combined with the fast emergence of the Internet as a reliable source of competitive data analysis has created a log jam for corporate business analysts. Because there is so much data to sift through, we need computers to perform the analysis for us. The process of using computer models and algorithms against internal and external organizational data to find hidden patterns in organization data is called *data mining*. Through the use of data mining techniques, businesses discover new trends and patterns of behavior that previously went unnoticed. Basically, businesses are finding the proverbial needle in the haystack.

There are two distinct uses of data mining: Predictive and Discovery. In the case of Predictive data mining, the algorithm tries to predict the behavior of an entity, person, or object based on given parameters and previously recorded data. For example, a predictive data-mining algorithm can be used in a banking application to approve or decline issuance of a credit card to a specific applicant by analyzing parameters, such as age, credit score, income, total debt, bank account balances, and previous payment behavior. These parameters can be compared to payment patterns of customers with similar characteristics at this bank.

Discovery algorithms, on the other hand, allow organizations to identify patterns and, or exceptions and deviations in data that are not evident to business analysts. For example, a retail organization might utilize a data-mining algorithm to identify products that are purchased together by a specific customer segment. Such pattern discovery can result in shelf placement of products, co-marketing of products, or providing coupons for one product if another one is purchased alone.

Rule-Based Analytics

Like data mining algorithms, rule-based systems are designed to either predict or discover undetected behavior based on a set of parameters and previous set of data. However, unlike data mining algorithms, rule-based analytics are focused on solving a specific problem at hand. Rule-based systems are fairly simplistic, containing little more than a set of if-then-else statements that try to solve a specific problem, and therefore, can be adapted to a variety of applications and industries. Expanding on the banking example for which the data mining algorithm can identify whether to offer a credit card to the applicant, the rule-based analytics would determine the type of card (regular, gold, platinum, and so on) and the annual percentage rate associated with the card. Another example of rule-based analytics systems can be found in hospitals and health maintenance organizations (HMO) at which the invoices are automatically scrutinized based on certain rules to ensure the procedures and medication have been charged appropriately and with the correct amounts. The systems do have the option of amending the bill when a charge is missing or of notifying an administrator when this discrepancy is discovered.

Balanced Scorecard

Balanced scorecard (BSC) was developed in the early 1990s to provide a clear prescription as to what companies should measure to "balance" their financial perspective. BSC enables organizations to clarify their strategy, translate them into short-term and long-term goals, and then translate those goals into tasks, create metrics on each task, and measure against the metrics. Organizations cannot improve what they cannot measure, and therefore, such metrics are a significant part of this approach. This is when a sound BI approach supports the efforts of the whole organization through BSC. By providing clean, consistent, and timely data into the BSC metrics, organizations can measure the success of each and every strategic and tactical project at any level of the organization, and organizations can make fast and accurate decisions. Because BSC normally includes both internal and external factors (such as customer satisfaction), the sound BI platform can help members of the organization capture and analyze various customer satisfaction points (such as surveys, complaints, loyalty, and so on) to provide a broader set of information to BSC.

Digital Dashboard

Resembling an enhanced automobile dashboard, digital dashboards organize and present information in a way that is easy to comprehend. Unlike a scorecard, which is often presented as a matrix of dozens or hundreds of metrics, a digital dashboard is an executive tool with a limited number of metrics displayed as dials, charts, or alerts. An organizational digital dashboard is interactive, allowing users to drill down and across to find the exact reason for a problem. Digital dashboards are now mostly portal-oriented, and therefore customizable based on the role, function, and preferences of the person using it. For example, the corporate chief operating officer (COO) might be interested in daily measurements including sales by each division on the previous day and its comparison with average sales for the past year. On normal days, the digital dashboard could present a green light under the sales measurement. On days when sales drop by more than 5 percent, the COO could set the dashboard to display a yellow light, and on days when sales drop by a measurement of greater than 10 percent, a red light can be set to display. On such days, the COO can quickly click on the red light, see the sales by each division, identify the problematic division, drill down to the specific store, and find the problem immediately.

On the other hand, the manager of a local store of the same organization can set the digital dashboard to display her specific measurements, allowing her to identify problematic areas and resolve them proactively prior to receiving a call from the COO notifying her of a problem at her store.

The digital dashboard plays an important role in the balanced scorecard approach for an organization by providing an easy-to-use and interactive presentation tool that can easily be incorporated as part of the organizational portal.

As you can see, a digital dashboard is meaningless without a sound BI strategy that can feed data for the quick consumption of various decision makers across the organization.

EMERGING TRENDS AND TECHNOLOGIES

Several trends and new technologies currently utilize BI to either increase revenue or decrease the cost in an organization. In this section, we describe some of these technologies and their use of BI to enhance an organization's performance.

Mining Structured and Unstructured Data

Earlier in the chapter, we discussed data mining and its advantages. However, as you will see in Chapter 11, "Managing Unstructured Data," about 85 percent of data in an organization is unstructured. That means that so far, data warehousing and BI applications have been able to harvest information from only 15 percent of organizational data. The current trend in data mining is to mine both structured and unstructured data. At the time of writing this book, most of the advancements in mining unstructured data have resulted from mining textual data, such as email, documents, or spreadsheets, as opposed to other types of unstructured data, such as video, audio, or pictures.

What can you gain by mining both structured and unstructured data? In the United States, the Federal Bureau of Investigation (FBI) has announced that it is planning to deploy business intelligence software to support a new FBI data warehouse that consists of a terrorism intelligence database and an information-sharing data mart. FBI agents will be able to analyze multiple document repositories that house more than one billion documents. The FBI has recognized that by utilizing mining algorithms on both structured data and unstructured documents, it can capture criminals faster and hopefully prior to them committing the crime.

Auto manufacturing organizations focus on mining both structured and unstructured data to measure defects in their vehicles and the cause of such defects. By capturing information from manuals, internal memos, and call centers in addition to utilizing structured information about vehicle and external information, a mining algorithm can identify patterns of part failures in a type of vehicle and predict the type of problems that might happen in a new model. This allows organizations committed to quality programs, such as Six Sigma or Total Quality Management, to improve the quality of parts as well as vehicles, and it allows them to maintain and increase customer brand loyalty.

The trend will continue to include audio, video, and picture files as part of the data mining algorithms. In a few years, a bidder on a Picasso painting might realize (by using a BI platform) that Picasso paintings with a blue background are a better investment historically than all others, and the investor can then make a decision on how much to pay for the painting. The FBI can mine structured data, documents, phone conversations (in any language), and pictures of terrorists to discover a plot against the homeland.

Radio Frequency Identification

Radio Frequency Identification (RFID) is a method of identifying unique items using radio waves. Typically, a digital reader communicates with a tag, which holds digital information in a microchip that is attached to the item. Although RFID has been in use in a variety of cases since 1945, there is a proposed new use that is interesting for this discussion. Today, as you pick up various items in a supermarket and go to the check out counter, the cashier scans the Universal Product Code (UPC) of the item and charges you for the product. There is a move in the retail industry to replace UPC codes with RFID by the year 2015. Wal-Mart is planning to introduce items equipped with RFID on its shelves as early as January, 2005. Utilizing RFID in place of UPC codes will unleash the power of BI, especially in retail organizations.

Imagine it is the year 2020 and you enter your favorite retail supermarket to do your weekly grocery shopping. As you enter, you choose a shopping cart and scan your customer loyalty card on a scanner installed on the cart. As you pass through the aisles of the store, you pick up an item and drop it into your shopping cart. At this moment, several things happen including the following:

- The signal from the item's RFID notifies the shopping cart of the item you just put in the cart. By utilizing the organization's BI platform, a targeted ad is displayed on the monitor and a coupon is printed on the printer (both installed on the shopping cart) about a companion product to the item that you just chose.

- The signal is transmitted to the back room where a computer tallies the total number of units of the products that have been picked up from shelves. Utilizing the organization's BI platform, an order is generated (at the optimal time and requesting the optimal quantity of the product). The order is placed directly with the supplier, facilitating the supply chain.

- The same BI platform—based on the number of units of the same product in the inventory, seasonal parameters, number of customers in the store, product's shelf life, competitor's information, and so on—will calculate the optimal price for the item and automatically update the point-of-sale computer, which will in turn change the price displays at the store.

- You continue to travel through the aisles and pass an item that you buy once every two weeks on average. Because it has been more than 2 weeks since you bought the item last, the organization's BI platform recognizes this fact and displays a note on the monitor that reminds you to purchase the item.

- When you are ready to check out, you will not have to stand in any lines. As you roll your shopping cart past the bagging stand, the total amount of your purchases is calculated and charged to your credit card (if on file) or your can pay in cash. At this moment, the BI platform kicks in again. It updates your profile, your customer segment, and your purchase habits based on your purchases.

This retail grocery store example demonstrates a simple RFID relationship to BI. Regardless of the industry, RFID will play a big role in capturing clean, consistent, and timely data, the main ingredient of all BI platforms.

BI MYTHS AND PITFALLS

Unfortunately, there are some myths and pitfalls associated with BI that hinder delivery of an optimal BI platform to an organization. Avoiding these mistakes can save thousands of hours of work, millions of dollars, and a lot of heartache in development and implementation of a successful BI project.

Following are the most common myths associated with BI:

Myth 1: There is a magic BI pill.

It is a myth to think that purchasing specific BI software (CRM, OLAP and presentation tools, dashboard products, and so on) will solve all of an organization's analytical problems. You have to remember that BI is part of a process. It requires modifications to business processes and modifications to the computer components. Such tools might be able to solve a specific problem in the organization, but delivery of a sound BI platform should involve a holistic approach to the problem.

Myth 2: ERP-related data marts are complete BI solutions.

Every major ERP package includes a module that allows for analysis of the data captured by the ERP system. Although these modules are excellent tools for analysis of that specific subject area, they are not designed to interface with other systems and therefore cannot provide a 360-degree view of the business. Such tools are a part of the total BI solution, but not the complete BI solution.

Myth 3: BI is too expensive.

A common perception among both business and IT executives is that BI is too expensive. The truth is that BI can be expensive, but it does not have to be. Planned, outlined, and implemented correctly, BI can pay for itself many times over, and the initial investment does not have to be outrageous. We have implemented many BI projects by delivering the system in phases, whereby the ROI becomes evident before expanding further on the BI platform or before expanding into other parts of the organization.

Myth 4: Organizations can be too small to take advantage of BI.

Many small- and medium-sized organizations view BI as a platform used only by the Fortune 500 companies. This is a detrimental misconception. The truth is that with a much smaller investment than that of a large organization, small- and medium-sized businesses (SMB) can also benefit from BI. In some cases, we believe that BI is more vital for the SMB organizations than the large organizations. Because not all SMBs utilize BI, doing so can provide a major competitive advantage to those that do take advantage of it.

Pitfall 1: Starting your BI project without a sound roadmap.

You'd never build a house without a blueprint. So, why would you build a BI platform without a roadmap? Developing and implementing a BI platform requires analysis, planning, and budgeting by utilizing a sound methodology. In addition, a sound roadmap should take all business process improvement activities into account. Utilizing such a roadmap can save hundreds of thousands of dollars in budget costs and hundreds of hours of rework.

Pitfall 2: Waiting for a few years to realize the first ROI.

While developing the roadmap, you need to emphasize the delivery that part of the project that provides a fast ROI to the line-of-business clients. Waiting for years to see the fruits of a project is discouraging for business users and uninspiring for developers and implementers.

Pitfall 3: Purchasing tools prior to completion of the roadmap.

Often, organizations purchase data transformation, OLAP, and other presentation tools prior to putting a roadmap in place. Some problems associated with this approach are as follows:

• An investment is made prior to the full analysis of the short- and long-term requirements of the project based on the roadmap (for example, the number of users, access types, exact needs of the project, and so on).

• Purchased tools might not fit the roadmap. The roadmap might not require the use of these tools in the short term or long term. Now, two things can happen:

  • The roadmap's recommendation is used, which can result in products being shelved and the loss of the investment.

  • The roadmap's recommendation is ignored, which could result in problems in the long term.

Pitfall 4: Tool experts are not necessarily BI architects.

An expert in data transformation, OLAP, or other presentation tool is not necessarily a BI architect. A BI architect must have a deep knowledge of systems on a variety of platforms. In addition, the architect should understand data and its flow through an organization. Finally, but certainly not least, is the architect's understanding of the business. The architect should be able to discuss and understand the needs and wants of the line-of-business decision makers from a line manager all the way up to the executive team.

CONCLUSION

As demonstrated, BI is an integral part of any overall data strategy for an organization. It will not only help organizations transform into a data-centric places, but it will yield to better decisions that can enhance the bottom line of the organization.

REFERENCES

IDC, October 2002.

Adelman, Sid and Larissa T. Moss. *Data Warehouse Project Management*. Boston, MA: Addison-Wesley, 2000.

Fayyad, Usama M. et al. *Advances in Knowledge Discovery & Data Mining*. Cambridge, MA: MIT Press, 1996.

Gartner, Business Intelligence Summit. Amsterdam, Netherlands, February 2004—http://www.in-sourced.com/article/articleprint/1273/-1/1/.

Kimball, Ralph et al. *The Data Warehouse Lifecycle Toolkit*. New York: John Wiley & Sons, 1998.

Marco, David. *Building and Managing the Metadata Repository*. New York, NY: John Wiley & Sons, 2000.

Moss, Larissa T. and Shaku Atre. *Business Intelligence Roadmap: The Complete Project Lifecycle for Decision-Support Applications*. Boston, MA: Pearson Education, 2003.

Verton, Dan. "FBI Begins Knowledge Management Facelift." *Computer World*, 2003.

CHAPTER 11

Strategies for Managing Unstructured Data

"Knowledge is of two kinds. We know a subject ourselves, or we know where we can find information on it."

—Samuel Johnson (1709–1784), quoted in *Boswell's Life of Johnson*

Any discussion about organizational data strategies is incomplete without formulating a tactic for maintaining unstructured data. Unstructured data (UD) focuses on data types that cannot be normalized and stored in a typical relational, network, or hierarchical database, but should nonetheless be organized, categorized, stored, retained, archived, deleted, searched, and delivered. We all work with this type of data on a daily basis: emails, documents, spreadsheets, reports, pictures, audio files, video files, and general content.

In the past several years, in some circles, the word "content" has become synonymous with Web content, which is only a form of unstructured data. In this chapter, we focus on the broader definition of the term, embracing all types of unstructured data, and we focus on strategies for managing content in the organization. The challenges in dealing with unstructured data are no different than the challenges of dealing with structured data. We just utilize different methodologies in solving the problems and introduce new technologies that directly relate to unstructured data types.

WHAT IS UNSTRUCTURED DATA?

As mentioned before, UD is defined as data that does not fit a certain normalized format. A data modeler cannot break down an electronic spreadsheet and identify its logical and physical or primary and foreign keys. We do not have to identify its type nor its size, and there is no reason to maintain it within the confines of a table.

We can, however, gather some metadata from unstructured data and use this metadata to organize this object (for lack of a better word) into categories. We can provide some security procedures around viewing and, or updating this object and also maintain various versions of the object as it changes. We can also define the rules regarding its retention, expiration, and deletion across the organization.

There are many types of UD, and with a sound strategy, you should not have to worry about the type. The object can be a picture, a text file, a Microsoft Word document, an electronic spreadsheet, an audio file (such as music or voice mail messages), a video file, an email, electronic forms, instant messages, and other types that are continuously added.

A Brief History

Ever since computers became a necessary part of business processing, information technology professionals have been looking for ways to provide "structure" to data. After all, how could machines process data if it were not stored in a file and formatted as records?

When using the word "structure," we mean applying categorization procedures to records that eventually evolved into normalization techniques. We first identify each atomic piece of data into columns (data elements or fields); then we categorize logically related columns into specific rows (records); identify a logical or physical key for the record; collect logically similar records into a table (file); and create a database by collecting a set of related tables and creating logical or physical relationships between them. Although the previous description mostly relates to relational or flat file models, it is not much different from other topologies, such as hierarchical or network in which one collates similar segments into a database and creates one-to-many or many-to-many, parent-child relationships between the segments.

In the process, any data that might have been structured was, and all other data types were typically ignored. As a result, the word "data" became synonymous with "structured data" and terms such as data processing, data management, database, data quality, and data strategies referred—and even today continue to refer—to structured data.

It was not as if organizations did not have other data types. These data types have been around much longer than the computers. Organizations have created reports, spreadsheets, pictures, audios, movies, memos, mailings, and other internal and external documents for years. A small number of organizations and corporations, mostly the larger ones, had the requirements to capture and store some of the reports, documents, and pictures and display them in either a Microfiche or, recently, a digital format. They just did not consider these documents to be data. Even more importantly, there was never a systematic and centralized strategy to capture and maintain such data. Each department and section within the organization maintained its own method of capturing content and often without any centralized management of the content.

In the late 1980s, most of the relational database management systems (DBMS) started recognizing the need to carry some unstructured data as part of the relational model and added various types of Large Objects (LOB) as a data type and as part of the relational record. Some examples are Binary Large Objects (BLOBs) and Character Large Objects (CLOBs). Some DBMSs carry Memo fields for smaller CLOBs. Utilizing LOBs, database modelers and administrators were able to include pictures or text blocks into the relational record, and in later years, audio and video files. There were several problems with this approach, which we discuss later in this chapter, but at least somebody recognized the need for inclusion of other data types as data. Earlier applications allowed displaying a picture along with a record (such as an employment record with the employee's picture attached to verify authenticity).

Also in the late 1980s and early 1990s, a large number of organizations started capturing reports in a digital format and sharing them with their users. For example, customer service representatives in various industries needed to view the same report in the same format as the customers. In a typical scenario, a customer would call with a problem on page 7 of her previous month's phone bill and the customer service representative needed access to an exact copy of the report printout to adequately reference the customer problem. Such requirements focused some attention on the matters of unstructured data, although the big picture was not there yet.

With the increase in the processing power of personal computers, the decrease in processor and storage prices, and the wide use of the Internet, more and more people and organizations started to capture unstructured data—or content—in a digital format especially in the cases of websites, emails, photographs, and digital audio and video files. In addition, for the first time, the Internet provided a medium for sharing and displaying content to a huge number of users. Imagine a large multinational organization developing a message and delivering it via its websites in 20 languages and in 50 different countries. All of a sudden, and in a short period of time, there was an explosion of volume in data (both structured and unstructured), and the number continues to grow at a maddening pace. According to a 2003 study by the University of California at Berkeley, about 5 exabytes (an exabyte is roughly the equivalent of 1,000 petabytes, 1 million terabytes, or 1 billion gigabytes) of unique analog and digital information were produced worldwide in 2002, twice the amount produced in 1999. That's a data explosion equivalent to half a million new libraries the size of print collection of the Library of Congress. With more and more organizations moving toward a paperless environment or digitalizing their unstructured data, this number will continue to expand exponentially.

Why Now?

Why is it that after all these years, organizations suddenly focus on UD? The Berkeley study is one reason, but there are several other factors to consider. IBM estimates that about 85 percent of data in an organization is unstructured and about 50 percent of the unstructured data is duplicated (see Figure 11.1). This huge volume of duplicated data costs organizations money in storage and backup costs.

In addition, in most cases, because there is not a central strategy for managing and retaining this content, it continuously gets duplicated. This is where the actual hidden cost should be calculated: productivity loss. For example, an engineering organization—an ISO-9000 shop—designed the same part 19 times, and some other parts were reengineered ranging from 2 to 17 times because the

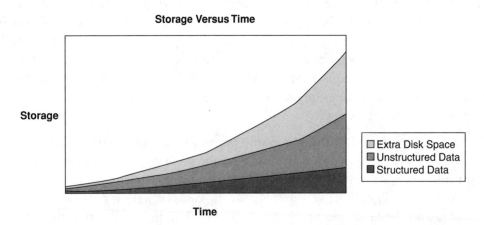

Figure 11.1: Storage Versus Time

organization did not realize they had already manufactured those parts. How could they not know? How could they design, test, set up the line, produce, and deliver the part without realizing that they already had it in stock? The answer is simple if you look at it from a data perspective: The organization had manufactured over 5,000 parts for various clients, and although the specifications and designs were maintained on digital format, there was not a centralized strategy for maintaining and searching designed parts. So when the order came from a client to create a similar part, the engineering department did a cursory search only through the client's previous orders. When they did not find any matching the specifications, they re-engineered the same part. Just imagine the duplicate cost for design, production line setup, quality assurance, raw material, salaries, packaging, and delivery, when there was already the same part—although it was with another name and for another client—in the inventory.

Although somewhat extreme, this example provides a glimpse into the state of unstructured data in organizations. Organizations in various industries—engineering and manufacturing, legal, financial, automotive, biotech, and others—have an immediate need for a central strategy for capturing content, but a much larger need to perform an intelligent search on the organization's content using certain search parameters.

Another major reason for the push to develop centralized content strategies is the Sarbanes-Oxley Act of 2002. There are two sections in the Act that relate to reports and documents: One is Title VIII, which makes it a felony to knowingly destroy any documents to "impede, obstruct, or influence" any existing or contemplated federal investigation. The other section makes it a crime for any person to corruptly alter, destroy, mutilate, or conceal any document with the intent to impair the object's integrity or availability for use in an official proceeding. Because an organization and its employees can be criminally liable for destroying documents, all public corporations must ensure that relevant documents are maintained in electronic format for 5–7 years, and readily available for scrutiny by various governmental entities.

In addition to the Sarbanes-Oxley Act, other legislations in the U.S., European Union, United Kingdom, Australia, and other governments have forced public organizations to maintain all electronic data (including documents, reports, publications, and even email for up to 7 years). In one case, a major financial organization estimated having 350 terabytes of just electronic mail in multiple languages that needed to be stored, retained, and searched if and when regulators requested. An example of such request can contain a search for email documents produced by "Joe Smith" between January and March, 2001 that contain the word "bribe" as part of its content.

Imagine the time that it would take an organization to respond to such requests having had no strategy, except for the basic backup of shared drives and email servers. Even if the search involved one email server and one shared drive, it would take months to restore, search, and find every piece of document and, or email produced by a specific person in that period and containing a certain text string. CTOs, and more importantly, legal departments cannot wait that long. They need a strategy and they need it now.

Current State of Unstructured Data in Organizations

In simple words, UD in most organizations is in a state of chaos. In most cases, there are no central strategies for creating, managing, retaining, and delivering these objects at the enterprise level.

In most organizations, UD is created and maintained in content silos where content authors work in isolation from others in the organization. Such content silos force the recreation of the content over and over within the organization and even within the same content area. For the reasons described in the previous sections of this chapter, such isolation causes redundancy, poor communication, lack of standards, and higher costs for creation of the content. In addition, the search and consumption of such content is harder and more costly for both internal and external users because the content sitting in isolated silos is not necessarily inventoried and, or accessible to consumers.

A UNIFIED CONTENT STRATEGY FOR THE ORGANIZATION

As level, size, and types of data increase in the organization, it becomes apparent that a central strategy for managing this data is the key component of a successful data-oriented organization. In this section, we focus on important components of central strategy as it relates to unstructured data.

Definition of a Unified Content Strategy

Ann Rockley, one of the leading consultants in the area of enterprise content management, describes a unified content strategy as, "a repeatable method of identifying all content requirements upfront, creating consistently structured content for reuse, managing that content in a definitive source, and assembling content on demand to meet your customers' needs."

Although an excellent definition, we believe that the organization's information strategy should anticipate that new data types, content requirements, and data sources—both structured and content—will be added in the future. As such, the strategy should be standardized to remove the risk of content silos as described in the previous section, and yet be flexible enough to embrace various new types of internal and external data.

Components of such a strategy are described in the following sections in more detail.

Storage and Administration

In the past 30 years, the world of structured data has evolved from disparate files into central databases administered by database management systems or DBMS. Although the historical evolution of the databases is out of the scope of this chapter, all DBMSs have been designed to perform the same certain tasks, regardless of whether they are in a hierarchical, network, object, or relational format. Regardless of topology, they have methods for storing, manipulating, searching, and retrieving records. In addition, they have allowed database administrators to manage data better by allowing for systematic backups and restores, data reorganizations, index management, and performance management. Another major functionality of the DBMS has been to secure its records from unauthorized access for viewing, modifying, and deleting.

As UD goes mainstream in organizations, we expect the same evolution to happen in managing UD objects. As discussed before, UD is—for the most part—spread throughout an organization's networks without any centralized plan for securing and administering data. The recognition of UD as a vital corporate asset has forced leading IT departments to utilize enterprise content management systems (ECMS) for managing all nonstructured data objects. Such systems allow for storing, administering, searching, securing, and retrieving content from a centralized base in the same method that a DBMS allows for administering structured data. ECMS systems—for example, DB2 Content Manager™ (IBM), Documentum™ (EMC), IFS™ (Oracle), and Filenet™ Content Manager (Filenet)—provide a repository for unstructured objects, allow for capturing metadata for each object for future searches, and create relationships among objects. They also provide centralized check-in, check-out functionality, backup, restore, and disaster recovery capabilities, and they enable users to search across various objects, and secure objects from unauthorized access. Such systems often provide tasks that fall outside of the scope of structured DBMSs, such as versioning, retention, and archiving. All the previously mentioned products—either by out-of-the-box functionality or by utilizing a companion product—also provide electronic workflow management capabilities to end users. Electronic workflows often simplify routing of documents and other electronic objects in the organization. A great example is used in a mortgage company when an applicant submits an application online. The next step on the workflow—after electronic evaluation—is for a mortgage processor to review the application and then electronically forward it to the manager for approval.

Why not use a DBMS to manage UD objects? This is a question that is frequently asked of an enterprise content management specialist. After all, most DBMS packages allow for capturing LOBs. Why can't we just increase our IT investments into DBMS to capture these objects?

There are several reasons for not utilizing these packages. First and foremost, these packages are not designed to manage content. They are structured data management tools designed to relate relational sets of tables and columns. UD objects do not fit into tables and columns. After all, how does one store many sections of a manual (including pictures, diagrams, indexes, foot notes, fonts, and formats) into tables and columns?

Secondly, DBMS packages are not designed to manage versioning, retention, and archiving of objects. We realize that they could be designed to perform these tasks, but such functionality is an embedded function of an ECMS.

Another reason is the size of database and its management. There are usually two ways to store LOBs in a DBMS: store it in the database or store it on the file system and store the link for the LOB in the DBMS. If one uses the first technique, the size of the database is huge and basic functionalities, such as backup and restore, take a lot of time. If the second option is chosen, the integrity of the database is compromised because the typical DBMS does not put a restriction on viewing, changing, or deleting the object file, and therefore, an unauthorized person can effectively view or remove a secured file. Again, we recognize that this activity can be protected by utilizing network security, but we argue that it should be managed from a centralized source.

Interestingly enough, most ECMSs utilize a form of a relational DBMS to capture and maintain metadata for each object and object type. Almost all of them allow for extension of such tables to include custom-designed metadata.

Archiving

Archiving is an important function in the UD world. The administrators of UD objects should plan for a time when the active objects (or old versions) should be archived and, or removed from the repository. Archiving methods are slightly different for UD than its structured relative. On the structured side, archiving is usually an after-thought. Several years after deployment of the original system, we are requested to archive data in a format that can be retrieved later. With a typical DBMS, there is no out-of-the-box way to archive the basic records. In ECMS, there is usually an archive flag associated with each object that signals the object to be archived.

Retention

The subject of record and object retention is not new. It has applied to nonelectronic records for years. Several governmental, internal, and external corporate rules, regulations, and standards manage and retain objects. Records retention varies from organization to organization, department to department, and even document (object) type to document type. For example, an organization might have a requirement to retain a financial report for 7 years and another requirement to maintain employee records for 3 years after dismissal, retirement, or death of an employee.

The same requirements have now been expanded to include electronic documents. These documents include financial reports, employee records, electronic manuals, advertisements, and even email. At times, some objects, such as corporate annual reports, must be retained indefinitely.

In the old days, nonelectronic reports, records, memos, and other documents were stored in file cabinets or were placed in boxes and shipped to long-term storage facilities. As you can imagine, retrieval and views of these records would have been a small nightmare.

In this electronic era, corporations need to ensure the retention of required electronic objects as well as the nonelectronic ones. To reduce the risk of deleting required records, the current approach is to generally remove the responsibility for retention of an object from all employees and to centralize it in a small group with only a few administrators. Utilizing specialized records retention software tools, the administrators create various categories and subcategories that are several layers deep. They can then set up retention rules for each bucket. The rules vary from a certain period after the creation of the object to a number of years after the termination of its author to dependency on another object. The same records retention software is used to identify—implicitly and, or explicitly—the new and changed files in the network drive (or email server) and then to group them into categories and sub categories (automatically or with the help of administrators). This software utilizes internal security to prohibit everybody—except authorized users (including the file's author)—from deleting the object.

Any modifications or additions to the object will take place in the form of a new version and are subject to all mentioned scrutiny. Interestingly enough, all the major ECMSs have introduced their own version of records retention components that not only allow for centrally managing the content, but also the management of the retention rules.

On a daily basis, the retention management systems review catalogues and identify records that are ready for archiving or deletion. The system administrators are notified and after reviewing the rules, they decide whether the selection was performed correctly or not. The archiving and deletion decision is electronically sent to the ECMS (or shared network) and the file is automatically deleted or archived (if in ECMS).

Content Reusability

One of the most important components of an organization's content strategy is the need to reuse an organization's existing content components in a new object. For example, an organization needs to create a website and printed marketing material; however, it does not need to create content for each of the objects separately. It can create a set of content for one, and then use paragraphs, pictures, graphs, and even sentences from one in the other. Utilizing this method, a content change to a specific object automatically changes the content on another, ensuring the consistency of the message across the organization.

Search and Delivery

Data is stored to be searched, manipulated, and viewed. UD objects are no different. A component of the organization's content strategy should be to implement methodologies for easy access, search, and delivery of content from various ECMS tools in the organization. Because the Google™ search engine has become a household name synonymous with searching the internet, an organization's content strategy should provide means for a Google™-type search across all content in the organization.

All enterprise-level ECMS tools allow explicit and implicit capture of metadata to enhance future searches. They also provide application programming interfaces (APIs) for application programs to search the metadata of a specific object. Keyword searches are performed by various search engines that have integrated functionalities in the ECMS.

Most ECMSs provide caching methods for faster search and delivery of the content to the users. In some instances, the ECMS can be configured to cache data to a variety of servers in various locations for faster access based on users' geographical position. In addition, as part of the organization's content strategy, an organization should recognize the fact that users are not limited only to their PCs for accessing data. Our information consumers utilize office workstations, home computers, lap tops, PDAs, and cell phones to access all types of information. The strategy should ensure that regardless of the type of tool utilized to access and present data, its search and delivery methods are standardized.

Combining Structured and Unstructured Data

In many organizations, the need to combine structured and unstructured data to provide a full view of data to users has risen. As part of an organization's data strategy, we should implement methods for searching structured and unstructured data simultaneously.

Many information consumers require the display of both structured and unstructured data on information portals to efficiently perform work. This information is merged through metadata, search criteria, or various other parameters, and its cleanliness and consistency is important in delivering the full picture to data consumers.

Another important use of combining structured and unstructured data is the ability to mine information across both types. For more information about data mining across structured and unstructured data, read chapter 10, "Business Intelligence."

EMERGING TECHNOLOGIES

Although content has been around for a long time, it's been just a short time since some organizations have started to consider it data. For that reason, there are few technologies related to unstructured data. At the same time, there are some emerging markets for such technologies and these promise a bright future for products and services in the complete enterprise data management market. The following is a list of just a few of these products and solutions and how they are used in various organizations:

Digital Asset Management Software

The relationship between digital asset management (DAM) software and ECMS is like the relationship of application software (Enterprise Resource Planning, CRM, and so on) to its DBMS. ECMS is the heart and sole of a DAM system. DAM contains applications that resolve a specific operational—and in the future, analytical—need of an organization by providing automatic batch entry, manual entry, workflow, and of course search, retrieval, and archiving of digital content from an ECMS.

A great example of DAM is a software developed for the entertainment industry in which the detailed aspects of a movie—including screen play (and all its subsequent changes), story boards, still photographs, daily shoots, edited versions, sound tracks, songs, marketing posters, interviews, junket clips, and so on—are loaded into a central repository regardless of where the shoot takes place around the world. In this case, the director, the producers, and the entertainment organization executives can track and view the daily work performed by all teams associated with the movie from the comfort of their homes or offices. In addition, the software allows for a complete archive of all digital information related to a movie in one central place, assuring availability of the data associated for a movie for future generations.

Another example of DAM software is used by several leading educational and religious organizations. It allows organizations to collaborate on creating lectures, essays, books, pictures, seminars—in all media (audio, video, print formats)—and store the objects as digital assets in a central repository. These systems allow the easy integration and harvesting of metadata by the users for each of the objects, enhancing and speeding up the experience of scholars, researchers, and students within the organization as well as all outside organizations that need the information. In addition, because all objects are centrally available, the information can be more easily disseminated to a geographically distributed set of users.

A large suite of DAM applications that will solve specific operational problems in the arena of digital asset management for various industries will be introduced in the next few years. We will see a large move to develop new systems, and at times, integrating digital assets into existing applications that already manage structured data in the organization. In addition, business intelligence tools and data mining methods will be enhanced and developed to take advantage of vast amounts of data in the enterprise and allow the easy analysis of the hidden information in the unstructured objects.

Digital Rights Management Software

Copyright laws in the United States and most of the world allow the author or rights holder of a document to have a say in reproduction of her material and allows her to be paid royalties and licensing fees associated with its use. Digital rights management (DRM) software utilizes technological methods to enforce these rights.

You have probably heard of the old Napster.™ The problem with the original Napster™—and any file-sharing engine—was that it allowed people to share copyrighted material without allowing its rights holders to enjoy royalties from the people who downloaded the music files.

The amount of losses experienced by software, music, and video industries due to piracy has been astronomical for the past few years: $29 billion in software piracy in the U.S. and $4.2 billion in music file piracy in the U.S. for 2003 alone. DRM software focuses on allowing only the users who have the right to utilize specific software to listen to a song or watch a video for as long as they maintain the right.

DRM software provides technical components that maintain and manage relationships between objects (digital assets), users (the person utilizing the object), and rights. These components can vary from object security to financial transactions to resource location. In a detailed example, imagine the scenario of purchasing a ring tone from the Internet for your cell phone. You go to the website and the website allows you to download and listen to the ring tone on your cell twice—or for 2 days—for free. After the second time—or second day—you will not be able to use the ring tone until you pay the full price for it. DRM software will handle the contract between you and the website from the standpoint of rights management. It will maintain the usage count (or days) or use and will stop you from utilizing the object when the contract expires. It will establish a new contract—without having to download the software again—when the full amount is paid.

DRM software products focus on much more than just software, audio, and video files. They also focus on any digital asset that needs to be protected from unauthorized usage, including competition-sensitive corporate assets. Imagine a corporate executive downloading a confidential report on to his laptop to work from home over the weekend. Now imagine losing the laptop. The person who finds or steals the laptop can break into the system and view the contents of its files. How does DRM protect against these problems? In this scenario, the contract between the user (the executive) and the object (the document) can be maintained and is always checked through a corporate license server. When the laptop is lost, the executive will notify a corporate security officer who will (as part of the normal procedure) remove the rights on all sensitive files from the executive's laptops.

We think DRM is an emerging technology that you will see a lot more of in the next decade. Securing all types of digital assets and maintaining short- and long-term contracts for various users of these assets has created an extensive market opportunity for various software organizations.

Electronic Medical Records

A typical and much needed example of DAM software is electronic medical records (EMR) software. This application allows medical offices and hospitals to maintain information about patients in a digital format and communicate that information between doctors and other clinics via an electronic format. In addition, the information can allow researchers to access detailed information about a patient and analyze patterns in treatments to suggest better methods of treatment for future patients with the same disease.

The *Boston Globe* reported in July, 2004, that the U.S. Department of Health and Human Services started to appoint a panel to analyze the cost of converting all hospitals, pharmacies, medical offices, and other practitioners to digital media. Based on the same report, such conversion can reduce errors that save the lives of up to 98,000 patients per year.

As you can see, the importance of these systems is truly measured in saving lives. We expect EMR to grow to a mainstream set of systems and in the future allow data mining across various databases to identify patterns of disease and treatments among a large patient sample.

CONCLUSION

Unstructured data plays a major role in an organization, and utilizing it correctly will improve processes and directly enhance the bottom line. As such, the need to capture UD and make it available to other parts of an organization must be an important part of any organization's data strategy.

REFERENCES

Rockley, Ann et. al. *Managing Enterprise Content*. Indianapolis, IN: New Riders Publishing, 2003.

Reimer, James Ph.D. and Chief Architect. "Enterprise Content Management Products," IBM in Content Management and WebSphere Portal Technical Conference, 9 June 2003.

CHAPTER 12

Business Value of Data and ROI

Some of the ideas in this chapter were derived from the Teradata white paper titled "Measuring Data Warehouse Return on Investment," by Sid Adelman.

Organizations have data on customers and suppliers, and they have transactional data that captures the guts of the business, the purchases, sales, customer calls, activities, and financial data. This data has value, meaning it is an asset that is just as important, if not more important, than the buildings, the inventory, accounts receivable, and equipment assets of the organization. When a company gets evaluated for purchase, evaluated as a merger candidate, or appraised by Wall Street, the notion of a going concern includes the value of the data as an asset. Rarely has this data asset ever been shown on the company's books, but it is there sometimes as goodwill, and sometimes it is partially reflected in the price of the stock.

THE BUSINESS VALUE OF DATA

You might question why we would need to assign value to data when an organization cannot exist without the data that supports its applications. The reason is that budgets and resources are limited, and it might be difficult for a person attempting to get the required budget and the right people resources. By showing the business value of data, the budget and the right staff should be easier to acquire.

"If the value of data was truly understood, it would be reflected on a company's balance sheet."

The following sections discuss specific industry circumstances in which the value of data should be apparent, and convincing management of the importance of data should be easier.

Companies that Sell Customer Data

A number of companies sell information about your customer, both wholesale and retail customers. Some of this is credit data that includes income, demographics, (age, gender, and race), credit experience, and credit scores. These companies sell data that is gathered when you fill out a warranty card. Companies also collect information about your buying habits from infinity or loyalty cards.

Internal Information Gathered About Customers

Organizations have the capability to electronically capture data on what customers are buying, which ones are returning merchandise, and what services they use. In addition, your organization has a customer relations department that should capture the concerns, kudos, suggestions, and complaints of the customers who either care enough to tell you what they like and what they don't like about your products and services or are so angry, they take the time to tell you why they are abandoning you. It is estimated that for every customer who expresses him or herself to you, there is a much larger number of customers who have the same opinion. This multiplier, of course, depends on how easy you make it to give you feedback. Smart and agile companies have taken the feedback and introduced new and successful products. The ones that don't bury their heads in the sand are alert to impending problems and quick to fix the problems. A number of companies miss the signs of dissatisfaction and the response to problems is slow, expensive, and the result is a public relations disaster.

Call Center Data

Many organizations with call centers capture data for types of calls, requests for information, problems, complaints, suggestions, and requests for services and products. By analyzing this data and integrating it with customer data, organizations can take appropriate action that might stop a customer from leaving for a competitor, making the organization more proactive to problems that can quickly escalate. The data analysis also helps the organization effectively target market an individual customer and identify opportunities for new products and services.

Click-Stream Data

Your organization has a website that is available to your customers, potential customers, partners, suppliers, and competitors. You may have asked them to sign in with their names, addresses, email addresses, comments (including complaints), and areas of interest. Your website might be able to capture how they navigate through the site, where they click, what information they ask for including financial information, products, and literature that you provide online. This click-stream data is a wealth of data that you can analyze for potential problems, marketing trends, and potential sales leads. This data can give you insights into what your customers are considering.

Demographics

Demographics include gender; age; income, assets; whether you are a homeowner or you rent; interests and hobbies; education level; number and age of children; where you live; if you have a second home; investments and your investment preferences; and what magazines you read. The data you have on your customers might not be so inclusive, but it should include the types of data that will make a difference in how you market to and serve your customers.

Channel Preferences

Most companies allow their customers to use various channels to transact business. Rarely are the channels mutually exclusive; you can use more than one. One of the more expensive channels might have an associated cost or there might be an incentive to use one that is less costly. The idea is to move customers into the less costly channels or to offset expenses by charging for the more expensive options. Banking customers have a number of options available to them and many use more than one channel. Some banking customers like to transact most of their business on the Internet, including balance inquiries, money transfer, and bill payment. Telephone bill paying has been with us for some time and some banking customers find this way of transacting business convenient with the added benefit of not having to buy as many stamps or get paper cuts on their tongues. Others prefer the ATMs for cash withdrawal, deposits, and balance inquiry. Some banking customers like to speak with a customer representative, whereas others prefer to come into the bank. Airlines have been able to significantly reduce reservation costs by offering online reservations.

Most organizations are in a position to learn the customer's channel preferences. This gives the organization the information to focus on the customer by continuing to make the preferred channel easily available and affordable. This helps keep the customer and makes them more likely to use a wider array of the organization's services.

Direct Retailers

The companies that send you catalogues need to know what you have bought in the past, your propensity to purchase only specials, and the specific types of items you are interested in. Many of these direct retailers send out specialty catalogues that target, for example, women's clothes. With some exceptions (men buying for their women partners and men who like to wear women's clothes, and so on), the direct marketer is wasting money and print by sending catalogues to those who have little or no interest in those targeted products. Accurate data is critical to these direct marketers.

Loyalty Cards

These cards are alternatively called "membership card," "loyalty card," "club card," and even "preferred savings card." Some retailers connect their loyalty cards to the shopper's checking account to capture not just the bank information, but also a driver's license number, home phone number, and social security number. With loyalty cards, retailers can capture purchasing information, market basket data (what's in the customer's market basket when they check out), and then integrate that data with coupon usage and the customer's demographics to better understand, for example, price sensitivity to promotions for premium dog food for shoppers over 55 years old. The retailer can issue personally tailored coupons, cash payroll checks, and provide special offers to lock in the customer. Purchasing information along with the demographics of the purchasers is of great interest to the retailers' suppliers, and they are willing to pay for it.

Travel Data

Travel data is captured by the airlines, hotels, and travel websites (Orbitz, Travelocity, and Expedia). They know what flights you have taken, your status with the airline (Premier, Gold, and 100K), if you flew business or coach, how you purchased your ticket, your seat preference, special meals, and if you've been flying with your prize Yorky, Fang. The hotels know how many nights you spend in their hotel, if the stays are at resort locations, if the stay was for a conference, if you eat in the hotel restaurant, what amenities you use (message or room service, for example), and what films you watch and how long you watch them. The car rental companies know your automobile preference, how often you use the service, your accident history with their rentals, and if the rentals are business or pleasure.

This incredible wealth of data allows the airlines, the hotels, the travel websites, and the car rental companies to target market to your preferences, your needs, and the ways you like to be serviced.

ALIGN DATA WITH STRATEGIC GOALS

Every organization—be it a publicly traded company, a private for-profit company, a non-profit organization, a governmental agency, or a quasi-governmental entity—has strategic goals. At minimum, the for-profit companies want to increase profits and more organizations have as primary goals, customer service and a high level of financial integrity.

ROI Process

Measuring return on investment (ROI) is relevant because an organization's cost justifies potential applications. It is also relevant for post-implementation evaluation. Many of the same procedures and equations can be used for both purposes. This chapter provides an approach to cost justify the value of data.

Expected ROI should be a major determinant in evaluating options and making decisions about which architectures to employ, which vendors to choose, and which projects to pursue, and how they should be prioritized. In addition, some companies measure their managers' performance based on the success of projects, and bonuses are often tied to the ROI of those projects. These managers want their projects to be fairly and fully represented and measured.

The project to be measured might be a new project, a re-implementation of an unsuccessful or partially successful system, or an existing project for which the ROI has never been established. It's important to establish expectations for both costs and benefits *before* a new project is launched. By establishing these expectations, organizations can determine if the project was successful. Measures should *never* be recast in an attempt to show success regardless of the actual outcome.

ROI can be demonstrated through a variety of means. This chapter presents three of the most commonly used techniques: payback period (or break-even analysis), net present value, and rate of return (or yield).

THE COST OF DEVELOPING A DATA STRATEGY

Developing a data strategy is not free. It takes significant time from some highly paid staff and might include the cost of consultants. The people who develop the data strategy will come from the upper echelons and from highly paid members of your technical staff. After the data strategy is developed, there might be requirements for additional software. These are some of the costs associated with implementing a data strategy:

- **Data quality**—The data strategy should include dealing with data quality issues, so a tool to profile the data might be recommended. Even if the profiling is performed with a tool, the effort is extensive.

- **Metadata**—A data strategy should include a metadata capability, which could be built in-house or purchased. Either way, there is a cost involved. Capturing metadata both automatically and manually (automatically is cheaper and less error-prone) involves cost and effort. Maintaining the metadata—depending on the size of the organization and which metadata is included, the tool used, and how automatic the process is—is usually a full-time job.

- **Security and privacy**— As it becomes apparent that there are holes in the existing security and privacy policies and the administration, you need to assign the staff to administer and audit.

- **Categorization**— The process to categorize your data and obtain management concurrence is labor intensive.

- **Data modeling**— Most organizations find that data modeling activities are insufficient to properly support a data strategy, and so a small investment in data modeling software and a significant effort to model the data must be included in the cost.

- **Performance and availability**—Supporting the SLAs for performance and availability addressed in the data strategy requires new processes and procedures, possibly new monitoring software and more hardware, and definitely experienced staff to develop and execute the procedures to maintain high levels of SLAs.

Data Warehouse

The expenses for any system vary widely. The cost depends on the size of the database, the number of users, the complexity and quality of the source data, the software tools employed, the need for consultants and contractors, the capabilities of the team, and how well the system is supported and maintained.

It's necessary to understand how to account for costs. Some costs are expensed immediately, and others are amoraterized over the expected life of the system. Costs appear in different accounts, and all of these factors become important when the actual total costs are tabulated and the ROI is calculated.

When there is uncertainty about costs or to validate your cost estimates, call references to find out what costs they experience in each of the cost categories. This not only helps you estimate your costs, but also helps explain the costs to management.

Hardware

For the data warehouse, you need CPUs, disks, networks, and workstations. The hardware vendors can help size the machines and disks. Some hardware vendors have benchmark capabilities that will help you estimate your hardware requirements. Be aware that unanticipated growth of the data, increased numbers of users, and increased usage will explode the hardware cost. Some vendors, such as Teradata, usually bundle the hardware along with the DBMS.

The amount of the disks required depends on the raw data and on the number and size of the indexes required to satisfy performance requirements. It also depends on the need and usage of summary tables and on the need for working disk storage. The multiplier can vary up to six times the amount of raw data. The need for indexes and summary tables is highly dependent on the DBMS. Some have no performance requirement for either.

If existing desktops and laptops are adequate to support end users, no additional costs should be charged; however, if upgrades or new machines are required, the additional cost should be assigned and depreciated over the expected life of the system. Three years is often used as the expected life, even though the system will probably last longer. The calculation is the cost to purchase or upgrade multiplied by the number of anticipated users.

Do not ask the query tool vendor for the minimum desktop configuration; ask for the *recommended* configuration.

Software

The data warehouse always needs a DBMS. The way the DBMS is priced (by node or by the number of users) can influence the cost of the DBMS. End-user access and analysis tools, such as Business Objects, Cognos, and MicroStrategy, usually price by the number of registered users or by server. A new tool might not be required, but an upgrade or add-on to user software may be necessary.

Most products have base prices and many add-ons. Many installations choose an extract/transform/load (ETL) tool, such as Informatica or DataStage, rather than write their own ETL code. Add-ons with the ETL tools can include additional costs for each different type of source file or target database. These tools are often priced based on the operating system and size of the machine. Additional tools are often needed for data cleansing and performance monitoring. An organization might decide to pass on buying one of these tools, but should consider the additional cost of developing and maintaining code.

Personnel Costs

You will probably determine that your existing staff is inadequate to properly support your data strategy.

Internal Staff

The fully burdened rate (salary plus taxes, benefits, support costs, and so on) for the IT folks associated with the project should be included in the project cost. Business personnel are usually not included in calculations for personnel costs, but any help desk staff in the business organization should be. Management will spend significant time devoted to the projects, but management time is rarely included in the cost calculation.

Internal people get paid regardless of whether or not you use them on this project. Why should you include their cost in the budget? There is an opportunity cost of assigning them to this project versus another project. Include the fully burdened cost of the people on your project. Your project should, at minimum, include the costs for a data modeler (data administrator), DBAs, and a business analyst.

Consultants and Contractors

Consultants are engaged to help determine requirements, help plan the project, create the scope agreement, cost justify the project, help select the software, and establish the initial and long-term architectures. Consultants are typically more expensive than contractors, but they usually don't remain on projects as long. Contractors are brought in to supplement technical skills, specifically for software such as the DBMS. A primary role of the contractors should be to transfer their skills to the organization's employees. The cost for contractors depends on how deficient the organization is in the required skills, how fast the organization needs the system implemented, and how long it will take to transfer skills after the implementation is complete.

Training

IT training will be required for the DBMS. Your organization may already have DBAs trained and experienced in online transaction processing (OLTP) usage, but you might require data warehouse-specific training, such as the data structures, security, data models, data placement, DBMS tuning, and different types of user data access. IT personnel will need enough time to work with the products to become proficient in their use. The vendor cost of training is sometimes included in the price of the tool. The more knowledge transfer you receive from the vendor, the lower your ramp-up costs.

The cost for IT training should include:

• Registration fees

• Travel and living expenses

• Fully burdened personnel time including class time, preparation time, travel time, and time to become proficient with the product.

Operations and System Administration

This is a grab-bag of roles and costs that includes monitoring the system performance, executing backups, administering security, administering the metadata repository, dealing with the vendors, and assigning charge-backs. These categories of cost are higher in the initial implementation, but they exist for the life of the system. Consultants can provide suggestions on how to estimate this cost category, but organizations similar to your own can give you the best idea of what these costs will be.

Total Cost of Ownership

The total cost of ownership (TCO) goes beyond initial implementation. Most organizations focus on the cost to implement the initial application, but they give little thought to ongoing expense. Over a period of years, the continuing cost will likely exceed the cost of the initial implementation. The annual cost for the maintenance of the system often runs between 40 percent and 60 percent of the initial implementation cost. Maintenance must be sustained for every year the system delivers service to your users. The cumulative TCO is particularly onerous for installations with multiple siloed applications that require extensive interfaces. Chief financial officers (CFOs) usually allow benefits to be calculated for only three years, but the TCO extends for the life of that system. It's like a mortgage you must pay until you abandon your house.

Maintenance includes the contractual maintenance cost of the hardware and software (usually 15 percent to 25 percent of the software retail or purchase price). If the hardware was purchased, the depreciation of the hardware should be included. For leased hardware, the cost of leasing must be included. New or upgraded software and hardware might be required if the system does not perform as expected or if the usage and complexity go beyond initial estimates. Technical personnel are always required to establish and run backup and recovery procedures, to monitor and tune the system, and with the normal turnover, there is an additional cost with the introduction of new technical people. There are always requirements for, and costs associated with, assimilating new data, new capabilities, and new users.

The database will not remain static. Anticipate growing your environment. The growth will be in the number of users (Web delivery can significantly increase the number of users), the requirement to perform more complex queries, an extension to users beyond your enterprise (for example, customers and suppliers through an Internet capability). New data will be added, sometimes more than for the initial implementation. The design most likely will change, and the database will need to be tuned. Additional historical data will increase CPU and disk requirements. New software will be introduced, new releases will be installed, and some interfaces will have to be rewritten. As systems grow, organizations will have to upgrade the hardware and network.

At some point, you might need to migrate to a more robust and better performing platform. Migration is always costly. The lost time and opportunity cost of not having the system deployed and available can far exceed the money wasted on a prototype or "phase one" implementation. Migration should never be considered an alternative to fully understanding how much capacity and capability will eventually be needed or as an alternative to implementing a scalable configuration in the first place. All these factors must be considered in the TCO. Balancing the cost and value so that the resulting ROI is significant is important to achieving a successful implementation.

BENEFITS OF A DATA STRATEGY

Data strategy metrics for measuring the value of the data strategy need to be agreed upon in advance of implementation to avoid confusion over what value they bring. This section details some of these metrics for measuring the benefits of a data strategy.

The Data Warehouse

The majority of tangible benefits from a data strategy can be derived from the decision-support capability of the data. The data warehouse used primarily as a report generator has little inherent benefit. However, a data warehouse can enable analysis that provides information and knowledge to generate more and better leads, identify valuable trends, improve asset management, or negotiate better prices. That knowledge coupled with new programs and effective action is what generates the value, and it must be recognized that the data warehouse is a necessary enabler, thus a major contributor to cost savings or increased revenue.

Estimating Tangible Benefits

The tangible benefits are those that have hard dollars associated with them. The following sections discuss examples of such tangible benefits.

Revenue Enhancement

Improved marketing can result in more revenue per customer, resulting from increased spending and a greater share of the customer's wallet. As a side benefit, the increase in wallet share is at the expense of competitors. Selling higher margin products, focusing on the more profitable customers, and turning unprofitable customers into profitable ones enhance revenue.

Cash Flow Acceleration

Accelerating cash flow always results in more effective use of working capital which, in turn, results in greater profit to the organization. The data warehouse can accelerate cash flow by more efficiently managing the supply chain including inventory management, increasing inventory turns, managing suppliers, managing product shipments, backlog control, more accurate demand forecasting, and managing cancellations. Cash flow is accelerated with improved control of accounts receivables with an emphasis on time to collect.

Analyst Productivity

In the past, business users, analysts, and knowledge workers had to spend 80 percent of their time gathering data with only 20 percent left over to perform the analysis. With some data warehouses, those numbers are reversed. Depending on the degree of consolidation, integration of the data, and the availability of useful metadata, analysts now may spend only 20 percent of their time gathering the data. This does not mean firing analysts. Instead, they can now address the backlog of questions that were left unanswered and, in many cases, not even asked. It also means the questions can be answered in a more timely fashion. To make comparisons, it's important to measure the productivity both before and after. A rough metric is the number of queries, reports, or analyses performed per day; however, this measurement does not account for the value or complexity of the analyses which should be considered elsewhere.

A major factor associated with productivity is query response time. If a query takes too long, the effectiveness and productivity of the analyst may be severely impacted. This is particularly true for iterative queries for which the result of one query generates ideas for the next query. For the data warehouse to truly deliver its promised productivity, response time must satisfy the response time service level agreement (SLA). Some queries need a response time within seconds, (for example, call-center inquiries), whereas for others, minutes or even hours are acceptable (for example, monthly sales reports).

If the fully burdened rate for an analyst is $100,000 per year, and the productivity improvement is estimated at 25 percent, the annual estimated value of the data warehouse for analyst productivity is $25,000, muliplied by the number of analysts using the data warehouse.

Cost Containment

Although revenue must be balanced with the cost required to produce that revenue, cost savings flow directly to the bottom line. The data warehouse can help to control costs in a number of areas. In each area, the organization must know its cost of doing business, estimate the savings per situation, and extrapolate the cost savings. The following are industry and general business examples of areas in which costs can be significantly contained:

- **Retail**—Having a better understanding of customer purchasing patterns, timing of purchases, and the specific products that will be purchased gives an organization the capability to minimize its inventory.

- **Distribution**—Correcting name and address data reduces the fines from shippers who charge for incorrect zip codes.

- **Internal corporate costs**—There are many benefits of containing internal corporate costs including:

  - Knowing more about employees, their productivity, and their contributions to profit puts management in a better position to negotiate contracts with unions and puts mangement in a better position to make Human Resource decisions regarding head count and use of temporary services.

- Having better information about employees and their financial position and desires allows management to structure more cost-effective pension and retirement plans and better negotiate contracts with health maintenance providers.

- Improving the quality of products and services reduces warranty and service costs.

- Having more accurate and complete knowledge of operations helps reduce governmental fines and contractual penalties from suppliers and customers.

- **Customer relationship management (CRM)**—Knowing more about customers allows organizations to minimize the number of promotional mailers and still achieve target sales. It also uses more cost-effective channels to deliver services (through the Web and telephony, for example).

Demand Chain Management

The data warehouse should improve demand forecasting, and with this capability, companies can reduce inventory costs. Knowing inventory carrying costs, companies can calculate the cost reductions attributable to the data warehouse.

Fraud Reduction

The data warehouse and data mining have been used to detect fraudulent insurance claims and fraudulent credit card usage. Analysis of claims has identified fraudulent health and workers' compensation claims coming from specific doctors and lawyers. The types and patterns of the claims alert the investigators, who then conduct a more thorough audit to uncover fraud and abuse. Mining current and historical data together has identified profiles of usage that can indicate that a credit card is stolen sooner than it would be detected through simple transaction monitoring.

Customer Conversion Rates

When a marketing solicitation results in a sale, the prospect has been converted to a customer. The effectiveness of the marketing or sales effort is measured as a conversion percentage. Better understanding the customer and targeting the prospect with the right products, channels, and incentives can dramatically improve the conversion rate.

Customer Attrition and Retention Rates

By knowing which customers are likely to leave, and knowing their relative profitability, you can take appropriate action to control attrition. The value of retention programs is a function of the percentage of increase in retention.

Marketing Campaign Selection and Response Rates

Marketing campaigns associated with advertising and give-aways are expensive. Some campaigns are successful, as measured by the response to the campaign, the revenue generated from the campaign, and the number of new customers. Profits can be improved by avoiding ineffective marketing programs. By testing out different marketing campaigns with different customer segments, marketing can find the right approach for each customer segment. This reduces marketing costs and generally results in successful marketing and sales campaigns.

Better Relationships with Suppliers and Customers

The data warehouse provides an organization with the means of communicating needs and product status with suppliers and customers throughout the supply chain. Manufacturing and retail organizations are giving their suppliers selected access to a data warehouse, so that the suppliers can track inventory levels, sales, and product quality. This gives the suppliers the information they need to minimize stock-outs, trim inventory, reduce overproduction, and improve asset turns and product quality. This also gives the data warehouse owner the ability to negotiate favorable terms, conditions, and discount levels, which should flow directly to the bottom line.

Suppliers are giving their wholesale customers selected access to a data warehouse, so that the customers can track inventory, orders, and shipping information. This information capability helps to lock in customers who find the data warehouse information available only from this supplier. It also minimizes stock-outs and better on-time delivery, resulting in more products sold to these customers. In addition, this capability lowers the customer's overall costs and gives the customer better information to help them manage their end of the supply chain.

Data Mart Consolidation

As seen in the section on costs, maintaining data marts is expensive. The cost includes the cost of the multiple hardware platforms and DBMS licenses, including maintenance and upgrades, internal personnel to support the multiple systems and redundant ETL processes, increased network costs, additional software, outside consultants and contractors, costs associated with operations and systems administration, and maintaining redundant data. Redundant data typically accounts for 50 percent of the data in data marts and this percentage goes up as the number of data marts increases. The cost specific to each data mart is a function of the size of the data mart, the number and complexity of the source files, the cleansing required, the number of users, and the DBAs assigned to the data mart. Studies show the annual costs to be between 1 and 2 million dollars to maintain each data mart.

In addition to the obvious costs of maintaining multiple, disparate data marts, carrying redundant data on customers and suppliers results in a costly and disruptive operation: synchronizing data and the reconciliation of different outcomes. No one has studied or measured the cost and frustration associated with the question from management, "Why are these numbers different? Would someone please tell me what are the true results?" Although not all data marts can be consolidated (there will always be political, regulatory, or security reasons to keep some separate), an organization can significantly reduce the ongoing data mart costs by consolidating.

Estimating Intangible Benefits

Intangible benefits are, by definition, difficult to quantify. The following sections list examples of intangible benefits.

Public Relations, Reputation, and Impact on Shareholders

When an organization is in crisis, it's always embarrassing if it can't answer questions about the critical situation. It's also embarrassing if it doesn't have enough information to tell the press and to inform employees about how they plan to deal with the crisis. A data warehouse can provide those answers and give upper management the information needed to respond to the crisis. A manufacturing quality problem may go unnoticed. As the news is disclosed, it becomes apparent that senior management is unaware of the situation. The question is always why upper management doesn't know what's going on. The data warehouse can provide an early warning system to alert management about these soon-to-be-uncovered disasters.

Organizations are evaluated in a number of ways. The quality of management is given great weight as Wall Street analysts determine a company's value. The technological capability and the ability of an organization to make effective use of information has become a major topic in computer and industry publications, and this has had a strong impact on the organization's reputation. The price of a company's stock is strongly affected by analysts who read these articles. A number of CEOs have indicated that the way they are measured is by the price of the stock. The data warehouse is a vehicle for providing information effectively and has been identified as both a competitive edge for certain companies and as an indicator of the strength of the company's technological capabilities and of management's competence.

Competitive Effectiveness

Competitors who use the data warehouse effectively put you in peril. They are in a position to steal your best customers and produce higher quality products at a lower cost. Competitors with a financial data mart can tap the capital markets more effectively and deliver a higher price earnings ratio on their stock. Your competitors can develop successful products and get them to market more quickly than you can. Companies that provide meaningful and accurate data analysis to employees across the organization enable employees to make optimal decisions and improve productivity, effectiveness, and morale. It is difficult to quantify the edge you would have to relinquish to the competition, but it is definitely a major factor in many decisions involved in initiating a data warehouse.

A handful of companies in the healthcare industry have integrated claims data warehouses and provide data at the detail level. Due to centralized efficiency, they can easily achieve early HIPAA (Health Insurance Portability and Accountability Act of 1996) compliance and they credit their data warehouse with providing competitive differentiation by streamlining costs while maintaining and even improving healthcare quality.

Better and Faster Decisions

If decision makers had better access to more accurate and more timely information, would they be able to make better decisions and would they make these decisions more quickly? Would these decisions result in more sales, more revenue, and more profit? Would responding to a customer quickly close a sale that might otherwise be lost? Although we may not be able to quantify these results, most of the people who now get this more complete, higher quality, and more up-to-date data believe it is highly valuable.

Organizations sometimes operate without sufficient timely information about their operations. Lack of information about product profitability, quality control, customer satisfaction, competitive pricing, and other critical information robs the organization of what they need to make the tactical and strategic decisions that spell the difference between profitability and loss. Questions that need to be answered in a timely manner means in time for them to take effective action. Management often doesn't even bother asking IT people or their analysts for answers because they know that by the time the question is answered, it is too late to act. There is usually a visible backlog of unanswered questions and an even bigger backlog of questions that have not been posed.

A baseline measure of user satisfaction should be taken before the data warehouse is rolled out to the user community. Three months after the roll out, the questionnaire should again be distributed and should continue to be sent out twice a year as long as the system is in place. We have seen significant increases in user satisfaction, but your own measurements point out where you are doing well and where you can improve. The questionnaire should include questions about comfort with the access and analysis tool, adequacy of training, and perceptions of data quality, performance, availability, and user support.

Better Customer Service

Most people are sensitive to the service provided by his or her bank, broker, auto mechanic, retailer, airline, doctor, and financial adviser. We choose our providers based on cost, but also on how we are treated. We want to believe that the provider knows us and is able to accommodate our specific needs and satisfy our desires. Better customer service translates into improved customer satisfaction, higher retention, and an increase in cross-sell and up-sell ratios.

Employee Empowerment

By giving employees access to better information, the employees become more productive and the requirement for supervision decreases. Employees always feel better about their jobs and the organizations they work for when they are given the right tools and the right information. This can lead to suggestions from employees for additional ways to leverage the data warehouse, which can also result in additional tangible benefits.

Post-Implementation Benefits Measurement

As part of cost justification, an organization should measure its benefits after the system has been implemented—it's important to know just what those benefits actually were. This measurement is crucial in determining the ROI from the project and helping with future goal setting, benefits estimates, and proposed expansions or enhancements. The measurement can highlight areas in which benefits were overestimated and it can uncover benefits that were serendipitous and not anticipated. The intangible benefits are difficult to measure, but all the stories and testimonials associated with those stories should be captured, documented, and disseminated.

It would be unusual if the resulting benefits were as predicted. It is important to review the benefits to determine the accuracy of the predictions. Armed with the results of the review, more accurate predictions can be made in each category, and the prediction process can be improved with more accurate benefits projected for future projects. The data warehouse lends itself to iterative development, which allows us to measure the costs and benefits of each new iteration. More accurate benefits analysis can aid in prioritizing data warehouse projects. Even if you don't estimate costs and benefits, post-implementation measurement is still beneficial. You can still determine if your project has a positive ROI and you can still determine if existing data warehouses should be abandoned.

CONCLUSION

In an age when almost all new ventures must show a value to the business, a data strategy initiative must also project a significant value. Because the project will take many months or even years to accomplish and since the strategy must be maintained in perpetuity, cost justification is an absolute requirement to support the project and sustain the necessary management commitment and protect it from cost cutters and short-term solutions that would undermine the strategy.

REFERENCE

Adelman, Sid. "Measuring Data Warehouse Return on Investment." www.teradata.com, 2003.

ROI Calculation Process, Cost Template, and Intangible Benefits Template

Some of the ideas in this appendix were derived from the Teradata white paper titled "Measuring Data Warehouse Return on Investment," by Sid Adelman.

The three most common methods of calculating Return on Investment (ROI) are net present value (NPV), rate of return (yield), and payback period (break-even analysis). The example presented in this section shows all three methods. They are not mutually exclusive—all three are used for evaluation. Although each is valid, the usefulness of any one method alone is limited. For example, payback does not include a measure of value after the investment has broken even. Assumptions are embedded in each model. Net present value assumes that you'll reinvest cash flows at the cost of capital. Internal rate of return assumes that you'll reinvest cash flows at the internal rate of return. It is advisable to use a combination of discounted cash flow techniques to ensure that you get as complete a view as possible.

COST OF CAPITAL

An understanding of the cost of capital is necessary for determining the rate of return and net present value. Every project must earn a return that's greater than its cost of capital; otherwise, the project diminishes the organization's value. Organizations with good credit ratings are blessed with a lower cost of capital than those on the verge of bankruptcy. Expressed as a rate of interest, it is a number the chief financial officer (CFO) in your organization fully understands and will want you to use as you perform ROI calculations; be sure to ask. For the purposes of illustration, we use 10 percent as the cost of capital or the discount rate.

RISK

Risk is only important in the cost justification process. After the system is in, running, and is being measured, most bullets have already been dodged. There are substantial risks to any data warehouse project. Cost justifications must consider the following risks:

• The system doesn't go in at all.

• The project is over budget.

• The schedule slips.

• Important functions are not delivered.

• The system does not perform.

• The users do not make effective use of the system.

• The expected benefits do not materialize.

Estimates of benefits should include the expected range of improvement. A conservative approach that helps manage expectations dictates using estimates in the lower range of improvement. If the expected yearly cost savings from improved inventory management ranges from $500,000 to $1,000,000 with a most likely savings estimate of $800,000, it is wise to use a lower number such as $700,000 for the ROI calculation. It's always better to deliver more than you promise.

ROI EXAMPLE

The examples given make some simplistic assumptions about the timing of the expenditures and the timing of the benefits. The primary, simplistic assumption is that all the expenditures will be spent halfway through the year and all the benefits will be realized halfway through the year.

Our example has an initial estimated outlay of $1,000,000. The yearly benefit is $800,000, but the cost to maintain the system will be $300,000 for every year the system is in production. This leaves a net benefit of $500,000 per year. Because of a demanding CFO, the system is estimated to survive for only three years following delivery.

Net Present Value

The present value is equal to the sum of the net yearly benefits ($500,000) discounted by the cost of capital (10 percent) for three years.

Net Present Value = Σ (Year 1 Benefits – Costs) / (1+discount rate) + (Year 2 Benefits – Costs) / (1+discount rate)^2 + (Year 3 Benefits – Costs) / (1+discount rate)^3

For example, the equation translates into the following for our example:

$500,000 / (1+.10) + $500,000 / (1+.10)^2 + $500,000 / (1+.10)^3 – $1,000,000

$500,000 / 1.10 + $500,000 / 1.21 + $500,000 / 1.331 – $1,000,000 =

$454,545 + $413,223 + $375,657 – $1,000,000 = **$243,425**

The ROI as represented by the net present value of this project is $243,425.

Internal Rate of Return

The internal rate of return (IRR) is the discount rate for which the present value of the benefits is equal to the amount of the investment. In other words, the IRR is the discount rate that produces an NPV equal to zero. The easiest way to determine the rate of return is to use a spreadsheet with financial functions such as those found in Microsoft Excel. There are other alternatives including a calculator with financial functions, an IRR, and NPV, or a book that contains tables with "present value of $1 received per period."

We used Excel's IRR function with the argument = IRR (A1:A4), as shown in the following chart:

A1	$(1,000,000)
A2	$500,000
A3	$500,000
A4	$500,000

The IRR for this example is 23.38 percent.

Payback Period

The payback period (break-even analysis) is the easiest to calculate and to explain. It resonates well with management and is the most frequently used measure of ROI for any IT applications. It's the time required for the cash stream that results from the investment to equal the original cost of the project. Management usually rejects applications that have a payback period that exceeds a predetermined number of years. As with the other methods, management will use the payback period to rank project alternatives. In this example, it's equal to the cost of the investment ($1,000,000) divided by the proceeds or net benefits per period ($500,000). The payback period for the example is two years ($1,000,000 / $500,000).

COST CALCULATION TEMPLATE

Use the following template to itemize the costs for this project. You will need to know the costs when management asks.

Cost Category	Calculation	Dollars
Hardware		
Maintenance		
Internal personnel costs		
Network		
Maintenance		
Internal personnel costs		
Desktops/Laptops		
Maintenance		
Internal personnel costs		
Software		
DBMS		
Maintenance		
Internal personnel costs		

Cost Category	Calculation	Dollars
Modeling Tools		
Maintenance		
Internal personnel costs		
Query/Report		
Maintenance		
Internal personnel costs		
ETL		
Maintenance		
Internal support		
Other tool #1		
Maintenance		
Internal support		
Other tool #2		
Maintenance		
Internal support		
Contracting		
Consulting		
Help Desk Support		
IT Training		
User Training		
Operations and Systems Administration		
Other Cost #1		
Other Cost #2		
Other Cost #3		
Total Cost		

Use this template to calculate *all* of your tangible benefits. Don't be shy. This can make the difference in the "go, no-go" decision.

Tangible Benefit	Calculation	Dollars
Revenue enhancement		
Cash flow acceleration		
Analyst productivity		
Customer conversion rates		
Customer attrition/retention rates		
Marketing campaign selection and response rates		
Cost containment		
Fraud reduction		
Data mart consolidation		
Demand chain management		
Better relationships with suppliers and customers		
Other Tangible Benefit #1		
Other Tangible Benefit #2		
Other Tangible Benefit #3		
Total Tangible Benefits		

INTANGIBLE BENEFITS CALCULATION TEMPLATE

Although the intangible benefits may not satisfy the accountants, their importance will not be lost on senior management. Identify as many as you can. Be descriptive in your explanations, and if you can, assign any dollar benefits that may derive from the project.

Intangible Benefit	Explanation or Narrative	Dollars or Other Benefit
Public relations, reputation, and shareholder value		
Competitive effectiveness		
Better and faster decisions		
Better customer service		
Employee empowerment		
Impact on internal champion		
Other Intangible Benefit #1		
Other Intangible Benefit #2		
Other Intangible Benefit #3		
Total Intangible Benefits		

REFERENCE

Sid Adelman, "Measuring Data Warehouse Return on Investment," www.teradata.com, 2003.

APPENDIX B

Resources

PUBLICATIONS

Adelman, Sid and Larissa Terpeluk Moss. *Data Warehouse Project Management.* Boston, MA: Addison-Wesley, 2000.

Adelman, Sid et. al. *Impossible Data Warehouse Situations.* Boston, MA: Addison-Wesley, 2003.

Beyer, Mark. "Metadata: The Compliance Get-Out-of-Jail-Free Card?" *Enterprise Analytics Strategies*, 26 October 2004.

Brackett, Michael H. *Data Resource Quality: Turning Bad Habits into Good Practices.* Boston, MA: Addison-Wesley, 2000.

Brackett, Michael H. *The Data Warehouse Challenge: Taming Data Chaos.* New York: John Wiley & Sons, 1996.

Codd, Edgar F., Dr. "A Relational Model of Data for Large Shared Data Banks," *Communications of the ACM*. Volume 13, Number 6, 1970.

Cook, Melissa A. *Building Enterprise Information Architectures: Reeingineering Information Systems.* Upper Saddle River, NJ: Prentice Hall, 1996.

Domanski, Bernie. "Simulation versus Analytic Modeling in Large Computing Environments: Predicting the Performance Impact of Tuning Changes," A White Paper from Responsive Systems Company, 1999. `

Duncan, Karolyn and David L. Wells, "Rule-Based Data Cleansing," *The Journal of Data Warehousing*, Fall 1999.

Eckerson, Wayne W. "Data Quality and the Bottom Line," *TDWI Report Series*, 2003.

English, Larry P. *Improving Data Warehouse and Business Information Quality*. New York: John Wiley & Sons, Inc., 1999.

English, Larry. "New Year; New Name; New Resolve for High IQ," *DM Review*, Volume 13, Number 1, January 2003.

Fayyad, Usama M. et al. *Advances in Knowledge Discovery & Data Mining*. Cambridge, MA: MIT Press, 1996.

Hall, Curt. *BI Advisory Service, Executive Update Vol. 4, No. 6*. Andover, MA: Cutter Consortium, 2004.

Haughey, Tom. "Is Dimensional Modeling One of the Great Con Jobs in Data Management History? (Parts 1 and 2)" *DM Review*, March and April 2004.

Hoberman, Steve. *Data Modeler's Workbench: Tools and Techniques for Analysis and Design*. New York: John Wiley & Sons, 2001.

Hubel, Martin. "Tuning PeopleSoft Applications for the DB2 OS/390 Environment," 1999, www.responsivesystems.com/papers/peoplesoft/peoplesoft1.pdf.

Imhoff, Claudia, Nicholas Galemmo, and Jonathan Geiger. *Mastering Data Warehouse Design*. New York: John Wiley & Sons, 2003.

Imhoff, Claudia, Lisa Loftis, and Jonathan G. Geiger. *Building the Customer-Centric Enterprise*. New York: John Wiley & Sons, 2001.

Inmon, W.H., Claudia Imhoff, and Ryan Sousa. *Corporate Information Factory*. New York: John Wiley & Sons, 1998.

Inmon, Bill.

—"Data Mart Does Not Equal Data Warehouse," *DM Review*, May 1998.

—"The Problem With Dimensional Modeling," *DM Review*, May 2000.

Killelea, Patrick. "Speeding up the Web," *Web Performance Tuning*, 2nd Edition. Sebastopol, California: O'Reilly Publishing, 2002.

Kimball, Ralph et. al. *The Data Warehouse Lifecycle Toolkit*. New York: John Wiley & Sons, 1998.

Kimball, Ralph.

—"A Dimensional Modeling Manifesto," *DBMS Magazine*, August 1997.

—"Bringing Up Supermarts," *DBMS Magazine*, January 1998.

—"Is ER Modeling Hazardous to DSS?" *DBMS Magazine*, October 1995.

—"The Matrix," *Intelligent Enterprise*, December 1999.

—"There Are No Guarantees," *Intelligent Enterprise*, August 2000.

Levy, Evan. Baseline Consulting Group. "Architectural Alternatives for Data Integration," TDWI FlashPoint, September 22, 2004.

Linthicum, David. *Enterprise Application Integration*. Boston, MA: Addison Wesley, 2000.

Loosley, Chris, and Frank Douglas. *High Performance Client/Server*. New York: John Wiley and Sons, 1998.

Loshin, David. *Business Intelligence: The Savvy Manager's Guide*. San Francisco, CA: Morgan Kaufmann Publishers, 2003.

Loshin, David. "Customer Care, Consistency and Policy Management," *DM Review*, Volume 13, Number 8, August 2003.

Loshin, David. *Enterprise Knowledge Management—The Data Quality Approach*. San Francisco, CA: Morgan Kaufmann, 2001.

Marco, David, and Michael Jennings. *Universal Meta Data Models*. New York: John Wiley & Sons, 2004.

Marco, David. *Building and Managing the Meta Data Repository: A Full Lifecycle Guide*. New York: John Wiley & Sons, 2000.

Millsap, Cary and Jeff Holt. *Optimizing Oracle Performance*. Sebastopol, CA: O'Reilly Publishing, 2003.

Moss, Larissa T., and Shaku Atre. *Business Intelligence Roadmap, The Complete Project Lifecycle for Decision-Support Applications*. Boston, MA: Addison-Wesley, 2003.

Moss, Larissa and Steve Hoberman. "The Importance of Data Modeling as a Foundation for Business Insight," Teradata.com, 2004.

Moss, Larissa. "Data Quality Is Not Optional," Business Intelligence Advisory Service Executive Report Vol. 3, No. 11. Cutter Consortium, 2003.

Moss, Larissa. "Organizational and Cultural Barriers to Business Intelligence," Business Intelligence Advisory Service Executive Report Vol. 1, No. 7. Cutter Consortium, 2001.

Pendse, Nigel and Richard Creeth. "Responsive Systems," www.responsivesystems.com.

Porter-Roth, Bud. *Request for Proposal: A Guide to Effective RFP Development.* Boston, MA: Addison Wesley, 2002.

Reimer, James. "Enterprise Content Management Products," IBM in Content Management and WebSphere Portal Technical Conference, June 9, 2003.

Rockley, Ann et. al. *Managing Enterprise Content.* Indianapolis, IN: New Riders Publishing, 2003.

Tannenbaum, Adrienne. *Metadata Solutions; Using Metamodels, Repositories, XML, and Enterprise Portals to Generate Information on Demand.* Boston, MA: Addison-Wesley, 2002.

Thibodeau, Patrick. "Data Problems Thwart Effort to Count H-1Bs," *Computer World*, 6 October 2003.

Verton, Dan. "FBI Begins Knowledge Management Facelift," *Computer World*, 2003.

WEBSITES

Business Intelligence—www.businessintelligence.com

Computer Measurement Group—www.cmg.org.

> The Computer Measurement Group, commonly called CMG, is a not-for-profit, worldwide organization of data processing professionals committed to the measurement and management of computer systems. CMG members are primarily concerned with performance evaluation of existing systems to maximize performance (response time, throughput, and so on) and with capacity management where planned enhancements to existing systems or the design of new systems are evaluated to find the necessary resources required to provide adequate performance at a reasonable cost.

Data Administration Management Association (DAMA)—www.DAMA.org

DB2 Journal—www.db2magazine.com

DM Review—www.dmreview.com

Gartner, Business Intelligence Summit, Amsterdam, Netherlands, February 2004—www.in-sourced.com/article/articleprint/1273/-1/1/

The OLAP Report—www.olapreport.com

Oracle Magazine—www.oracle.com/oraclemagazine

Professional Association for SQL Server (PASS)—www.sqlpass.org

SQL Server Magazine—www.sqlservermagazine.com

Sybase Magazine—www.sybase.com/about_sybase/magazine

Teradata Magazine—www.teradatamagazine.com

Teradata—www.teradata.com

Index

Register Your Book

at www.awprofessional.com/register

You may be eligible to receive:

- Advance notice of forthcoming editions of the book
- Related book recommendations
- Chapter excerpts and supplements of forthcoming titles
- Information about special contests and promotions throughout the year
- Notices and reminders about author appearances, tradeshows, and online chats with special guests

Contact us

If you are interested in writing a book or reviewing manuscripts prior to publication, please write to us at:

Editorial Department
Addison-Wesley Professional
75 Arlington Street, Suite 300
Boston, MA 02116 USA
Email: AWPro@aw.com

Addison-Wesley

Visit us on the Web: http://www.awprofessional.com

Also available from Larissa Moss, Sid Adelman, and Addison-Wesley